The Book of Job
Aesthetics, Ethics, Hermeneutics

Perspectives on Jewish Texts and Contexts

Edited by
Vivian Liska

Volume 1

The Book of Job

Aesthetics, Ethics, Hermeneutics

Edited by
Leora Batnitzky and Ilana Pardes

DE GRUYTER

ISBN 978-3-11-055394-9
e-ISBN (PDF) 978-3-11-033879-9
e-ISBN (EPUB) 978-3-11-039398-9
ISSN 2199-6962

Library of Congress Cataloging-in-Publication Data
A CIP catalog record for this book has been applied for at the Library of Congress.

Bibliographic information published by the Deutsche Nationalbibliothek
The Deutsche Nationalbibliothek lists this publication in the Deutsche Nationalbibliografie;
detailed bibliographic data are available on the Internet at http://dnb.dnb.de.

© 2014 Walter de Gruyter GmbH, Berlin/Munich/Boston
This volume is text- and page-identical with the hardback published in 2015.
Cover image: Source: http://www.zeno.org – Contumax GmbH & Co. KG
Typesetting: Meta Systems Publishing & Printservices GmbH, Wustermark
Printing and binding: CPI books GmbH, Leck
♾ Printed on acid-free paper
Printed in Germany

www.degruyter.com

Acknowledgments

This book had its beginnings in a conference on the Book of Job that was held at Princeton University in October 2012 as part of a collaborative project between the University of Antwerp, the Hebrew University, and Princeton University. We are grateful to the Program of Jewish Studies and the Department of Religion at Princeton University for hosting the conference. We also wish to thank Jeremy Schreiber for his fine copy editing, Katja Lehming and De Gruyter Press for their support, and Vivian Liska for her energetic intellectual leadership on this book series.

L. B. and I. P.

Contents

Leora Batnitzky and Ilana Pardes
The Book of Job: Aesthetics, Ethics, and Hermeneutics

The Book of Job has held a central role in defining the project of modernity from the age of Enlightenment until today. What makes the Book of Job such a prominent text in modern literature and thought? Why has Job's response to disaster become a touchstone for modern reflections on catastrophic events? What sort of answer (if any) can the Voice from the Whirlwind offer in a post-theological age? How have modern and postmodern thinkers and artists translated Job's social critique to address ethical and political concerns? What are the interrelations between traditional conceptions of Job as a parable and modern Joban parables? How does Job's aesthetic legacy function as a key element in defining the cry of modern witnesses? To what extent can aesthetic inquiries within religious realms modify our perceptions of religious texts and religious experience – and, vice versa, to what extent does religion allow or compel us to open up the concept of the "aesthetic"?

The Bible has not always been venerated as an aesthetic touchstone. The literary Bible emerged in the eighteenth century, in England and in Germany, as the invention of scholars and literati who tried to rejuvenate the Bible by transforming it from a book justified by theology to one justified by culture. The aim of this post-theological project was not quite to secularize the Bible – though it was now construed as the product of human imagination – but rather to reconstitute its authority in aesthetic terms. The Book of Job played a vital role in enhancing this transformation. Jonathan Sheehan goes so far as to trace what he calls a "Job revival" within the context of English and German Enlightenment, a revival that included numerous new translations and scholarly studies of the text.[1] Indeed, the Book of Job acquired so prominent a position as an aesthetic touchstone that Edmund Burke evoked it, in *A Philosophical Enquiry into the Sublime and the Beautiful* (1757), as an exemplary text for the exploration of the sublime experience in its relation to power and terror.

J. G. Herder, one of the German forerunners of the literary approach to the Bible, devoted an entire section of his renowned *The Spirit of Hebrew Poetry* (1782–1783) to Job. In response to Burke, Herder reinterpreted the sublimity of the Book of Job as pertaining to the realms of the heart, of vision, and of vivid

---

1 Sheehan, Jonathan, *The Enlightenment Bible: Translation, Scholarship, Culture*, Princeton University Press, Princeton 2005.

Oriental imagination. God's whirlwind poem, for Herder, is the poetic epitome of Job, for like the Oriental descriptions of nature "it awakens a love, an interest, and a sympathy for all that lives."

> What wretch, in the greatest tumult of his passions, in walking under a starry heaven, would not experience imperceptibly and even against his will a soothing influence from the elevating contemplation of its silent, unchangeable, and everlasting splendors. Suppose at such a moment there occurs to his thoughts the simple language of God, "Canst thou bind together the bands of the Pleiades," etc. – is it not as if God himself addressed the words to him from the starry firmament? Such an effect has the true poetry of nature, the fair interpreter of the nature of God. A hint, a single word, in the spirit of such poetry often suggests to the mind extended scenes, nor does it merely bring their quiet pictures before the eye in their outward lineaments, but brings them home to the sympathies of the heart.[2]

Alongside the interest in Job's sublimity in the age of Enlightenment and beyond, one can trace a growing preoccupation with the text's genre. The pivotal question in this respect was whether the Book of Job should be defined as a tragedy. Robert Lowth, a prominent advocate of the literary Bible within the English context, included in his renowned *De Sacra Poesi Hebræorum* (1753) a substantive comparison of the poetic form of Job with that of Greek tragedy.[3] Lowth compared Job with the tragedies of Sophocles and concluded that, despite certain similarities, the biblical work does not rely on the type of plot that would establish it as tragic.

Defining the Book of Job as a tragedy became prominent in nineteenth-century biblical criticism. Thus, Wilhelm Martin Leberecht De Wette, in his *Einleitung*, regarded the Book of Job as a "Hebrew tragedy," which unlike Greek tragedy represents "the tragic idea by words and thoughts, rather than by action."[4] Neither Lowth nor De Wette linked the tragic in Job to the question of impatience. Only in twentieth-century criticism does one find a consideration of Job as an impious tragic figure whose mode of suffering resembles that of tragic heroes in Greek drama, most notably in Richard B. Sewall's reading of

---

2 Herder, J. G., "God and Nature in the Book of Job" (from *The Spirit of Hebrew Poetry*), in: *The Dimensions of Job: A Study and Selected Readings,* ed. Nahum N. Glatzer, Schocken Books, New York 1969, 154.

3 For a discussion of Lowth's contribution to the rise of the literary Bible, see David Norton, *A History of the Bible as Literature: From 1700 to the Present Day,* Cambridge University Press, Cambridge 1993, 59–73.

4 De Wette, Wilhelm Martin Leberecht, *A Critical and Historical Introduction to the Canonical Scriptures of the Old Testament,* Volume 2, trans. Theodore Parker, D. Appleton and Co., New York 1864, 555.

Job in *The Vision of Tragedy* (1959), a reading that, interestingly, relies on Melville's Ahab.[5]

Among twentieth-century Jewish critics, however, the tendency was to reject any attempt to define the Book of Job as tragedy. Baruch Kurzweil, a prominent Israeli critic, sees no affinity whatsoever between the Greek tragic worldview and the belief in redemption, the very core of biblical monotheism. What is more, that Job has no flaws and is hailed as blameless actually renders him the antithesis of the Aristotelian designation of the tragic hero. A "biblical tragedy," Kurzweil concludes, is not a possibility.

The most influential avowal of tragedy within Jewish thought is that of George Steiner, in his *Death of Tragedy* (1961). Steiner's opening declaration in this work revolves around the Book of Job:

> Tragedy is alien to the Judaic sense of the world. The book of Job is always cited as an instance of tragic vision. But that black fable stands on the outer edge of Judaism, and even here an orthodox hand has asserted the claims of justice over tragedy: "So the Lord blessed the latter end of Job more than the beginning: for he had fourteen thousand sheep, and six thousand camels, and a thousand yoke of oxen, and a thousand she-asses." God has made good the havoc wrought upon His servant; he has compensated Job for his agonies [...] The Judaic spirit is vehement in its conviction that the order of the universe and man's estate is accessible to reason. The ways of the Lord are neither wanton nor absurd.[6]

Ariel Hirschfeld's "Is the Book of Job a Tragedy?" – the first essay in this volume – relies on new perceptions of tragedy in its reading of the Book of Job. Instead of a chasm between Hebraism and Hellenism, Hirschfeld calls attention to unexpected similarities between Greek tragedies and the Book of Job. While acknowledging the unmistakable differences between biblical and Greek traditions, Hirschfeld argues that the Book of Job's vision of the divine shares an essential element not with the pagan vision as a whole, but specifically with the tragic view of the gods – namely, a lack of understanding, a palpable detachment, between the human and the divine. Hirschfeld also offers a reconsideration of Job's alleged perfection and traces a streak of hubris in his blameless world.

Moshe Halbertal's essay, "Job, the Mourner," similarly shifts the reader's attention away from questions of theodicy. Rather than posing philosophical and theological questions about God's justice and the suffering of the innocent, Halbertal examines the Book of Job from the stance of the mourner. Like the

---

5 Sewall, Richard B., *The Vision of Tragedy*, Yale University Press, New Haven 1959.
6 Steiner, George, *The Death of Tragedy*, Faber & Faber, London, 1961, 4.

mourner, Job is an outcast who finds the world as he knew it destroyed. In presenting the perspective of the mourner, Halbertal's reading of Job highlights the abusive response of Job's friends to his suffering. The challenge of the Book of Job, and the challenge of the experience of evil and loss, is to bring the mourner back into the web of life and human relations. The Book of Job suggests that the mourner can return to the world only when he is able to care for others, as does Job, in Chapter 42, when he prays for his friends.

Naphtali Meshel's "Whose Job Is This? Dramatic Irony and *double entendre* in Job" similarly complicates any attempt to read the Book of Job as providing a straightforward theological or philosophical worldview. Writing from the perspectives of biblical studies and philology, Meshel focuses on a specific type of *double entendre* used in key passages of the Book of Job – a mode of *double entendre* that formulates two diametrically opposite expressions via a single phonetic and/or graphic sequence. Through careful philological analysis, Meshel illustrates that the Book of Job's choice of language intentionally embodies the ambiguity of any attempt to resolve the problems of divine justice and human suffering.

Yosefa Raz's "Reading Pain in the Book of Job" considers the somatic experiences depicted in the Book of Job, specifically, the experience of the body in pain. Drawing upon Elaine Scarry's work, Raz offers a reading of the Book of Job in which pain is intimately related to the formation and shattering of both language and power. She critiques Scarry's presupposition that the Bible provides a coherent representation of God as torturer and argues that the Book of Job sustains multiple perspectives on the question of pain. Thus, the final speeches from the whirlwind suggest a divinity whose creative forces are not only based on diminishing and wounding the bodies of human believers, and as such attempt to re-fashion the very structure of belief.

While these first four articles represent new perspectives on major aesthetic and ethical questions in the Book of Job, the following six articles consider different moments of reception within the realm of literature. The resonance of Job in modern literature can hardly be exaggerated. Indeed, some of the key literary texts of modernity revolve around the biblical sufferer. The following articles explore different Joban adaptations in a whole array of cultural contexts, including American literature, German literature, and modern Hebrew Literature.

In "Melville's Wall Street Job: The Missing Cry," Ilana Pardes explores Herman Melville's insistence to reinvent Job as he moves from *Moby-Dick* to "Bartleby." Melville's Wall Street Job, Pardes argues, is bleaker than the *Pequod* Jobs – even more than tragic Ahab. Yet this dark rendition of the plight of the biblical rebel does not lack a peculiar sense of stubborn vitality that owes much to the audacity with which Melville probes new aesthetic possibilities. A closer translation of Job into modern times, Melville intimates in "Bartleby," would entail the invention of a sufferer whose fate is so bleak that he is not even granted the privilege of expressing his grief, misery, and protest in grand poetic form. Pardes closes her reading with a consideration of "Bartleby" as a precursor of Franz Kafka's Jobs.

Vivian Liska's "Kafka's Other Job" focuses on the Kafka-Job connection. The most general and far-reaching parallels between Job and Kafka, Liska argues, were drawn in the late 1920s and 1930s by a group of German-Jewish thinkers who echoed and contested each other's work. Liska discusses the evocations of the interrelations between Job and Kafka in the writings of Margarete Susman, Max Brod, and Gershom Scholem, calling attention to the ways in which this nexus allows them to conceptualize modernity. Rethinking the foundations of Judaism in the face of the rupture with tradition, these thinkers probe the possibilities and impossibilities of a divine order after the "death of God." Liska offers her own understanding of Kafka's "other Job" through an analysis of two Kafkaesque accounts of "other Abrahams."

In "Joban Transformations of the Wandering Jew in Joseph Roth's *Hiob* and *Der Leviathan*," Galit Hasan Rokem explores the interconnections between the Book of Job and the legend of the Wandering Jew in Joseph Roth's *Hiob* (*Job*, 1930) and "Der Leviathan" (*The Leviathan*, 1938). Job and the Wandering Jew configure a central tension in Roth's literary oeuvre: the tension between European universality and Jewish particularity, with special attention to the problem of human suffering. Resonating both Roth's personal tribulations and the anguished historical circumstances between the two World Wars, these two texts illuminate multiple aspects of the ancient question regarding the suffering of innocents. Hasan Rokem's reading also entails a consideration of the folkloristic dimension of Roth's poetics.

In "Hebrew Poems Rewriting Job," Robert Alter examines three Joban poems by the contemporary Israeli poet Natan Zach. "For Job It Was a One-Time Thing" carries out a familiar modernist strategy in its drawing a strong antithesis between the ancient story fraught with cosmic drama and the predicament of a modern average person whose afflictions are trivial banalities. "Sometimes He Misses" teases from the biblical tale an element of empathy and divine compassion strangely missing from the scriptural text. "Man As the Grass His Days" evokes phrases from Job and from Psalms that become a haunting meditation on mortality. Alter ends with a poem by Zelda, "Be Not Far," highlighting its disturbing mirroring of the distance between every person and someone plunged in suffering.

The reception of the Book of Job in Israeli culture is further adumbrated in Freddie Rokem's "The Bible on the Hebrew/Israeli Stage: Hanoch Levin's *The*

Torments of Job as a Modern Tragedy." Rokem's article considers the ways in which the Bible has been used in Israeli culture as a source of avant-garde art. He explores the cultural and ideological background of Levin's play, arguing that it upsets the presumed harmony, in Zionist and Israeli culture, between the Bible and the State of Israel. Setting "The Torments of Job" in the context of Levin's reaction to the 1967 Six Day War and its aftermath, Rokem offers an analysis of Levin's play as a modern tragedy.

Leora Batnitzky's essay, "Beyond Theodicy? Joban Themes in Philip Roth's *Nemesis*," turns to the American Jewish writer Philip Roth, and considers how literature, as opposed to philosophy or theology, might avoid the pitfalls of theodicy when approaching the Book of Job. Roth's *Nemesis* has been compared to Sophocles' "Oedipus Rex"; however, as Batnitzky argues, Bucky, the protagonist of Roth's novel, rallies against God, just as Job does (and as Oedipus does not). Job's rallying against God upsets the piety of his day – that the righteous are rewarded and the wicked punished – just as Bucky's rallying against God upsets the piety of his day – that the course of a person's life is largely determined by chance. Neither the Book of Job nor *Nemesis* answers the question of why the innocent suffer. Yet it is through this lack of resolution that literature, as opposed to philosophy or theology, avoids theodicy.

We end with a passage from Kafka's *The Trial*, where K. and the priest discuss the parable "Before the Law":

> Some people take this line of interpretation even further and hold that the words "you are insatiable" express a kind of friendly admiration [...] At any rate, the figure of the door-keeper is thus interpreted in a way that differs from your opinion' [...] Then K. said: 'So you think the man was not deceived?' 'Don't misunderstand me,' said the priest. 'I am only telling you the opinions which exist. You must not pay too much attention to opinions. The written word is unalterable, and opinions are often only an expression of despair. In this case there is even an opinion that it is the door-keeper who is deceived.'[7]

Jacques Derrida's renowned essay "Devant la Loi" positions the parable in the Cathedral as an exemplary text in its insistence on the impossibility of interpretation.[8] As Derrida notes, what emerges from the discussion between Joseph K. and the priest about the meaning of the parable is that all readings are necessarily misreadings. We shall never comprehend with certainty what lies behind the succession of guarded doors which divide us from the "Law." Following Derrida, Harold Fisch wonders whether the parable in the Cathedral is

7 Kafka, Franz, *The Trial*, trans. Idris Parry, Penguin Books, London 2000, 169.
8 Derrida, Jacques, "Devant la Loi," trans. Avital Ronell, in: *Kafka and the Contemporary Critical Performance*, ed. Alan Udoff, Indiana University Press, Bloomington 1987, 128–149.

specifically meant to question the very possibility of interpreting the Book of Job with its inexplicable trial.[9]

Kafka reminds us that modern literature has no leverage over traditional modes of exegesis in deciphering the Law or the mystery of the Book of Job. In fact, all the writers whose Joban works are addressed in this volume – Melville, Kafka, Joseph Roth, Zach, Zelda, Levin, and Philip Roth – have insisted, albeit in different fashions, on highlighting the complications of exegetical endeavors in the context of modernity. That hermeneutic enigmas problematize the efforts to unravel them, however, does not render them less alluring. Somehow it is the impossibility of fathoming the Book of Job that seems to compel these writers, with ever-growing drive, to engage and interrogate the biblical text. To quote the door-keeper's words to the man from the country: these writers are "insatiable."

Bibliography

Derrida, Jacques. "Devant la Loi". *Kafka and the Contemporary Critical Performance*. Trans. Avital Ronell, Ed. Alan Udoff. Bloomington: Indiana University Press, 1987.

De Wette, Wilhelm Martin Leberecht. *A Critical and Historical Introduction to the Canonical Scriptures of the Old Testament,* vol. 2. Trans. Theodore Parker, New York: D. Appleton and Co., 1864.

Fisch, Harold. *New Stories for Old: Biblical Patterns in the Novel*. New York: St. Martin's Press, 1998.

Herder, J. G. "God and Nature in the Book of Job". *The Dimensions of Job: A Study and Selected Readings*. Ed. Nahum N. Glatzer. New York: Schocken Books, 1969. 141–156.

Kafka, Franz. *The Trial*. Trans. Idris Parry. London: Penguin Books, 2000.

Norton, David. *A History of the Bible as Literature: From 1700 to the Day*, Cambridge: Cambridge University Press, 1993.

Sewall, Richard B. *The Vision of Tragedy*. New Haven: Yale University Press, 1959.

Sheehan, Jonathan. *The Enlightenment Bible: Translation, Scholarship, Culture*. Princeton: Princeton University Press, 2005.

Steiner, George. *The Death of Tragedy*, London: Faber & Faber, 1961.

---

9 Fisch, Harold, *New Stories for Old: Biblical Patterns in the Novel*, St. Martin's Press, New York 1998, 81–99.

Ariel Hirschfeld
Is the Book of Job a Tragedy?[1]

1

The question of the tragic dimension of the Book of Job cuts through the broad swath of issues that surround the terms "Job" and "tragedy." The juxtaposition of these two words evokes two primary symbols, representing two cultures that have supposedly stood in opposition for millennia. "To thee I come," says Shaul Tchernichovsky in his poem "Before the Statue of Apollo," "I am the Jew. Dost thou remember me? / Between us there is enmity forever!"[2]

If these two terms remain frozen in the pristine form of this symbolic configuration – if "Job" remains the symbol of Jewish faith, in its clearest expression; and if "tragedy" continues to represent a world founded wholly on "the beautiful" – then indeed there will be an everlasting battle between the "Jewish" and the "Apollonian." Faced with the fissure between the law of his fathers and the world of Apollo, Tchernichovsky is close to despair:

> The heavens and the boundless wildernesses
> Were short to bridge the wideness set between
> My fathers' children and thou worshippers [...]

Yet his poem maps a shift – "But among those that will return to thee / I am the first" – and closes with a primordial connection between the God of the Jews and the gods of the Greeks:

> I kneel to life, to beauty and to strength,
> I kneel to all the passionate desires
> Which they, the dead-in-life, the bloodless ones,
> The sick, have stifled in the living God,
> The God of wonders of the wilderness,
> The God of gods, Who took Canaan with storm,
> Before they bound Him in Phylacteries.

There is no need to accept Tchernichovsky's idealization at face value. The notion of the primordial splendor of the God of Israel, like the idea of the per-

---

1 This is a shorter version of my article "Ha-im Iyov hu tragedya?,' first published in Hebrew in: *Iyov: ba-mikra ba-hagut ba-omanut*, ed. Lea Mazor, Magnes Press, Jerusalem 1992, 145–51.
2 Tchernichovsky, Shaul, "Before the Statue of Apollo," trans. Maurice Samuel, in: *The Jewish Anthology*, ed. Edmond Fleg. Harcourt Brace, New York 1940, 326.

fect beauty of the Greek gods and culture, is a common Romantic yearning that has not survived the test of modern thought and scholarship, and has faded with other shades of centuries past. However, the idea that emerges from the radical symbol that closes the poem is more complex. It is, fundamentally, Nietzschean: Judaism, (like Christianity), has subjected the body to the spirit – symbolized by the phylactery straps – castrating its primeval vitality, and so condemning it to a historic withering, which the poem embodies in images of desiccated bodies – "corpses of people and the rot of the seed of man." The conceptual scheme that emerges as part of the act of return is fascinating: it is a dynamic symbol which faces the future, while hinting that the void separating the two cultures may be no more than a passing episode, caused by the conceptual imprisonment of Jewish thinking about the divine. In other words, Judaism's vision of itself and its God can be dynamic, open to the influence of the renewed relationship between body and spirit that the poem foretells. The cultural war may be long-lasting, but need not be eternal.

Twentieth-century biblical criticism widened the conception of the biblical text, opening new interpretive modes that would not have been possible at the close of the nineteenth century. Similarly, recent scholarship on tragedy has undermined many of the approaches that had been prevalent since the era of European neo-Classism and neo-Paganism. The concept of "tragedy" can no longer be seen as a simple symbol – neither for "Hellenism," nor for some kind of absolute, defined, and total essence that is the tragic genre. The question of defining the Book of Job as tragedy rests on far more complex foundations than it did in the days of "Before a Statue of Apollo," and even more so than in the era of Barukh Kurzweil's "Job and the Possibility of Biblical Tragedy." What is the Book of Job? Is it that perfection of 1070 verses, or is it a strained compilation of diverse texts, forced into uneasy coexistence so as to be included within the canon? And what is the relationship between these two views? Is the question of the Book of Job's tragic bent the same if we expunge its Conclusion or the Prologue? On the other hand, we need to ask: What is tragedy? We can no longer conceptualize this term through the Aristotelian prism, as does Kurzweil. Despite the fact that tragedy is one of the most distinct genres in the Western tradition, it is clear today that its definition is not fixed, that it is still – or again – comprised of an assortment of various features.[3] If the existing, surviving corpus of Greek tragedy (and not only *Oedipus* and *Antigone*) is an indicator of the original, now partially lost corpus of the Classic tragic genre, then the assortment of features that is tragedy underwent many varied modifi-

---

3 For more on this, see Oliver Taplin, *Greek Tragedy in Action*, Methuen, London 1978.

cations – modifications which, considered *in toto*, leave little of what Aristotle saw as so essential in *Oedipus Rex*.

The meaning of the question "Is Job a tragedy?" is no longer simple. It is open to new directions, which may reveal that the gaping chasm between these two realms of meaning – on one hand, Job's conception of human destiny and faith; on the other, the Greek understanding of fate as embodied in tragedy – is not a law of nature or a definitive necessity, and may not even be a chasm.

It seems we can no longer understand the story of Job without taking into account the critical tradition that developed around the genre of tragedy. Nonetheless, we must clearly differentiate between the features of tragedy – even if they are acknowledged as essential elements of the tragic genre – and the definition of a specific work as tragedy. It is important to recognize the threshold of minimal requirements needed to argue that a certain composition is a tragedy.

2

I will open with a selection of approaches to this question. I focus only on those written within the last fifty years, and only within an explicitly exegetic context – whether in regards to the Book of Job, or the scholarship on the tragic form.

Few consider the Book of Job an actual tragedy. Dorothea Crook's *Elements of Tragedy* is the most elaborate reading of this sort.[4] Crook follows in the footsteps of Sewall's masterpiece, which classifies the Book of Job as a "religious tragedy."[5] For Sewall, the Book of Job is linked to tragedy mainly through the concepts of "suffering" and "pathos." Not only are these integral elements of the plot, but they are also explicitly articulated in the Book of Job in a manner that is incredibly close to expressions found in several Greek tragedies. Crook views the concept of tragedy as a formal schema built of four consecutive sections: the "act of shame or horror"; "suffering"; "knowledge"; and the final "affirmation or reaffirmation of the dignity of the human spirit and the worthwhileness of human life."[6] In other words, she does not dwell on a single determinant factor like "suffering," but rather emphasizes the linkage and sequential development between "suffering" "knowledge" and "reaffirmation" as depicted in the Book of Job. Her key text is "Though he slay me, yet will I

---

4 Crook, Dorothea, *Elements of Tragedy*, Yale University Press, New Haven 1969.
5 Sewall, R. B., *The Vision of Tragedy*, Yale University Press, New Haven 1959, 9–24.
6 Crook, *Elements of Tragedy*, 8.

trust in him; but I will maintain my own ways before him" (13:15),[7] which she reads as expressing the all-consuming need to know the meaning of fate, even at the price of life. The "reaffirmation" comes via the Voice from the Whirlwind, which "consoles him from his suffering."

There is no problem identifying the stages of "suffering" and "knowledge" in the Book of Job, nor in tracing the fundamental linkage between them as a kind of *Agamemnon*-like "suffer and learn." The attempt to see the Voice from the Whirlwind as a "reaffirmation of the dignity of the human spirit" is more problematic, however. In the context of the Book of Job, this is not the straightforward reading Crook presents, but rather a very specific interpretation. More importantly, even if we accept Crook's schema, the Book of Job still does not account for the first stage of tragedy, the "act of shame or horror." What is Job's "shameful" action? And here we must consider: what is God in relation to the Greek gods? In focusing on the supposedly redemptive aspect of the concluding whirlwind speech, Crook ignores these fundamental questions.

I now turn to three critics who reject the possibility of reading the Book of Job as a tragedy: Barukh Kurzweil, Isaiah Leibowitz, and George Steiner.

Kurzweil sees the relation between the Bible and Classical tragedy as contrasting the sacred and whole with the secular, aesthetic and ruptured, where human destiny is embedded in a relativistic, subjective reality. Like Franz Rosenzweig, he views the tragic hero as "trapped within himself," in an inescapable mode of existence."[8] According to this understanding, there can be no tragedy within the biblical context, because human destiny is open to divine grace. "It is possible to take the biblical story out of context, removing it from its place, and imposing upon it the subjectivity of the secular autonomous artist," Kurzweil claims. However, "this tragic construction of the biblical figure is possible only if we completely disconnect the biblical story from its own world. Job, among other biblical figures, can be read as a tragic hero only by ignoring – whether knowingly or unknowingly – the sacred meaning of the text. These readings grow from a turn to secular fiction, in all its forms."[9]

Kurzweil here merges the "religious" with the "monotheistic," and, following this linkage, excludes the tragic from the realm of monotheistic religions. In this view, the divide between "Judaism" and "Hellenism" must remain in

---

7 The Hebrew here offers two alternate forms: the *kri*, the way the verse is traditionally read; and the *khtiv*, its written form. This verse can be read alternatively as "yet will I trust him" or "I will not trust."

8 Kurzweil, Barukh "Iyov ve-efsharut ha-tragedia ha-tanakhit" ("Job and the Possibility of Biblical Tragedy"), in: *Ha-maavak 'al 'erkhei ha-yahadut*, Schocken, Tel Aviv 1970, 11.

9 Kurzweil, "Iyov ve-efsharut ha-tragedia ha-tanakhit," 25.

place, and Kurzweil appoints himself its faithful watchman: "What is the value of those debates, trying to compare that which cannot be compared? [...]. Discussions such as these are based on an apologetic approach, which misses the fundamental point: namely, the acknowledgement of the essential difference between these two worlds – a difference that must be respectfully maintained, without any attempt at mitigation."[10]

In his essay "On the Tragic Elements in the Book of Job,"[11] Kurzweil adds yet another important objection to reading the Book of Job as tragedy. This objection rests on the famous Aristotelian requirement in Chapter 13 of the *Poetics* that the tragic hero not be *too* perfect, as such perfection would undermine the identification necessary for creating the effect of *catharsis*: "A good man must not be seen passing from happiness to misery [as the] ... situation is not fear-inspiring or piteous, but simply odious to us."[12] Job, as Kurzweil points out, is described as "perfect and upright, and one that feared God, and eschewed evil" (1:1).[13] He is therefore an inappropriate choice for a tragic hero, as he does not fulfill the central Aristotelian requirement that tragedy be cathartic. (It is worth mentioning here that Kurzweil found this argument in Mordekhai Hack's annotations to his translation of the *Poetics*. In a comment on the above-quoted sentence from Chapter 13, Hack observes: "for example, the story of Job cannot be a tragedy."[14])

Yet it should be noted that Kurzweil cites the Aristotelian requirement as proof for his argument, without acknowledging that this requirement is based on the assumption that the purpose of tragedy is catharsis – an affect that can be achieved only through a combination of "fear and pity." Kurzweil also ignores the fact that this passage in the *Poetics* does not deal with structure, but rather with the choice of material to fit into a structure. Aristotle is trying to establish the precise prescription for various emotional responses, while correlating them to a precise index of theatrical effects, measuring each in terms of the other.

Leibowitz, for his part, rejects a tragic reading of the Book of Job on the basis of a single fundamental principle: the relationship between the human

---

10 Kurzweil, "Iyov ve-efsharut ha-tragedia ha-tanakhit," 22.

11 Kurzweil "'Al yesodot ha-tragedia be-sefer iyov," in: *Ha-maavak 'al 'erkhei ha-yahadut*, 26–38.

12 Aristotle, *Aristotle on the Art of Poetry*, trans. Ingram Bywater, with a preface by Gilbert Murray, Clarendon Press, Oxford, 1920, Authorama, http://www.authorama.com/the-poetics-14.html (Last accessed 6 May 2014).

13 I have used the King James translation of the Bible throughout, except in specific cases where alternate reading of the Hebrew was required.

14 Aristo, *Poetika, 'al omanut ha-piyut*, Mahbarot le-sifrut, Tel Aviv 1964, 62.

and the divine, or between the biblical conception of humanity and the Classical one. The difference between "a religious belief which is based on man's sense of dependence on God, versus one based on man's awareness of his duty to serve his god, is the difference between *Job* and *Antigone*."[15] Leibowitz relates the conception of the "pagan gods" to the laws of nature, as well as to the Greek *Ananke* ("necessity"). Therefore, "Sophocles's belief in the gods is nothing more than his acceptance of himself and his nature," whereas "the author of the Book of Job is not dealing with issues between man and himself, or between man and nature, but rather the standing of man in the presence of God." God, in his whirlwind speech, tells Job that "being divine, Creation is completely inexplicable."[16] Leibowitz concludes: "What is the relation between Sophocles and the author of Job? The same as the relation between fearing God for ulterior motives, and fearing God out of an awareness of God."

Steiner, for his part, opens his *Death of Tragedy* by relating to the Book of Job in his grand declaration:

> Tragedy is alien to the Judaic sense of the world. The book of Job is always cited as an instance of tragic vision. But that black fable stands on the outer edge of Judaism, and even there an orthodox hand has asserted the claims of justice over tragedy: "So the Lord blessed the latter end of Job more than the beginning: for he had fourteen thousand sheep, and six thousand camels, and a thousand yoke of oxen, and a thousand she-asses." God has made good the havoc wrought upon his servant; he has compensated Job for his agonies [...] The Judaic spirit is vehement in its conviction that the order of the universe and man's estate is accessible to reason. The ways of the Lord are neither wanton nor absurd.[17]

In noting the difference between Hellenism and Judaism, Steiner states:

> The Judaic vision sees in disaster a specific moral fault or failure of understanding. The Greek tragic poets assert that the forces which shape or destroy our lives lie outside the governance of reason or justice. Worse than that: there are around us demonic energies which prey upon the soul and turn it to madness or which poison our will so that we inflict irreparable outrage upon ourselves and those we love [...] To the Jew there is a marvelous continuity between knowledge and action; to the Greek an ironic abyss.[18]

---

15 Leibowitz, Yeshayahu, "Ben iyov le-sophakles," in: *Yahadut, 'am yehudi, u-medinat yisrael*, Schocken Tel Aviv, 1975, 395–397.
16 Leibowitz, "Ben iyov le-sophakles", 397.
17 Steiner, George, *The Death of Tragedy*, Alfred A. Knopf, London 1961, 4.
18 Steiner, *The Death of Tragedy*, 6–7.

3

Today, we witness the emergence of a new perspective on tragedy – a view unconstrained by Aristotle's definitions of the genre. We can now include other issues and emphases in our consideration of the topic, which might finally liberate it from the conceptual quagmire in which it has sunk. In the following sections, I will highlight two central components of tragedy, while tracing their presence within the Book of Job. Both are connected to the interrelation between the human and the divine in the tragic world; both create a structure – a pattern of relationship – that precedes and subsumes any concrete (narrative) sequence. Both are necessary elements of tragedy, though only the second is both necessary and definitive

I do not wish to refute the unmistakable difference between the biblical and the Greek conception of the divine. Yet it is impossible to deny that, despite these differences, the Book of Job's vision of the divine shares an essential element, not with the pagan vision as a whole, but specifically with the tragic view of the gods – namely, a lack of understanding, a palpable detachment, between the human and the divine.

Steiner's avoidance of the verse regarding the return of Job's children in the Epilogue is symptomatic. It is interesting that the Sages could not ignore the problem inherent in the fact that God gives other children *in place* of those who died. They cannot but assert that the children returned to Job are the very ones he thought dead.[19] For the final blessing, like the disaster and bereavement that open the story, descends from above. It is unexpected and incomprehensible, expressing once again the disconnection and arbitrariness of the divine deed in relation to the human realm. The Epilogue solves nothing; it does not point to any sort of "marvelous continuity between knowledge and action" that supposedly characterizes the Judaic. While it might point to some kind of continuity, the Book of Job is far from aggrandizing or celebrating it. Leibowitz rightly does not attempt to bridge what cannot be bridged in the Book of Job: namely, the lack of comprehension dividing the human and the divine. The God who demands of Abraham "Take now thy son, thine only son Isaac, whom thou lovest" (Genesis 22:2) understands Abraham's life and world. He recognizes the full meaning of the relationship, the depth of the pain, that He is evoking in his request for sacrifice. The God of the Book of Job understands nothing.

It is possible to accept Leibowitz's approach (which is essentially a variation of Maimonides's), that the irrelevance of God's whirlwind speech is pre-

---

19 See Amos Hahamm, *Sefer iyov (da'at mikra)*, Mosad ha-rav kuk, Jerusalem 1970, 331, note 108.

cisely the point (or part of the point). To quote the *Guide for the Perplexed:* "there is a difference between God's rule, providence, and intention in reference to all natural forces, and our rule, providence, and intention in reference to things which are the objects of our rule, providence, and intention [...] we should not fall into the error of imagining His knowledge to be similar to ours, or His intention, providence, and rule similar to ours."[20] But it is impossible not to see that the Book of Job juxtaposes the word of God with the questions of Man, calling attention to the chasm between them. Job poses questions that arise from a rich, complex, human world, which God neither relates to nor understands.[21]

The gap of comprehension separating the divine and the human is one of the most fundamental elements of Classical drama, and it is explicitly expressed in the tragedies of Euripides, albeit in a condensed, terse form. Consider the words of Artemis at the closing of *Hippolytus*, when, she looks down from on high at Hippolytus's dismembered body: "I see you, but can shed no tears."[22] The final, harrowing scene of the *Bacchae* expresses a similar idea. The god Dionysus appears on stage, entering the city of Thebes to stand before the people he has destroyed – the elderly Cadmus and the queen, Agave, who still clutches the body of the son she had slaughtered while in a frenzy of possession by Dionysus.

> *Dionysus:* It is I who announce these dooms, I, Dionysus, born not of mortal father, but of Zeus. And if you had chosen to be wise when you did not choose it, you would have acquired Zeus's son as an ally, and would now be happy.
> *Cadmus:* Dionysus, we beseech you, we have sinned.
> *Dionysus:* You have learned too late; you did not know it when you should have.
> *Cadmus:* Now I understand, but your punishment lacks all mercy.
> *Dionysus:* True. I am a god.[23]

More striking than any difference between Euripides's tragedy and the Book of Job's respective perceptions of the divine is the shared insistence on a terrible gap between, on one hand, the complexity of fate, depth of emotion, and power of endurance within the human realm, and, on the other, the simple, almost

---

20 Maimonides, *Guide to the Perplexed*, trans. M. Friedländer, Routledge & Kegan Paul Ltd., London 1904, Part III, Chapter 26, 303, *Sacred Texts*, http://www.sacred-texts.com/jud/gfp (last accessed 6 May 2014).
21 See Paul Ricoeur, "The Wicked God and the 'Tragic Vision' of Existence," in: *The Symbolism of Evil*, trans. Emerson Buchanan, Beacon Press, Boston 1969, 211–227.
22 Euripides, *Hippolytus*, line 1396. Translation based on Ariel Hirschfeld's translation to Hebrew.
23 Euripides, *Bacchae*, line 1340–1348. Translation based on Ariel Hirschfeld's Hebrew.

blank, divine perception of itself in relation to humanity. "*Thus* did my father Zeus approve it long ago,"[24] says Dionysus to Cadmus, rather than offering any explanation. "Where wast thou when I laid the foundations of the earth? declare, if thou hast understanding" (Job, 38:4), God asks, in response to Job's questions. His rhetorical questions surely provide no answer.

Even if the frame-story was not originally an integral part of the Book of Job, but rather attached at a later date to integrate the book with the theology of the Bible, this fundamental gap between the human and the divine still stands. For it is specifically this frame-story that was attached to this specific poem. In other words, it is possible that this same gap might exist between the theology of the Bible and the poem included within the frame-story.

4

Let us turn to the second component of tragedy: namely, hubris, the key concept that defines the notion of human destiny as presented in the works of the Classical tragedians. This complex term – which can be translated as "arrogance," "pride," "haughtiness," "complacency" and "innocence" simultaneously – is far more encompassing than might seem from the writings of Aristotle. According to Aristotle, "hubris" is one of the structural constituents of a plot that includes a fall, which in turn engenders a response of *catharses* – the supposed purpose of the genre as a whole. Hubris catalyzes the *hamartia*, the famous fatal flaw that leads to the *todainon*, the shameful action. Yet hubris is actually connected to a much broader, cyclic principle, which extends well beyond the closed framework of the cathartic effect. It is part of a rhythmic pattern associated with the outer limits of the concept of *dike* – not justice in the moral sense, but rather the realignment of forces that have been set off balance.[25] These forces can be, amongst others, the intellectual versus the emotional; the divine versus the human; the cultural versus the savage; the refined and complex versus the primal and simple; the masculine versus the feminine. The balance that is attained at the end of Aeschylus's *Oresteia* between Athena and the avenging goddesses in determining the fate of Orestes (he and his destiny are the loci of the struggle and negotiations) is an equilibrium achieved through an entire sequence of states of hubris, each of which is eliminated or

---

24 Euripides, *Bacchae*, line 1349.
25 See Walter Burkert, *Greek Religion: Archaic and Classical*, trans. John Raffan, Harvard University Press, Cambridge 1985, pp. 130, 185, 249.

adjusted in the course of the trilogy. These states of hubris gradually progress, slowly ascending the ladder of cultural development, until they eventually enable the hero of the trilogy to bridge the opposition between the various forces that have been set askew. This pattern does not necessarily lead to catastrophe. It is only Aristotle who makes catastrophe the definitive structural element of tragedy. Disaster can actually be considered a single component of a broader, rhythmic framework, a temporary and secondary stage.

The tragic trajectory thus traces the progression of the *hubris-dike* sequence. It uncovers the trauma inherent in this progression when it occurs within the life of a human being; yet it also points to the unfolding of life, the formation of personality, and the achievement of maturity. The divine force in tragedy embodies this process as an inescapable law. The reach of this law, however, as well as its implementation, impact, and meaning, are found in the human realm. The experience of the gap between the human and the divine – which, as we have seen, is a prominent aspect of the Book of Job – is enwrapped with the person's dawning awareness, when faced with *dike,* of the gap between law and life, a gap which reflects the gap between a word and its meaning (a word: mark, sentence, prophecy; meaning: presence, action, affinity). The person comprehends the failure, or refusal, of the divine to understand or pity at the very moment that his endurance becomes strong enough to bear the consciousness of his utter solitude. This moment is often the peak of suffering, and is occasionally marked by the act of cursing life, cursing the day of birth.

Only the prevalence of the Aristotelian approach to the tragic could conceal the prominent presence of the definitive principle of "hubris-leading-to-*dike*" in the Book of Job. Job is in fact a spectacular example of hubris: the supreme hubris of perfection. Few heroes of Greek tragedy approach this hubris, and perhaps only one resembles Job: namely, Alcestis. Yet we must remember that even among the surviving texts to which we have access, there are almost no duplicate forms of hubris. Job is "perfect and upright ... feared God, and eschewed evil" (1:1), yet his children feasted every day, and Job would wake each morning to offer sacrifices to the number of his children, lest "my sons have sinned, and cursed God in their hearts. Thus did Job continually" (1:5). Job creates a perfect structure to "eschew evil" – not only for himself, in his own life, but even for those closest to him. He tries to impose it upon his sons to the point that he can control even their inner drives. On a moral level, this might seem an image of perfection. Yet it discloses a fundamental warpage: Job views his children not as separate people but rather as an extension of his own identity. This is a distinctly omnipotent mode of belief, for Job does not truly acknowledge the power of evil, of physicality, of flesh, of urges and of drives.

The imbalance between good and evil is echoed perfectly in the mirror version of the story in the divine realm, where the Adversary says "Hast not thou made an hedge about him, and about his house, and about all that he hath on every side? thou hast blessed the work of his hands, and his substance is increased in the land" (1:10). The Adversary exposes the artificiality – indeed, the falseness – of Job's perfection. This is why his words trigger God's response: "Behold, all that he hath is in thy power" (1:12). God's words reflect the moment when perfection collapses into its opposite. The continuity between hubris and *dike* perfectly explains the particular relationship between God and the Adversary in the Book of Job. The Joban Adversary is neither a demon nor an embodiment of evil; he does not persecute Job but rather questions his mode of perfection. Only Christianity and post-biblical Judaism could exaggerate the figure of the Adversary in the story in this way, thereby damaging the delicate exactitude of his characterization and of his moral and theological position.

This is where the textual structure of the Book of Job, with its development, sequencing and unique phraseology, must be taken into account. It is specifically here, in the system of internal linkages, that the Book of Job's original, precise conception of the divine is embodied – a conception that the midrashic extrapolations of the Sages have blurred and concealed.

With meticulous, exacting literary analysis, Meir Weiss, in his magnum opus "The Story of Job's Beginning,"[26] uncovers a precise parallel between what happens on earth and what happens in the heavens in the first chapter of the Book of Job. Moreover, he demonstrates that the shifts on earth chronologically precede the events in the heavens within the narrative sequence:

> A full parallel of the two descriptions – that of heaven, and that of earth – would demand not only that Job's "sending" for his sons have some echo in the gathering of the "sons of God"; but also that the gathering be in response to a sudden doubt in an exacting father's heart regarding the righteousness of his sons. And indeed this is the case, except that the author *embodied* the skepticism in the figure of The Adversary.[27]

In this argument, Weiss comes close to Maimonides's approach to the relationship between God and humanity. Like Maimonides,[28] he defines the Adversary by interweaving two exegetic approaches. First, an analysis of the phraseology that is unique to the Joban Adversary (from the level of sentences; to words;

---

26 Weiss, Meir, "Ha-sipur 'al reishito shel iyov," in: *Iyunim* 40 (1969). In English: *The Story of Job's Beginning: Job 1–2: A Literary Analysis*, Magnes Press, Jerusalem 1983.
27 Weiss, 41.
28 Maimonides, *Guide to the Perplexed*, Part III, Chapter 22, 297 onwards.

to sound patterns). Second, through a comparison to related scenes in other parts of the Bible, which leads Weiss, like Maimonides, to relate the Book of Job's Adversary with Zachariah's concept of the angelic.

> Both in Zechariah and in Job, The Adversary is a hypostasis. Not of actual opposition to God, but rather of one of His opposing characteristics. He is the embodiment of the ambivalence of God himself.[29]

The Book of Job's virtuosic play on the word *blessing* (Hebrew root *brkh* ברכ), which continuously turns into *curse*, is only a single aspect of a perfection that continuously approaches its opposite. It is no coincidence that the Adversary's declaration that "he will curse [*ye-varkh-kha* יְבָרְכֶךָ, literally, 'he will bless'] thee to thy face" (1:11) echoes Job's own words: "It may be that my sons have sinned, and cursed [*verkhu* בֵרְכוּ, literally, 'blessed'] God in their hearts" (1:5).

Weiss's essay is a wonderful example of the type of process implemented by Tchernichovsky in his poem, a process indicative of the change and development that the conception of the divine can undergo within the Jewish and Hebrew discourse. This development paradoxically leads to a more primordial connection, as Weiss's literary approach (which draws upon modern scholarship) allows the original text to speak with the inherent power and gravity embodied in its "aesthetic" narrative structure. It reveals how the religious function interacts with, and is dependent upon, the aesthetics of the specific text. A comparison between Weiss's and Maimonides's analyses of the Adversary illuminates this point. Maimonides, who well understands the unique nature of the Joban Adversary, nonetheless connects him to, on one hand, the Aristotelian conception of matter and form, and, on the other, the Sages' traditional view of the Adversary on the other. This deprecates the figure of the Adversary, pushing him to an extreme that disconnects him from his unique Joban role as an element of the divine. He becomes instead a personification of "matter," as opposed to divine "form"; and he is also, to quote Reish Lakish in the Talmud, the "evil inclination and the angel of death."

From this perspective, the Voice from the Whirlwind sounds like a series of questions revolving around the control of the forces of nature – forces which are ultimately embodied in the two great beasts of sea and land that appear at the closing; it is a declaration of the cache of powers that stand in opposition to the simplicity of the original care to "eschew evil" – the Stygian forces of matter, energy, flesh, urges and drives. Thus, the Address indeed responds to something that precedes the question of actions and their consequences. God

---

29 Weiss, 42.

presents Himself as the primal power that contains and balances the various elements and forces that man could only imagine to control.

Job, as he stands facing the divine, says, "Wherefore I abhor myself, and repent of dust and ashes" (42:6). God declares that he has now spoken the "thing that is right [*nekhona*]" (42:7). The term *nekhona* refers to "appropriateness," "correctness," "suitability," the balancing and adjustment of two elements. Job's initial simplicity at the opening of the story was not *nekhona*; it was not finely calibrated. It was a "blessing" that necessarily contained its opposite, as a denied, contradictory force. The Job of the closing is no longer simple.

The Epilogue that closes the Book of Job is no stranger to the spirit of Classical drama. The divine unity of the final address – a unity that contains contrasting forces, as opposed to the split Being we encounter at the opening of the book – resembles the change that takes place in Erinyes at the closing of the *Oresteia*, where the goddesses of revenge turn into the *Semnai* – the "kindly ones."

5

Clearly, the disparity between the monotheism of the Book of Job and the polytheism of classical tragedy is fundamental. The multiplicity of the Greek conception of the divine demands the involvement of various gods, representing different forces, for the establishment of *dike*. By contrast, in the Book of Job, the various forces are united within a single divinity that encompasses and exceeds the sum of its parts. The Book of Job, more than any other book in the Bible, presents the divine as the unity of the manifold. God's absolute mastery over the universal (monstrous) forces of nature establishes Him as above and inclusive of them. The Greek gods, in contradistinction, remain in continuous struggle with the destructive forces of nature. To quote Aharon Shabtai:

> The Olympian gods (who represent the interactive, constructive aspect of power) subjugate the archaic gods, the Titans (who represent the destructive, uncaring, aspect). But the victory of Zeus is achieved only on the organizational side of the cosmos. The archaic powers (the Titans and the female descendants of Night) are not annihilated. They remain a part of the tragic structure of the world and of society.[30]

---

30 Shabtai, Aharon, "Introduction", in: *Aeschylus, Agamemnon, Schocken Books* Tel Aviv 1990, 9.

Moreover, the Greek conception of the divine posits a twofold existence. The gods are both personalities with a physical presence, and abstract universal forces that act within the world, nature, and the human soul. This conception is the source of much of the dramatic tension between humans and gods in tragedy. The gods are the cause both of hubris and of its destruction; they are simultaneously without and within.

The biblical conception of God does not allow this kind of psychologization of the divine. Yet in the Prologue and throughout the progression toward the whirlwind speech, the Book of Job constructs an equivalent configuration. Anomalously, the divine happening is, as we shall see, regarded not only as synchronic with the earthly realm, but also as a magnified, externalized parallel to human psychology. In the initial exchange in the Heavens, the Adversary intimates that God is responsible for Job's supposed perfection: "Hast not thou made an hedge about him?" (1:10). This reveals that God is also the embodiment of the core of the personality, or – to be more precise – that He symbolizes and protects it: "only upon himself put not forth thine hand" (1:12), God initially commands. When the Adversary returns, God becomes more specific, insisting on one boundary that is not to be crossed: "Behold, he is in thine hand; but save his life-spirit [nefesh]" (2:7). The nefesh, the life-force, the soul, is the fundamental connection between matter and spirit. Nefesh is life and vitality: "and the Lord God ... breathed into his nostrils the breath of life; and man became a living soul [nefesh haya]" (Genesis 2:6). It is a cognate of breath (neshima), of life, and also refers to the most unique, hidden, aspects of the self: "With my soul [nefesh] have I desired thee in the night; yea, with my spirit within me will I seek thee early" (Isaiah 26:9); and "the soul of Jonathan was knit with the soul of David, and Jonathan loved him as his own soul [nefesh]" (Samuel 1:18). The idea of *physical desire* is an extension of this linkage of matter and spirit: "thou mayest eat grapes thy fill at thine own soul [nefesh]" (Deuteronomy 23:24). So too is the conception of *will* – "If it be your mind [nefesh]" (Genesis 23:8); and emotion that is separated and opposed to the body – to quote the Book of Job: "But his flesh upon him shall have pain, and his soul [nefesh] within him shall mourn" (Job 14:22). Thus, Maimonides's argument that the nefesh in the Book of Job represents *only* the spiritual, as opposed to the physical, is untenable:

> This is expressed in the words, "But keep away from his soul" (Job. ii. 6). I have already shown you the homonymous use of the term "soul" (nefesh) in Hebrew (Part I., chap. xli.). It designates that element in man that survives him; it is this Portion over which the Adversary has no power.[31]

---

31 Maimonides, *Guide to the Perplexed*, Part III, Chapter 22, 298.

The drama of the Book of Job is the clash between the opposing forces in the universe, within humanity and within the human body, in the meeting of matter with spirit. God's words imply that the Adversary *can* impact even the *nefesh* itself – except that in this case God intercedes to protect the *nefesh* from utter annihilation. This protection is a crucial component of the dramatic structure of the Book of Job as tragedy.

The concepts of "spirit" and "matter" are the primary symbols in the process Job undergoes. In the opening, Job curses life as a whole (the inversion of the initial "blessing"), nullifying the value of human existence: "Let the day perish wherein I was born, and the night in which it was said, There is a man child conceived" (3:3). This undoing of birth leads to a longing for a primordial, earlier form of human existence – that of a fetus in the womb – an existence that precedes any consciousness or conflict: "Why died I not from the womb? why did I not give up the ghost when I came out of the belly? / Why did the knees prevent me? or why the breasts that I should suck? / For now should I have lain still and been quiet, I should have slept: then had I been at rest" (3:11–13). In the course of the Joban *pathos*, Job's mind gradually connects between this curse of life and the disaster, so that the curse transforms into a kind of awareness. It is no longer internal turmoil, but rather the *awareness* of turmoil, that causes the total breakdown of the mind: "Though I were perfect, I know not my soul: I despise my life" (9:21) and especially "My soul is weary of my life; I will leave my complaint upon myself; I will speak in the bitterness of my soul" (10:1).

From this point onwards, Job constructs a new conception of the interrelations between the body and the spirit. This conception is fashioned, segment by segment, throughout the section running from Chapter 10 to Chapter 28 – from the description of God's embodiment of man in matter (10:8–12) to the account of the human capacity to rule over the material world, be it in the domain of natural resources or agriculture (28:1–11). This involvement in the question of the interaction of spirit and matter seems a minor philosophical issue until Chapter 28, but eventually becomes (through the connection between Chapter 28 and Elihu's speeches) the primary stage in the growth of Job's awareness, leading to his full recognition of God's response. This process is incredibly complex, and plays out in two divergent modes and expressions, whose affinity is not always readily apparent. One aspect is figurative; the other philosophical. Their mode of depiction is also opposed: one is synthetic; the other analytic.

6 The Figurative Aspect: "Dust and Ashes"

The figurative depiction of this process spans the entire book, and revolves around the ever-changing implications of the phrase "dust and ashes." Its appearance in Chapter 30, in Job's retrospective summation of his life, is indicative. In this final response, Job reviews the course of his life and unfurls the complete structure of the development of his story: Chapter 29 is dedicated to the lost wholeness of his former existence – an existence as protected as that of a fetus in the womb, but now transformed into hubris. Chapter 30 turns to the breakdown, which is presented as a complete inversion: the preserved good and excessive honor are transformed into shame. The central verse here is 30:15: "Terrors [*balahot*] are turned [*ha-hefakh*] upon me: they pursue my soul as the wind: and my welfare passeth away as a cloud." This verse – Job's most exact articulation of the disaster – is also an accurate definition of the tragic catastrophe, which is structured as a *peripateia*, a "turnabout." (The unique configuration *ha-hefakh*, a verb form of the root *h-f-kh*, "reversal," "opposite" can be seen as relating to the form *balahot*, "terrors," as in "the terrors turned and fell upon me." However, the structure of the parallelism opens the possibility of a more complex reading: "the good of my life turned [*ha-hefak*] to terror," with the subject of the verset missing but implied.) This verse leads Job to restate his situation in the present, in a reiterated series of descriptions and questions thrown at God. Each series of questions revolves around a single verse describing Job's bodily state. In the first cycle, the verse – which flows directly from the description of the catastrophe – is 30:19: "He hath cast me into the mire, and I am become like dust and ashes."

Reading the Book of Job in sequence, one is struck by the recurrent presence of a series of phrases constructed around these two symbols of matter: "Dust and ashes" (*afar ve-efer*) represent here, and in the Bible as a whole, the opposing, complementary forces to "soul" and "spirit" in a human entity.

> "And he took him a potsherd to scrape himself withal; and he sat down among the *ashes*." (2:8)
> "My flesh is clothed with worms and clods of *dust*; my skin is broken, and become loathsome." (7:5)
> "... for now shall I sleep in the *dust*; and thou shalt seek me in the morning, but I shall not be." (7:21)
> "He hath cast me into the mire, and I am become like *dust and ashes*." (30:19)
> "Wherefore I abhor myself, and repent of *dust and ashes*." (42:6)

First, the appearance of the phrase "dust and ashes" in Chapter 30 establishes the pairing as a structural element of the story. It becomes a marker indicating the domain defined by the catastrophic shattering. Second, a close look at the five uses of these terms reveals a process which revolves around the changing relationship of the "I" (within the human realm) and the pairing of "dust and ashes." In the beginning, the "I" is literally mired in the ash, in accordance with the accepted mourning customs. The ash here has an entirely realistic meaning that is nonetheless connected to its external, accepted symbolism. In Chapter 7, the dual meaning of dust – both as an image for the color and texture of Job's infected skin, and as an expression heightening the sensation of disease in the body – works to create an intense experience of *death in life*. The reiteration of the word "dust" in verse 21 further amplifies this feeling: there is a dramatic, fully spatial, perception that death is a fast-approaching event within the speaker's consciousness. Through the links between Chapters 2 and 7, the author creates a situation in which the phrase "dust and ashes" is happening in actuality, with Job literally sitting within the ashes.

Towards the end of the process, Job's growing awareness connects these two words, in two different relations. The first connection is through figuration or simile – "I am become *like*"; the second is of identity or metaphor – "I repent of dust and ashes." The "dust and ashes" can be read here as an apposition, establishing an equivalence to the "I": I repent myself, that I am dust and ashes. "Dust and ashes" has now become a state of consciousness, unfurling the awareness that was initially present without being fully understood. This progression of consciousness is constructed in explicitly spatial terms, as a movement from the outside in; it is a gradual internalization. We move from the outer environment, through the skin and the body, into figuration and then into the very "I," into the center of the *nefesh*. This internalization closes the gap between "skin" and "soul"/*nefesh* that is present in the Adversary's words at the opening of the story: "Skin for skin, yea, all that a man hath will he give for his soul [*nefesh*]" (2:4). The journey towards identification with "dust and ashes" breaks down the primal opposition between dust and soul, creating full awareness of the metaphysics embedded within matter. The *nefesh* is embedded in the body, and the body as a whole both contains and represents it. Replacing the word "I" with "dust and ashes" to the point that any connecting word ("like" or "I will become") disappears is a complete identification of the *nefesh* with "matter" – a merging which is similar to the identification of God with the powers of nature in the whirlwind speech. In both cases, the supremacy of spirit over matter (or the divine over the world) is rendered tangible through the ability to *verbalize*. In other words, the *nefesh* is the ability to say "dust and ashes" as a signifier and not a signified. In the Book of Job, as we have seen, the "signifier" is the realm of the divine.

7 The Philosophic Aspect: Elihu

The appearance of Elihu son of Barachel is a profoundly important event in the tragic structure of the Book of Job. His entrance is a necessary step in building the tragic equilibrium that is achieved in the aftermath of God's whirlwind speech. Indeed, his words are a kind of human prefiguration of God's own, both in content and in how they interrupt the predictable sequencing of the dialogues forming the "pathos" section of the story. This structure is broken first by Job, when he "moreover continued his parable" (27:1), rather than clearing the stage for the next round of responses. Instead, Job continues to discuss the issues he raised in his last "parables" – issues to which his former friends no longer respond. Elihu is the first outsider to enter and reply to a mechanism already in place, and which had actually been summed up in Job's previous speech. Elihu also departs from the basic assumptions that have implicitly governed the discussion up to this point (and which still crop up at the closing of Job's words) – namely, that fate is set in response to sin, punishment and righteousness (in its most palpably moral sense); he even ironically cites Job's own self-perception regarding his "cleanness" and "innocence" (33:8–11)! "I am young," (32:6) states Elihu, thus removing himself from yet another set of assumptions: it is not empirical life experience that is needed here, but rather a sudden breakthrough – or leap – of awareness. It is worth noting that Elihu's name is formed of two phrases: Eli-hu ("He is my God") and Barakh-El ("Bless God"). In terms of the plot structure, Elihu plays the role of the messenger, or mediator, between man and knowledge. It is a role similar to that of Neoptolemus in *Aias*: Neoptolemus is the pure youth who stands between the swindling, corrupt Odysseus, and heavenly revelation (represented by Herakles, who appears from on high and reveals to Aias the future impact of his decision to aid his people).

The thrust of Elihu's speech, the pivotal point that causes the "turn" (or *peripateia*, the reversal that moves "non-knowledge to knowledge," to use Aristotle's formulation),[32] is his significant contention regarding the revelation of the divine *within* the human. In his first address (33:15–30), Elihu declares that the divine is revealed to the human in two unique ways: in dreams, and in disease.

---

32 Aristotle, *Aristotle on the Art of Poetry*, Section II.

7.1 Dreams

In a dream, in a vision of the night,
when deep sleep falleth upon men, in slumberings upon the bed;
Then he openeth the ears of men,
and sealeth their instruction,
That he may withdraw man from his purpose,
and hide pride from man.
He keepeth back his soul [*nefesh*] from the pit [*shahat* שחת],
and his life from perishing by the sword. (33:15–18)

Elihu's initial contention is constructed in two stages: first, God reveals Himself in dreams; second, this revelation comes to undo actions and "pride" that would otherwise lead to "the pit" and death. The key point is that the revelation in dreams is private and individual, a knowledge that comes from within, rather than from holy writ or any other socially or culturally accepted forms of knowledge ("when deep sleep falleth upon *men*"). It is specifically this type of knowledge, which comes from the private and the hidden, that serves to balance pride and prevent the fall into the abyss lurking below.

The two stages create a twofold structure: waking versus sleep (which parallels "social" versus "private"); and the state of "pride," which is opposed to the "pit" of the underworld and to death. The social, or the "known," enables the kind of deeds and "pride" that will eventually lead to the "pit" of death. For the "social" allows only a partial, limited knowledge of the divine – a knowledge that must be supplemented by the private awareness that reveals itself in sleep. Only thus can death be prevented and life preserved. (Notice, in verse 18, the complementary relationship between the concepts of *nefesh* and life!)

It is not a stretch of the imagination to see here the principle of balance and equilibrium between different types of knowledge, and the deadly danger that awaits those who are misaligned, who are deaf to the voice of dreams. "Dreams," in this conception, can be seen as the eruption of the unconscious – as an alternative route to consciousness that breaks free of the ordinary, logical, and socially accepted, while providing direct conduit between that which is most subjective and personal and that which is most universal and encompassing.[33] It is worth noting that the Job of the opening is concerned only with

---

33 Elihu's model of dreams is fundamentally different than that of Eliphaz in Chapter 4, which opens with the same formulation: "In thoughts from the visions of the night, when deep sleep falleth on men" (4:13). Elihu speaks of dreams that play a part in every person's life by balancing the human soul, not a revelation aimed at a chosen few.

the knowledge of waking men – "[he] *rose up* early in the morning, and offered burnt offerings" (1:5) – this, even when it comes to his atoning for unknown (and possibly non-existent) actions ("It *may* be that my sons have sinned" [1:5]) committed while feasting!

7.2 Disease

Elihu's claim regarding the role of disease opens by positing a specific conception of illness: that it is a kind of message, and one of the divine modes of communication – "He is *chastened* also with pain upon his bed" (33:19). But the broader context of the verse creates a more complex claim: that disease comes in response to a more severe type of non-listening, of disconnection between man and knowledge. It is the dragging of the living man into "the pit," as indicated by the repetition of the word *shahat* שַׁחַת in the two claims:

> He keepeth back his soul from the *pit* [*shahat*],
> and his life from perishing by the sword. (33:18)

> Yea, his soul draweth near unto the *pit* [*shahat*],
> and his life to the destroyers (33:22)

> Then he is gracious unto him, and saith,
> Deliver him from going down to the *pit* [*shahat*]: I have found a ransom. (33:24)

Disease is presented here as a second-tier, drastic level of response to human non-listening, pride, and hubris. A man who knows how to listen to what is said within his dreams "keepeth back his soul from the pit"; however, he who closes himself off will fall ill, until he hears the divine speech within his very body and flesh. We see here a process of repression, a kind of atresia of consciousness, which drives content from the *nefesh* into the body in order to cause a shockwave powerful enough to crumble the barriers of consciousness. Illness, which draws the living man close to the experience of death in life (to use a variation of Job's own words), is understood as annihilating the flesh until it is barely visible (or as destroying its appearance until it cannot be looked upon): "His flesh is consumed away, that it cannot be seen" (33:21). Thus, it propels the power of consciousness from the flesh back to the spirit. The relationship between the body and the "I" is also a dialogue here.

Elihu's claim is an exact – but inverted – parallel to the dialogue between God and the Adversary in the Prologue. The fall into the "pit" is understood as resulting from a blockage that is an inversion of the divine "hedge" of protection in the Prologue ("Hast not thou made an hedge about him, and about his house, and about all that he hath on every side?" [1:10]). It is a block *against* the penetration of the divine word that emerges from the hidden (the dream). This is a reversed but complementary picture, which – like the dialogue between God and the Adversary, and the misfortunes that descend on Job – contains a two-pronged process: the dream and the disease, which are an appropriate, balancing inversion and that eventually lead to "uprightness" (33:23) by revealing the depths of the "pit."

This is the pivotal turning point, and verse 23 is the keystone on which everything rests. As with the Prologue, we have the sudden appearance of a quasi-divine figure: an angel (whose role is the opposite of the Adversary's), who comes (in complementary inversion) to "mediate" between the "deeps" at the nadir of destruction ("the pit"), and the "heights" of the divine. The central change is emphasized not only through the sudden appearance of the angel, who serves as man's champion (*melitz* – "interpreter," "mediator," – also implies "defender," "champion"), but also by the process that takes place throughout the verses describing the fall, and the escape from it – the climax being the turnabout between verses 22 and 23:

> 22: Yea, his soul draweth unto the pit,
> And his life to his destroyers.
> 23: If there is an angel for him,
> A mediator, one among a thousand,
> To show man his uprightness [יָשְׁרוֹ] [...]

The role of this suddenly present angel is to be understood through Elihu's allusion, via the phrase "one among a thousand," to Job's words in Chapter 9, when Job lamented "If He will contend with him, he cannot answer Him one of a thousand" (9:3). Job's earlier words can be read as referring to God, who, despite His immense, overwhelming powers, has chosen to "contend" with man. Already at this point in Chapter 9, the word *ma'ane* – "answer," "address" – is imbedded within the divine. True, it is presented in the negative, as a description of the divine's terrible powers, so far beyond any human ken. Nonetheless, it also contains the first intimations of dialogue and understanding. The number "one among a thousand," cited by Job in order to make palpable the excess of divine arguments that cannot ever be answered for overabundance, becomes, for Elihu, a positive possibility. This use of the conditional ("If there is"), which resonates with Job's formulation ("if he will contend"), is pregnant with meaning. It can be understood on two levels. The first, more obvious sense is: if the angel explains even "one of a thousand" of God's words, then "man" will respond with the first intimations of understanding. However, the parallelism between "angel" and *melitz* ("mediator," "defender") opens the door to a more extreme interpretation: "if there is an angel for him" –

that is, there may or may not be; *if* this man has an angel, one among thousands, who will serve as mediator to "show" God's "uprightness" – which ultimately is also his own.[34] This statement demonstrates the fragility and instability of the projected positive reversal. It is not at all clear that a man can rise from the fallen state of "death in life," ascending from the depths with an understanding of the "uprightness" of the divine. It can happen only if there is a small component, "one of a thousand" – whether in the *nefesh* or in the heavens that are its parallel – that is capable of connecting the shattered parts ("mediator ... to show"). *If* and only if such a component exists, it opens the door to the complete renewal described in the subsequent verses.

The phrase "to show man his uprightness" (*yoshro* יִשְׁרוֹ), which closes this fascinating verse, confers a double aspect on the word "uprightness" (*y'sh'r*). It is both the "uprightness" of God and the uprightness of man, of the upper and the lower realms together. The placement of the word "uprightness" here diverts it from its usual idiomatic connotation of "just" and "ethical," which is its usage at the opening of the story – "that man was perfect and upright" (1:1) – and in Bildad's words – "if thou wert pure and upright" (8:6). *Yashar* is restored here to its original, literal, meaning of "straight," a line that is not crooked, cognate of a flat "plane" (*mishor* מִישׁוֹר). It is the shortest line connecting between the high and low, the upper and lower realms; the perpendicular balancing plumb-line that appears in Amos 7:7 and Isaiah 40:12. This primary, geometric meaning of the word is defined through opposition to the "crooked." As such, it speaks of inherent tension and relationship, rather than of something that exists in and of itself. Within the context of Elihu's address, the word comes to connote the balance between opposing forces and dimensions: high and low; life and death; spirit and matter. Thus, it can be understood as the distillation of the divine power of "wisdom," the same power manifested in the archetypal concepts that God places before Job in His whirlwind speech: "Where wast thou when I laid the foundations of the earth? declare, if thou hast understanding. Who hath laid the measures thereof, if thou knowest? or who hath stretched the line upon it?" (38:4–5).

The crux of God's address is not the abundance of phenomena, substances and animals; it is the quiet harmony of adding them together. God enumerates myriad oppositions in various "measurements" of perception: large-small, hot-cold, predator-prey, high-low, solid-liquid, and matter-spirit, among others. Against them stands a single, harmonious power – a balancing (of the sum, beginning, end, dimensions, boundaries, etc.) that creates the whole.

---

34 In Hebrew, the referent of the "his," (i.e., the possessive ending of "*yoshro* יִשְׁרוֹ") is ambiguous.

The emergence of the angel from within the throes of physical suffering – the fateful conditional "if" that opens the verse – serves to remind us of the full danger that lies at the foundation of any tragic process. The Book of Job leads its hero through this dangerous progression. The reader, who is immersed in the story's unique dramatic irony and knows, from the opening, that Job's *nefesh* is being preserved by God, does *not* know – as Job does not – from whence will come the knowledge that can bring together the various pieces. This knowledge – God's whirlwind speech – comes, as it does in Elihu's words, from the body, from matter, from the proximity to death. Yet it also comes, in complete inversion, from the world – from the storm. Elihu himself, in the progression of his disquisitions, creates this reversal. His fourth "answer" is structured in parallel to his first, and argues that God is to be heard within the storms, for wind and thunder are a type of speech:

> Hear attentively the noise of his voice,
> and the sound that goeth out of his mouth.
> He directeth it under the whole heaven,
> and his lightning unto the ends of the earth.
> After it a voice roareth: he thundereth with the voice of his excellency;
> and he will not stay them when his voice is heard.
> God thundereth marvellously with his voice;
> great things doeth he, which we cannot comprehend. (37:2–5).

This address follows Elihu's answer to Job's contentions regarding God's rule of the world. It is structured around a detailed development of the idea that divine speech emerges from bodily suffering. It appears here in a more Classic formulation: the paradigm of the "exalted" (i.e., hubris) is a king whose suffering and fall ("cords of affliction" [36:8]) constitute an act of divine speech, a revelation. In verse 36:16, Elihu again turns to directly address Job, and once more constructs the spatial metaphor of height and depth that appears in his first speech. Here, he explicitly contends that Job's disaster is a divine act that comes to save Job from falling into the abyss. The final verses addressed to Job right before the final turn in 36:22 (which serves as an introduction to the storm) are constructed to mask a surprising revelation, and constitute a request for reprieve.

> Desire not the night, when people ['amim עַמִּים] are cut off in their place.
> Take heed, regard not iniquity: for this hast thou chosen rather than [literally, "from"] affliction. (36:20–21)

Verse 20 alludes to Job's own words in 7:2: "As a servant earnestly desireth the shadow ..." Yet here they develop new psychological depths, which can be read as: "Do not get carried away with longing for death, do not strive for the falling of the night, to lie beneath the rising darkness" – the Hebrew *'amim* עמים ("people") can also mean "murkiness" – "Rather guard yourself from the ease of this longing, which resembles the seduction of 'regarding [i.e., listening to] iniquity' Resist its blandishments, and turn to face what you have chosen from within your 'affliction.'" This phrase בָּחַרְתָּ מֵעֹנִי ("chosen from affliction") strikes the dominant chord of Elihu's words. The concept of "affliction" (*'oni*, עֹנִי) encapsulates the lack of material possessions (whether in body, property or power) while also distilling the state of the sufferer whose "flesh is consumed away, that it cannot be seen" (33:21). The conjunction of "chosen" (*baharta*, בחרת) and "affliction" (*'oni*) transforms "affliction" into a moral, spiritual force, a choice. Elihu dubs Job an "afflicted" (*'ani*, עֲנִי), and thus turns him into someone worthy of divine justice, according to the terms set forth in the opening words of this argument: "He ... giveth justice to the poor [literally, 'afflicted']" (36:6).

It is no coincidence that the Sages were uncomfortable with the character of Elihu, seeing in him an alien presence whose words border on idolatry, as he directs humanity to look for the divine within natural phenomena. Yet nor it is coincidence that Maimonides specifically cites Elihu's words as encapsulating "the principal object of the whole Book of Job," which is structured around a transformation of the concept of "knowledge": "This lesson is the principal object of the whole Book of Job; it lays down this principle of faith, and recommends us to derive a proof from nature, that we should not fall into the error of imagining His knowledge to be similar to ours, or His intention, providence, and rule similar to ours."[35]

Here, at the cusp of the divine response, let us return to Elihu's opening words, where he justifies his candidness. Elihu offers a long introduction to his disquisition (32:6–33:8), gradually building towards the unique approach with which he opens his main contention (36:7 onwards). It is important to analyze this introduction and its contents, and to see them in the context of the opening of the whirlwind speech that follows. Elihu sets out to make Job feel that he utterly identifies with him, so that his own words can change and shape Job's state of mind rather than engendering yet another dead-end philosophic battle. This progression, which takes place between 32:6 and 33:8, is perhaps the only "realistic" passage in the Book of Job, and its implicit psychological insight is impressive. Elihu creates a complex manipulation, based on a series of contrasts between himself and the older friends who preceded him, moving from there to an announcement that he speaks only from the intensity

---

35 Maimonides, *Guide to the Perplexed*, Part III, Chapter 23, 303.

of feeling rising within him: "For I am full of matter, the spirit within me constraineth me. Behold, my belly is as wine which hath no vent; it is ready to burst like new bottles. I will speak, that I may be relieved ..." (32:18–20). He then proceeds to apologize for his harshness. Yet it is specifically from this point on that he commences to directly earn Job's trust. Elihu addresses Job by name (he is the only friend to do so), connecting his own fate as a *man*, as a human being, to Job's. All of the ideas that will be developed in the course of his disquisition are implicit here in condensed form:

> Wherefore, Job, I pray thee, hear my speeches,
> and hearken to all my words.
> Behold, now I have opened my mouth,
> my tongue hath spoken in my mouth.
> My words shall be of the uprightness of my heart:
> and my lips shall utter knowledge clearly.
> The spirit of God hath made me,
> the breath of the Almighty hath given me life.
> If thou canst answer me,
> set thy words in order before me, stand up.
> Behold, I am according to thy wish in God's stead:
> I also am formed out of the clay.
> Behold, my terror shall not make thee afraid,
> neither shall my hand be heavy upon thee. (33:1–7)

This sequence already contains within it the fundamental elements of Elihu's central contention regarding the connection between the concept of "uprightness" (*yashar*) – the divine voice that is heard from within the internal human experience of being – and the "matter" from whence the "I" is formed. The similarity between these two concepts is implied in human empathy – which is why the inherent "terror" of this understanding does not cause one to be "afraid." Here we can see how far Elihu goes in order to awaken Job to the possibility of a divine response. God's whirlwind speech opens by referencing Job's masculinity – that is, his physical and sexual prowess: "Gird up now thy loins like a man" (38:3). A simple reading is that this is merely an opening salvo, encouraging Job to answer. Yet these opening words also serve as a reminder of the powers of life that flow from the loins – the power of procreation, the very same force cursed by Job at the opening of his words: "Let the day perish wherein I was born, and the night in which it was said, There is a man child conceived" (3:3). God's response is not a redeeming grace that flows from above, but rather a call to man to activate his full facilities.

> Gird up now thy loins like a man;
> for I will demand of thee,
> and answer thou me. (38:3)

The structure of the verse underscores the spiritual aspect of the procreative power: in the second half of the verse, fecundity (the "loins") is transformed into a mental ability to "answer." The reversal occurring here is multidimensional: from silence to speech; body to spirit; non-knowledge to knowledge. The address is a question, and one that demands an answer – and man's answer to this question is: "Thou." This completely undoes hubris. It turns out that the result of "gird up now thy loins like a man" is the utterance "Thou." It is the escape from the "I." The recognition of "uprightness," of one's fellow human beings, and of the entire world, with its mountains and eagles, emerges from the "I" and is aimed towards the ultimate Other – namely, God. It emerges from the most corporeal of elements – the loins – and aims towards the most spiritual. Yet nonetheless, it is conceptualized as a stand-in and continuation of that same power, that same vitality, of birth. From within the extreme expression of the powers of nature in turmoil – the storm – sounds the "word," the *logos*, which is presented as an address, that is, as a response to an other. The recognition of the divine is not the recognition of the nothingness of man. On the contrary, it is the ability to contain the immeasurably sublime divinity; the Presence that rests in the most physical and corporeal ("He is the first of the acts of God" (40:19) is said of the behemoth), and extends to the wisdom that rules it. And alongside this power is the ability to see the human as a presence that rests in the physical and bodily, and extends to the wisdom that links it to the divine response. God, here, is not nature, but rather the word-within-the-storm regarding nature; He is the "uprightness" formed of "wisdom" that provides wisdom to his creations.

Job indeed collapses momentarily in the face of this response, as evidenced by his fragmented speech in 42: 2,3,4. Yet, in the end, he finally succeeds in articulating himself. His words are not a cancelation of the self. True, he identifies the self with "dust and ashes" through an action termed "seeing" (42:5) – which can signify a non-causal, sudden insight rather than literal, physical sight. Yet this identification expresses his ability to contain the understanding that stands at the foundation of "dust and ashes" without being destroyed by it. The very act of making this declaration strips the "I" from the concepts of body and matter that surround it, yet the death of the body is *not* seen as the end of human identity. On the contrary, only thus can the divine and the universe finally be seen as truly separate addressees, as a Thou from which one can separate and say: "now mine eye seeth Thee" (42:5).

Here we see man standing singular and separated from the universe and from the divine, stripped of all his former childish "symbiotic" certainties regarding his ability to understand fate – whether his own, or his children's, or of his surroundings as a whole. Here, the hubris of Job offering sacrifices to atone for possible actions by his children while they were feasting becomes clear. The pretention of this preemptive defense (which parallels God's making "a hedge about") comes of not acknowledging the human "Thou," the separate, uncontrollable, other – the children; of not accepting his inability to contain the human forces that are a microcosmic reflection of the universe with its monsters. Job's hubris was to set himself up as a god.

The closing of the story (42:10–17) is not a divine miracle at all. Rather, what is at play here is the power mentioned by Elihu: the regeneration that stands at the basis of the human "I." True, the events are initially presented as divinely instigated, but the verses take care to mention that the praxis of this process unfolds in a completely realistic, sociological manner: Job's "brethren" and friends gather around him, bringing him "a piece of money" (42:11) – the initial property that sets him on the path to renewal.

The ceremony enacted by his family and friends at the closing of the story – "Then came there unto him all his brethren, and all his sisters, and all they that had been of his acquaintance before, and did eat bread with him in his house: and they bemoaned him, and comforted him over all the evil that the Lord had brought upon him" (42:11) – broadens Job's destiny until it again corresponds to the dimensions of human society, creating a new perspective of time and fresh memories. The recollection of suffering – which for a moment transforms God back into He who brought "all the evil ... upon him" – consolidates the entire story around the sense of movement and life – and the vitality of the painful memory of how they were formed. The presence of "evil" within renewal makes palpable the fecund balance that has been achieved by *dike*. Or, as explained in the opening of Aeschylus's *Oresteia*:

> [He] shows the perfect way
> Of knowledge: He hath ruled,
> Men shall learn wisdom, by affliction schooled.
> *In visions of the night, like dropping rain,*
> *Descend the many memories of pain*
> Before the spirit's sight: through tears and dole
> Comes wisdom o'er the unwilling soul –
> A boon, I wot, of all Divinity,
> That holds its sacred throne in strength, above the sky![36]

---

36 Aeschylus, *Agamemnon*, trans. E. D. A. Morshead, Macmillan, London 1928, *The Internet Classics Archive*, http://classics.mit.edu/Aeschylus/agamemnon.html (Last accessed 6 May 2014).

This essay was translated by Batnadiv HaKarmi-Weinberg.

Bibliography

Aeschylus. *Agamemnon*. Trans. E. D. A. Morshead. London: Macmillan, 1928. *The Internet Classics Archive*. http://classics.mit.edu/Aeschylus/agamemnon.html (Last accessed 6 May 2014).

Aristotle. *Aristotle on the Art of Poetry*. Trans. Ingram Bywater, with a preface by Gilbert Murray. Authorama. http://www.authorama.com/the-poetics-14.html (Last accessed 6 May 2014).

Burkert, Walter. *Greek Religion: Archaic and Classical*. Trans. John Raffan. Cambridge: Harvard University Press, 1985.

Crook, Dorothea. *Elements of Tragedy*. New Haven: Yale University Press, 1969.

Hahamm, Amos *Sefer iyov (da'at mikra)*. Jerusalem: Mosad ha-rav kuk, 1970.

Hirschfield, Ariel. "Ha-im Iyov hu tragedya?." *Iyov: ba-mikra ba-hagut ba-omanut*. Ed. Lea Mazor. Jerusalem: Magnes Press, 1992. 145–151.

Kurzweil, Barukh. "Iyov ve-efsharut ha-tragedia ha-tanakhit" ("Job and the Possibility of Biblical Tragedy"). *Ha-maavak 'al 'erkhei ha-yahadut*. Tel Aviv, Schocken, 1970. 11.

Leibowitz, Yeshayahu. "Ben iyov le-sophakles." *Yahadut, 'am yehudi, u-medinat yisrael*. Tel Aviv, Schocken, 1975.

Maimonides. *Guide to the Perplexed*. Trans. M. Friedländer. London: Routledge & Kegan Paul Ltd., 1904. *Sacred Texts*, http://www.sacred-texts.com/jud/gfp (Last accessed 6 May 2014).

Ricoeur, Paul. *The Symbolism of Evil*. Trans. Emerson Buchanan. Boston: Beacon Press, 1969.

Sewall, R. B. *The Vision of Tragedy*, New Haven: Yale University Press, 1959.

Shabtai, Aharon. "Introduction." *Aeschylus. Agamemnon*. Trans. Aharon Shabtai. Tel Aviv: Schocken Books, 1990.

Steiner, George. *The Death of Tragedy*. London: Alfred A. Knopf, 1961.

Taplin, Olivier. *Greek Tragedy in Action*. London: Methuen, 1978.

Tchernichovsky, Shaul. "Before the Statue of Apollo." *The Jewish Anthology*. Ed. Edmond Fleg. Trans. Maurice Samuel. New York: Harcourt Brace, 1940.

Weiss, Meir, "Ha-sipur 'al reishito shel iyov." *Iyunim* 40. 1969. [The esay takes up the entire volume.] (In English: *The Story of Job's Beginning: Job 1–2: A Literary Analysis*). Jerusalem: Magnes Press, 1983.

Moshe Halbertal
Job, the Mourner

The Book of Job was understood among philosophers and theologians as a great attempt to grapple with the metaphysical and theological challenges that the fact of evil poses. It was common therefore to interpret the book as an integral part of the discussion concerning the problem of evil and theodicy. Yet there is another, very different stance of addressing the encounter of evil, one not of the theologian or the philosopher; this is the stance of the mourner, which is adopted by the narrative framing of the Book of Job. The different statements of the protagonists in the book, statements that served as the canonical formulations concerning the problem of evil, occur in the particular context of Job's sitting in mourning while engaging in debate with his friends who presumably have come to comfort him. This particular setting – of the mourner and his comforters – is not mere decorative background to a theological debate. It is a far more serious context, constituting the particular stance in which the problem of evil is experienced and addressed in the Book of Job. In order to understand the full implications of the mourner's stance it is worthwhile to first outline the traditional theological and philosophical problem of evil and the varieties of responses that come under the heading of theodicy. The traditional project of theodicy will then serve as a contrasting background that will help illuminate what I think is at the center of Job's stance as a mourner, a stance that might touch deeper dimensions of the human experience of evil, and that helps to articulate what is at stake in the drama unfolding in the Book of Job.

1 The Problem of Evil

The problem of evil that philosophers and theologians have attempted to solve exists in the apparent impossibility of affirming the following three statements simultaneously: a) God is almighty; b) God is good; c) there is evil. If evil exists, God might be good only if he is not almighty and does not have power to prevent it, or he might be almighty and not good and does not care to prevent evil. In their attempt to reconcile these statements, the theologians and philosophers loyal to the monotheistic faith were determined to preserve (a) and (b), while focusing on the denial of (c) as the key to resolve the problem of evil. Two different paths can be discerned in that effort that leads to denying the existence of evil: one despicable and one downright silly (silly in a way only metaphysicians can be). The despicable path requires accusing the victim. To restore and maintain the moral order some religious and theological trends attempt to prove that the one who is struck by disaster is to blame for it. In this view of divine justice it is not necessary to point out the sin of the suffering person, as the suffering itself serves as proof of a hidden guilt made visible through suffering. In the Book of Job the response of the friends to Job's lament takes this form of *theodicy*, in that it transfers the guilt from God to the victim. In one such assertion Job's friends make the following claim: "Think now, who that was innocent ever perished? Or where were the upright cut off?" (Job 4:7).

To pass the guilt for Job's predicament onto Job is particularly vile here, given the context of the friends' accusations: that of a visit to a mourning man. Job is mourning his sons and daughters, who perished during a storm. The friends who come to comfort him end up delivering a number of moral lectures, each of which Job must respond to. Instead of comforting their distraught friend, the friends rub in the guilt, under the guise of a hypocritical defense of his faith and sincerity. There is not just maliciousness. The situation of interdependency between mourner and consoler is transformed into a situation of moral superiority. The sudden fall of the rich, strong Job confers his friends a sense of liberation, as if Job has received a portion of evil that was in fact meant for one of them. The accusation of the victim is ideally possible at moments of mourning, as at such times the mourner is inclined to accept blame anyway. In this sense, Job is guilty because he stayed alive while others perished and because he failed to protect his children. From here it is only a small step to his internalization that the deaths of his children were the result of his sin.

It is difficult to say who comes off as the worst character in this biblical book: Satan, God, or the friends of Job. Yet it seems that Job's friends earn the title, as they – in their hypocrisy – inflict a blow upon a bruise. As if Job's suffering is not enough, they would have him go to the grave with the conviction that he has sinned and thus brought evil upon his children.[1] Job feels twice betrayed, and with good reason. Once by God, who has inflicted his suffering, and once by his friends, who blame him for his own suffering. "My companions are treacherous like a torrent-bed, like freshets that pass away. (...) You would even cast lots over the orphan, and bargain over your friend," he protests (Job 6:15 and 6:27). Job is the hero of the book not only because he holds a courageous dialogue with God, but also because he refuses to absorb the blame his "consolers" attempt to impute on him. Throughout all the moods

---

1 What the friends do is called *honaātdevarim*, or "verbal abuse,"in the Talmud. Babylonian Talmud, treatise Baba Kama, folio 58b.

and dispositions Job undergoes, one fact remains: Job defends his innocence. The greatness of the Book of Job lies in the fact that God himself refuses to accept the simplest solution, that of accusing the victim. God even justifies Job's courage, raging against Elifaz and his friends: "My wrath is kindled against you and against your two friends; for you have not spoken of me what is right, as my servant Job has" (Job 42:7).

God's rejection of the answer proffered by Job's friends undermines an old Biblical logic of reward and punishment between humans and God. The friends, whose version of this project is rejected by God himself, represent the Biblical theology from before the Book of Job, according to which the sinner is punished and the just man is rewarded. This is what makes the canonization of this book within the biblical canon even more astounding. It even goes further than that: the Book of Job not only rejects the attempt of blaming the victim as way of resolving the problem of evil, it considers such an attempt an added evil in itself, since it entails inflicting further distress – feelings of guilt – on the sufferer. The theological attempt at theodicy does not resolve evil but instead increases it.

Apart from this attempt to pass God's guilt onto the victim, theodicy can take a second path to achieve its goal of denying evil. Here, the idea is that the victim is mistaken not because he fails to accept his guilt, but because he considers his suffering as an evil. Evil, we are thus told, only looks like evil because we do not see the bigger picture. As soon as the complete story unfolds, we will understand that in the long run a good thing was happening to us. In the historical-philosophical understanding of this idea, which might be called "the big picture argument," Hegel teaches us that evil is part of a dialectical movement of an inevitable progress, and is therefore not a real evil. Yet such sophisticated maneuvers seem objectionable. Why should a future good justify a contemporary pain? Why would we accept such a "consequentialist" justification, in which suffering of the one is considered a means for the future salvation of the other?

The denial of evil has a more refined version in the history of philosophy, namely that of the Spinozists. According to their position, there is no such thing as evil; instead, there are physiological experiences of pain and pleasure upon which people project categories of good and evil. The Spinozist ontology claims that there is indeed such a thing as reality independent of our mental states, but that it is neither good nor evil. Good and evil are external categories that are being projected upon a reality, which is in itself neutral. According to this version, humans project evil upon the world and consequently complain about the problem of evil.

To my understanding our consciousness of reality works the other way around. We perceive reality because of our experience of evil, not the reverse.

Our perception of reality as independent of our mind and self is a consequence of the fact that the world outside comes into collision with our aspirations and appears inconsistent with our view of what it should be according to our wishes. Nothing is more real than evil, for it reveals a world completely alien to our desires. In fact, if everything in the world happened according to our wishes, we would perhaps not have clear consciousness of a real world independent from ourselves. Among other things, the attraction of evil is a result of a perverse search for the concrete and real in some decadent environments, in which artificial and overly protected surroundings do not provide sufficient friction with the world to create the feeling of reality. In such cases pain is inflicted in an attempt to feel some sense of reality. Evil is not something we project onto reality; it is what – in a very harsh manner – allows for our notion of reality.

The Book of Job, as we have seen, rejects one strategy for denying evil, that of blaming the victim. In this rejection, however, the book teaches us that attempts to resolve the problem of evil can themselves contain much evil. The problem of evil is not to be resolved; it is to be *combated* and limited. It is here that we can address how Job's struggle is articulated beyond the sphere of the theological problem of theodicy.

2 The Theologian and the Mourner

Job's initial statement laid before his consoling friends captures the kernel of the mourner's response to evil. When his friends arrive, Job begins his lament with a death wish. "Let the day perish in which I was born, and the night that said, 'A man-child is conceived.' Let that day be darkness! May God above not seek it, or light shine on it" (Job 3:4). He laments further, "Why did I not die at birth, come forth from the womb and expire? Why were there knees to receive me, or breasts for me to suck?" (Job 3:11–12). Because of his suffering and outrage Job the mourner loses interest in the world and in his own existence. He curses that existence and expresses anger that he did not die in his mother's womb.

The death wish expressed in Job's initial reaction is intimately connected to the state of mourning. The nature of such a state of mourning must be examined closely in order to appreciate the meaning of Job's predicament in full. A central feature of mourning, and one essential to Job's predicament, is revealed in the surprising way by which the Talmud equates the mourner's condition with that of the outcast and banned. A Talmudic discussion[2] on mourning describes the structure of mourning rituals as follows: During the seven days after the funeral the mourner is not allowed to wash himself; wash his clothes; shave himself or cut his hair; wear shoes; show his face (he must cover it); anoint his head; greet anyone; study Torah; work; have sexual intercourse. In the first seven of these prohibitions (from shaving to offering greetings) the Talmud compares the mourner with the outcast. Like the outcast, the mourner loses his social persona: he cannot show interest in his surroundings via greeting people, and he is unwashed, unshaved, shoeless, and in dirty clothes.[3] The mourner becomes an asocial being, like the outcast.

Why is the mourner compared to the outcast? At the roots of this comparison are two deep issues that concern the existential consciousness of the mourner. The first is that the mourner feels excluded. The mourner has detached himself from the world, as that world does not reflect his inner condition. The sun rises after each painful night, and the busy day-to-day life of the workers and the noises from the street continue as if nothing has happened. The gap between the world of the mourner that has halted and the cruel, blind continuity of life and the cosmos isolates the mourner from his environment and makes him, in his own view, an outcast. Moreover, in our relation with the world, the bond with those we love serves as our link with the world. Love is our umbilical cord with reality and always takes the form of a particular attachment and bond. Thus, loss of the beloved person results automatically in our detachment from reality. In principle we are strangers in our environment, and the hand that is offered to us from the world is the hand of those we love. With the loss of a loved one, we lose that stretched-out hand. The rules of mourning, structured as a ritual acting out of that sense of exclusion, reflect the basic existential condition of the mourner in relation to his environment.

However, there is an important difference between the mourner and the outcast that must be noted. The mourner feels excluded, though society tries to include him again. This is reversed for the outcast, who is punished via the severing of all bonds and contact with society. The mourner is – or should be – comforted by friends and family who come with food and drink to console him.

---

2 I refer to the discussion in the Babylonian Talmud, tractate Moad Katan, folio 14b–16a.

3 The prohibitions imposed on the mourner in no circumstance reflect attempts to inflict pain or suffering upon him. The prohibition on sexual intercourse, washing, anointing, and wearing footwear correspond to the rules for Yom Kippur, save that the mourner is not required to chastise himself. Mourning is not an expression of pain; the mourner is allowed to eat meat and drink wine. In fact, there are many stories about excessive consummation of food and drink (to ease the pain and the suffering) occurring in the houses of the mourning.

The drama of the week of mourning is the complex interaction between the alienated perspective of the mourner and the attempt of his environment to draw him back into the world. The "work of mourning" is not about forgetting the loss and the slow separation from the dead, as Freud described it in his essay "Mourning and Melancholy." The mourner does not separate from the dead; rather, he internalizes the dead deep in his consciousness. The problem which the work of mourning is trying to address is the challenge of returning to the world after that loss is internalized. The mourning process is based on a strong ritualistic expression, enacted by the mourner, of the gap that has opened with the world; as the cycle of mourning continues, this expression is gradually moderated. This measured return to the world via the process of mourning is articulated in a Talmudic statement which carefully and physically crafts the norms of relocating the mourner into his world: "Our Rabbis taught: during the first week a mourner does not go out of the door of his house; the second week he goes out but does not sit in his [usual] place [in the synagogue]; the third week he sits in his [usual] place but does not speak; the fourth week he is like any other person" (Moed Katan 23a).

This view of the mourner as isolated and excluded teaches us a great deal about the situation of Job. It is no wonder therefore that Job's first reaction is a deep and bitter expression of a death wish. This view also magnifies the deep failure and betrayal of his friends, who instead of stretching their hands to Job so as to help him return to the world, blame him and thereby push him further and deeper into his already devastated state.

The problem of evil for the mourner in his state of isolation and banishment is not the question of whether or not he still can "believe" but rather if he still can "trust": Job does not question the existence of God; he simply *loses all trust* in him. Job's situation resembles that of a child punished violently by his father. We can ask for justification: what has the child done wrong that he is punished like that? But from the perspective of the child such justification is not the issue. For him, the problem is the loss of trust in a relationship that should provide security and an anchor. The mourner, in his confrontation with evil, does not attempt to defend metaphysical positions. For him, it is an existential problem, which expresses itself in depression and disinterest in a reality that appears alienating.

As related to the problem of evil from the perspective of mourning, the challenge the mourner faces is his loss of will to combat evil. Fighting evil requires love for the world (*amor mundi*), and it is exactly this love that is affected by evil. The experience of evil creates in us a stoic position, aimed at simply surviving the world and remaining unaffected by its whims. Such a retreat from the world is reflected in Job's attempt to be inconspicuous, to remain unnoticed and not to be tested. In the horror of his visibility, Job yearns for anonymity and admonishes God for being the guardian of humans: "Am I the Sea, or the Dragon, that you set a guard over me? (...) you scare me with dreams and terrify me with visions, so that I would choose strangling and death rather than this body" (Job 7, 12–15).

After all, Job's misery began the moment someone in heaven directed attention to Job, the moment God said to Satan: "Have you noticed my servant Job? There is no one like him on the earth, a blameless and upright man who fears God and turns away from evil" (Job 1:8). Being in the spotlight before power can be terrifying, even in something such as sending a complaint to the tax authorities: files maybe opened and the results are uncertain. In a negative assessment of the presumed piety expressed in vowing, the Talmud states: "Whoever initiates a vow his file is examined." The act of vowing as a voluntary act of acceptance of an obligation (a demand which is beyond the norm) draws dangerous attention.[4] Job is averse to this attention. He does not want to be noticed and he demands God avert his attention from him. In his most difficult moments, Job reminds us of the stoic nihilism of the book *Ecclesiastes*, which imparts on humans the cynical yet wise advice not to be noticed, in either a good or a bad way. From the point of view of the one who suffers, the world looks like a place one should try to avoid. Job's longing for death is not part of an interest to limit evil; it is an element of his desire to retreat from it.

While the problem of the theologian is only a problem for religious people who assume that God is good and almighty, the problem of the mourner is experienced by religious and non-religious people alike, for it is rooted in the gap between the world as it is and as we want it to be. Evil weakens the human will to fight it. And it is important to stress that the distinction between moral evil and natural evil is not useful here. Technological progress has made it highly difficult and problematic to establish a clear boundary between the two. Today, the distinction between what we can call *misfortune* and *injustice* is disappearing, as Judith Shklar has argued.[5] In the past, an earthquake was considered a natural injustice; however, with the advent of new building techniques, a death caused by an earthquake is no longer always considered a misfortune but instead may be termed an injustice. The increasing capacity to arm ourselves against natural disasters renders many earthquake-related deaths a matter of injustice and unequal distribution of goods.

---

4 Jerusalem Talmud, Nedarim 1:1, 36,4. A similar approach is expressed in the warning that appears in the Talmud against prolonging prayer and the fact that such practice might cause the recording of the petitioner's sins. See Babylonian Talmud, Berakhot 55a.
5 Shklar, Judith, *The Faces of Injustice*, Yale University Press, New Haven 1990, 51–83.

Evil has a numbing effect. It transforms us into survivors, people who protect themselves and at best are not interested in harming others yet have lost the confidence and care required to combat evil itself. The challenge of the Book of Job and the problem of evil is to make Job come alive again. After Job's opening speech, when he expresses his death wish, his friends begin to accuse him. The first step Job makes in the direction of life is expressed in his persistent attempt to establish his innocence before he goes to the grave. It is the malicious friends who paradoxically call him back to life. In the next stage of his awakening Job demands God to appear and account for Job's misery. God appears – yet his answer might be unsatisfying, and maybe the words God spoke to Job were not especially meaningful to him and did not really solve anything. But as we saw, the abused child does not demand explanation; instead, he wishes to be heard, and seeks the caring attention of the father in order to restore some degree of trust. The explanation that is actually provided by the father might in that case be marginal to the fact of his actual appearance and his need provide an explanation which in and of itself is important. In line with this quest, after the appearance of God, Job says "I had heard of you by the hearing of the ear, but now my eye sees you" (Job 42:5). The seeing, the direct encounter, is what makes the difference.

3 Evil, Mourning and the Shrinking of Horizons

But the problem of the evil of the mourner includes another element for which God's answer might have some intrinsic meaning. Extreme pain ordinarily leads us to focus on our own suffering and closes our capacity of attentiveness. The victim might tend to self-centeredness in his suffering. In one of his protests, Job cries, "O that my vexation were weighed, and all my calamity laid in the balances! For then it would be heavier than the sand of the sea; therefore my words have been rash" (Job 6:1–3). From the perspective of the victim his suffering and pain outweigh that of the whole world. Evil has not only a numbing effect but also a closing effect, in which the self is fully consumed by pain and need. The suffering and the consciousness of evil fill our inner screen and shrink our horizons.

Such deep tendency to self-centeredness manifests itself in Job's ongoing complaint that he has been treated unfairly, which implies that everything that occurs in the world happens either to his favor or to his disadvantage. When during a heavy storm his house collapses and his loved ones die, Job protests by asking: what did I do that this storm was sent to me? Maimonides has interpreted God's answer to Job as being an attempt to break this anthropocentric attitude. The shift away from anthropocentrism emerges in how God describes the immense cosmos and creation, a description rendered in different terms than in the creation narrative in *Genesis*. In *Genesis* the world is created as a house for humans, who are considered the crown of creation. This cosmological conception invites the locating of the human at the center of the cosmos. Following such an anthropocentric account, rain or drought in biblical literature is an unmistakable example of reward or punishment: rain falls in favor of and for the benefit of humans; if there is no rain, it is to make humans suffer. In contrast with this the Book of Job describes creation in quite different terms. Here, the crown of creation is the terrifying leviathan, not human beings.

The leviathan is described in God's speech to Job as follows: "On earth it has no equal, a creature without fear. It surveys everything that is lofty; it is king over all that are proud" (Job 41:33–34). God's speech also stresses that rain also falls on uninhabited places, implying that the blissful phenomenon of rain is not oriented solely to the needs humans: "Who has cut a channel for the torrents of rain, and a way for the thunderbolt, to bring rain on a land where no one lives, on the desert, which is empty of human life" (Job 38:25–26).[6] God says to Job: not everything in creation happens because of you – I have other, very different matters to be concerned with. God's answer, as many readers have noted, does not address directly the problem of evil; yet, in its denial of humanity's central place in the universe this answer is helpful in at least one respect, in that it challenges the anthropocentric assumption which tends to reinforce the self-centeredness of pain.

Job's overcoming of the shuttering condition of mourning and suffering emerges only towards the end of the book when he becomes able to perceive the needs of others. "And the Lord restored the fortunes of Job when he had prayed for his friends; and the Lord gave Job twice as much as he had before" (Job 42:10). In praying for his friends, in caring for them and their plight, Job breaks free from the prison of evil and ruptures the isolating self-centeredness of the victim. Such a caring gesture does not in any way imply resolution of the problem of evil in the way it was conceived as a problem of theodicy. Rather, it is a moment of reconciling with the world, which stands in a stark opposition to the starting point of Job's bitter journey – his death wish. The trajectory of

---

6 On the change in the conception of creation from Genesis to Job, see JisraelKnohl, *Mijir'a le-ahava – hassagat ha-emet ha-datit be-seferIyovu-betorat ha-kehoena* ["From fear to love – the religious perception of truth in the Book of Job and in the priestly codex"], in: *Iyov, ba-Mikra ba-hagutba-ommanoet*, Lea Mazor, ed., Magnes, Jerusalem 5655 (1995), 89–103.

Job's spiritual and existential path as a mourner is the move from the isolated seclusion of the mourner and its disinterest in the world, to the caring concern and attentiveness to the needs and pains of others.

The rejection of the theological version of the problem of evil and the project of theodicy implies that the question of evil should not be resolved. There lurks a certain evil in the human attempt to resolve the problem of evil. Evil must be combated, reduced, weakened. The problem of evil begins at the place where evil weakens our capacity to fight it. Evil as a problem of the mourner transforms us into isolated, enclosed beings; it numbs our capacity to moral *outrage*. It prisons us and locks us into the narcissism of victimhood and pain. Can we – with the aid of our friends and family – mobilize the necessary means to conquer this problem of evil? This is the difficult question of the Book of Job. It is also the true problem of evil in our society.

Bibliography

Babylonian Talmud. Treatise Baba Kama.
Babylonian Talmud. Berakhot.
Jerusalem Talmud. Nedarim.
Jisrael Knohl, *Mijir'a le-ahava – hassagat ha-emet ha-datit be-seferlyovu-betorat ha-kehoena* ("From fear to love – the religious perception of truth in the Book of Job and in the priestly codex"). *Iyov, ba-Mikra ba-hagutba-ommanoet.* Ed. Lea Mazor. Jerusalem: Magnes Press, 1995.
Shklar, Judith. *The Faces of Injustice.* New Haven: Yale University Press, 1990.

Naphtali Meshel
Whose Job Is This? Dramatic Irony and *double entendre* in the Book of Job*

בּוֹ בַיּוֹם דָּרַשׁ יְהוֹשֻׁעַ בֶּן הוֹרְקָנוֹס שֶׁלֹּא עָבַד אִיּוֹב אֶת הַמָּקוֹם אֶלָּא מֵאַהֲבָה
שנ' הֵן יִקְטְלֵינִי לוֹ אֲיַחֵל אֲדַיִין הַדָּבָר שָׁקוּל לוֹא אֲנִי מְצַפֶּה אוֹ אֵינִי מְצַפֶּה לוֹ[1]

On that day Joshua son of Horqanos expounded: "Job served God only out of love, since
it is said, *If he slay me, I will yearn for him* (Job 13:15). But still the matter is equivocal [as
to whether it means], 'I shall pine for him,' or 'I shall pine away.'"

1 Introduction

Two literary techniques long recognized as being highly developed in the Book
of Job are dramatic irony and *double entendre*.[2] These techniques are a common heritage of Biblical Wisdom Literature[3] and of ancient Near Eastern litera-

* I thank the participants of the conference, as well as Prof. Yohanan Grinshpon, Dr. Itamar
Kislev, Jessica O'Rourke-Suchoff, Ayelet Wenger, and the participants of the 2012 Weinfeld
Symposium of the Bible Department at the Hebrew University, for many valuable comments. I
thank Prof. Baruch Schwartz for discussing many details with me, and Prof. Gary Rendsburg
for reading a draft of this article and offering several insights.
1 *m Sot* 5:5, the nonstandard vocalization follows Ms. Kaufmann. Ironically, the scribe originally wrote לוֹא, thereby negating the yearning where he meant to affirm it and (unwittingly?)
underlining the very homophony upon which the text comments. The error was later discov-
ered and the א erased. The English translation offered here aims to capture a sense of the
ambiguity, at the price of diverging significantly from the original.
2 Standard translations of the text (JPS, SRSV) are used when there is general scholarly consensus on the translation of a verse. When scholarly consensus has not been reached or existing translations require deeper inquiry, alternate translations will be proposed and explained,
since these instances of non-consensus can indicate double-edged words at work.
3 Narrowly perceived, this category usually refers to Proverbs, Qohelet, Job, and some of the
Psalms; more broadly, it includes narratives considered to be influenced by Wisdom circles,
such as the Joseph narrative in Genesis.

ture more generally,[4] and had been recognized and reflected upon already in antiquity.[5]

In this article it will be argued that a specific type of *double entendre*, namely double-edged wording – the formulation of two diametrically opposite expressions by means of a single phonetic and/or graphic sequence – is used systematically in key passages in the Book of Job; and that it couples with dramatic irony to serve as an organizing principle of the book, allowing for two simultaneous, incompatible readings to coexist – one from the limited perspective of one or more of the characters; the other from the privileged perspective of the reader.

Recent scholarship on the Book of Job has highlighted the book's polyphonic character in the sense that it conveys a multiplicity of competing messages,[6] as well as its iconoclastic nature in the sense that it opposes classical

---

4 See Scott B. Noegel, ed., *Puns and Pundits: Word Play in the Hebrew Bible and Ancient Near Eastern Literature*, CDL Press, Bethesda 2000; in that volume, see particularly Victor Avigdor Hurowitz, "Alliterative Allusions, Rebus Writing, and Paronomastic Punishment: Some Aspects of Word Play in Akkadian Literature," 63–88.

On Janus parallelism in the Book of Job, with additional examples from other ancient Near Eastern works of literature, see Scott B. Noegel, *Janus Parallelism in the Book of Job*, Sheffield Academic Press, Sheffield 1996.

Seow's study of the defective spelling in Job demonstrates that homography in pre-masoretic manuscripts of the Book of Job was even more widespread, allowing for a larger array of *double entendres* (e.g., nn. 15, 19); see Choon Leong Seow, "Orthography, Textual Criticism, and the Poetry of Job," *Journal of Biblical Literature* 130.1 (2011), 63–85. Regarding the questionable applicability of the category "Wisdom Literature" in Mesopotamian literature, see Victor Avigdor Hurowitz, *Proverbs*, Am Oved and Magnes, Tel Aviv and Jerusalem 2012, 1.54–55. On the elaborate South Asian techniques of composing extended narratives that can be read consistently as relating two completely different stories, see Yigal Bronner, *Extreme Poetry: The South Asian Movement of Simultaneous Narration*, Columbia University Press, New York 2010.

5 See *m Sot* 5:5 cited in the epigraph; perhaps also b BB 16a *infra* (on אֵיּוֹב אֹיֵב, cf. the homograph אִיב that appears in 4QpalaeoJob[c]). The elaborate reversal of the hierarchies of knowledge in the Greek Testament of Job, where Satan does not know that Job was told in advance that he will be subject to a trial, suggests that the authors were well aware of dramatic irony. For the text see Robert A. Kraft et al., eds., *The Testament of Job*. Scholars Press for the Society of Biblical Literature, Missoula 1974.

6 See for example Robert Gordis, *The Book of Job: Commentary, New Translation, and Special Studies*, Jewish Theological Seminary of America, New York 1978, 239; Yair Hoffman, *A Blemished Perfection: The Book of Job in Context*, Sheffield Academic Press, Sheffield 1996; Edward Greenstein, "In Job's Face / Facing Job," in: *The Labour of Reading: Desire, Alienation, and Biblical Interpretation*, eds., Fiona C. Black, Roland Boer, and Erin Runions, Society of Biblical Literature, Atlanta 1999, 301–317; Carol A. Newsom, *The Book of Job: A Contest of Moral Imaginations*, Oxford University Press, New York 2003; James L. Crenshaw, *Reading Job: A Literary*

Wisdom Literature ideology with regards to the principles of divine righteousness and just reward.[7] The present study builds upon this literature, but its thrust is different. First, while it acknowledges the existence of a spectrum of readings in the Book of Job, it focuses on two extremes of this spectrum, suggesting that two opposite readings are systematically present throughout the book. Second, while the claim offers a new literary reading of the Book of Job based on forms of irony that were not identified in the past or were identified only in passing, the claim is not limited to the hermeneutical potential of the text. Rather, this study also aims to offer criteria for the identification of intentional use of double-edged words, suggesting that in the Book of Job one encounters a highly developed literary technique available in Wisdom circles.[8]

2 Double-Edged Words

2.1 Definition of a double-edged word

Israelite Wisdom Literature was notorious already in antiquity for offering contradictory advice.[9] A well-known example (*not* based on double-edged wording) is Proverbs 26:4–5:

אל תען כסיל כאולתו פן תשוה לו גם אתה
ענה כסיל כאולתו פן יהיה חכם בעיניו

> *Do not respond to an idiot in accordance with his stupidity lest you, too, become just like him.*
> *Respond to an idiot in accordance with his stupidity lest he consider himself wise.*[10]

Double-edged wording arises when two such expressions, rather than appearing in two consecutive utterances, are combined in a single phonetic (or graph-

---

and *Theological Commentary*, Smyth and Helwys, Macon, 2011; and David Frankel, "The Image of God in the Book of Job," *Shnaton* 22 (2013): 27–65.

7 See for example John Briggs Curtis, "On Job's Response to Yahweh," in: *Journal of Biblical Literature* 98. 4 (Dec. 1979): 497–511; Jack Miles, *God: A Biography*, Alfred A. Knopf, New York 1995; and Frankel, "The Image of God in the Book of Job."

8 *Contra* the approach advocated by Yair Hoffman, who claimed that "[w]hether this use of equivocal words was premeditated or accidental is of minor consequence." See Yair Hoffman, "The Use of Equivocal Words in the First Speech of Eliphaz," in: *Vetus Testamentum* 30 (1980): 114–118.

9 See for example *b Shab* 30b.

10 Regardless of the various solutions offered for these verses (for example, Hurowitz, *Proverbs*, 2.510), the example illustrates what constitutes "diametrically opposite" advice.

ic) sequence that is interpretable in two incompatible ways. Naturally, the two incompatible readings are rarely as neatly and completely diametrically opposed as Proverbs 26:4–5. Double-edged wording is thus a subcategory of *double entendre*, and like other *double entendres* it can be crafted by means of a variety of techniques, such as lexical homophony and homography, syntactic ambiguity, and Janus-faced parallelism. In the Book of Job, it also takes the form of rhetorical questions with two opposite implied answers.

2.2 Double-edged words in context: Proverbs and Ahikar

Let us turn to Proverbs 23:13, a verse that lends itself to two very different yet compatible readings.

אל תמנע מנער מוסר כי תכנו בשבט לא ימות

Do not withhold chastisement from a boy; if you beat him with a sprig – he will not die (13a)

At first glance, this statement appears to imply that:

> (1a) *even if* one beats one's son, the son shall not die (in other words, a good beating never killed anyone).

However, upon reading the second hemistich, "You should beat him with a sprig – and save his life from Sheol" (13b, אתה בשבט תכנו ונפשו משאול תציל), one realizes that the first hemistich could actually imply quite the opposite of what was initially apparent:

> (1b) *only if* one beats one's son, does one save him from (untimely) death.

That is, a father who *fails* to chastise his son effectively leads the child to an untimely death, for in raising a rascal he will effectively set his son on the path of lawlessness and violence.[11]

The same duality is found in the Aramaic version of Ahikar from Elephantine:[12]

---

11 On "retrospective patterning" see Barbara Herrnstein, *Poetic Closure: A Study of How Poems End*, University of Chicago Press, Chicago 1968, especially 10–14, 212. Seow summarizes retrospective patterning as "retrospective readjustment of interpretation as one progresses through a [text]." See Seow, "Orthography, Textual Criticism, and the Poetry of Job," 76.

12 Ahikar 177 (Column 12 [J] l. 3). See Bezalel Porten and Ada Yardeni, *Textbook of Aramaic Documents from Ancient Egypt*, The Hebrew University, Jerusalem 1993, 48.

If I beat you, son, you will not die　　　הן אמחאנך ברי לא תמות
but if I leave you be [you shall not live][13]　　והן אשבקן על לבבך [לא תחיי]

At first glance, the first hemistich appears to imply (1a) – "you will live *even if* I beat you" – however, upon reading the second hemistich it becomes evident that the first hemistich implies quite the opposite – (1b) "you will escape death *only if* I beat you."[14]

The fact that the very same duality is found in Ahikar and in Proverbs – though the duality is expressed by different syntactic means and in two different languages – coupled with the fact that Wisdom literature is notoriously diffusive[15] – suggests that the play on words is probably not mere coincidence and that we are dealing here with a shared technique, the analysis of which belongs to the realm of the study of literary conventions in antiquity.

Let us now consider Prov 19:18:

יסר בנך כי יש תקוה ואל המיתו אל תשא נפשך

This verse, too, can be read as (1a) *Chastise your son since there is [still] hope but do not strive to kill him!*[16]; or as (1b): *Do not seek to have your son killed – chastise him while there is still hope!*[17]

In all three examples – two from Proverbs and one from Ahikar – readings (1a) and (1b), though quite different in nuance, do not offer opposite advice: both encourage generous application of the rod as a proactive educational device. However, Prov 19:18 also allows for a third, diametrically opposite reading:

(2) *Beat your son while there is still hope, and pay no heed to his whining!*

---

13 "Leave you be" – literally, "leave you to your heart." See also n. 14.

14 The Armenian version spells out the logic of this verse: "Son, spare not the rod to thy son [...] if thou leave him to his own will, he becomes a thief; and they take him to the gallows and to death, and he becomes unto thee a reproach and breaking of heart." See F. C. Conybeare et al. *The Story of Ahikar*, Cambridge University Press Warehouse, London 1898, 27.

15 See James C. Vanderkam, "Ahikar/Ahiqar (Person)," in: *The Anchor Bible Dictionary*, Volume 1, ed. David Noel Freedman, Doubleday, New York 1992, 113–115; and Vanderkam, "Ahiqar, Book of," in: *The Anchor Bible Dictionary*, 119–120

16 Fox, Michael V., *Proverbs 10–31: A New Translation with Introduction and Commentary*, Yale University Press, New Haven 2009, 656–657. The progression from chastisement to (nearly) killing is also found at Ps 118:18. The text implies that a father may have the urge to do so.

17 While reading (1b) may seem somewhat strained (the order of the hemistichs is inverted in English for the sake of clarity), it is allowed by the grammar of the verse, and is accepted by many ancient and modern commentators, perhaps because it dovetails with Proverbs 23:13–14 (and Ahikar).

Since the ancient manuscripts were unvocalized, הַמִּיתוֹ is a homograph, which may be read either as הֲמִיתוֹ "the killing of him" – an infinitive construct of the *hiph'il* of מו"ת, with a 3.m.sg. objective pronominal suffix, as in readings (1a) and (1b) – or as הֶמְיָתוֹ, the substantive הֶמְיָה with a possessive pronominal suffix, "his [pleading] voice" (see Ps 55:18).[18] This alternative reading is possible also in the vocalized Masoretic text if we consider הֲמִית to be a noun derived from המ"י and equivalent to הֶמְיָה ("[pleading] voice") precisely after the manner of שְׁבִית (= שְׁבָיָה, שְׁבִי, from שב"י) and בְּכִית (= בְּכִי, from בכ"י), forms that are attested in Biblical Hebrew.[19]

It is essential to recognize that readings (1) and (2) are both grammatically unlikely. Reading (1) is grammatically awkward, since infinitive constructs are never preceded by the preposition אֶל.[20] Had the author wished to convey reading (1) alone, one would have expected him to use either ולהמיתו אל תשא נפשך (with an infinitive construct),[21] or ואל מותו אל תשא נפשך (with מות perceived as a substantive, מָוֶת, not as a *qal* infinitive) – but not the hybrid אל המיתו. Reading (2), on the other hand, is problematic, since נָשָׂא נֶפֶשׁ אֶל does not denote "take heed of," but rather "long for."[22] Had the author wished to convey this reading alone, one would have expected some other phrase, using שמע or האזין with שועה or תחנונים (cf. Ps 28:2, 31:23, 143:1 *et passim*). However, the more natural grammar for (1) would spoil reading (2); and a more natural formulation of (2) would lead to the loss of readings (1a) and (1b).

2.3 Identifying a double-edged word

The fact that both readings are grammatically awkward (yet acceptable, with a stretch of the grammar)[23] suggests that certain constraints were at play. The

---

18 Several commentators – modern as well as medieval – follow this reading (see Jäger, Baumgartner, Ralbag and Nahmias cited in Fox, *Proverbs 10–31*, 657).

19 See Yehudah Ḳil, *Sefer Mishlei*. Mossad Harav Kook, Jerusalem 1983, 128–129.

20 The only exception of which I am aware is אל הלקח ארון האלהים (twice – in 1 Sam 4:19, 21), which is altogether different. אל there is either used in the sense of על, or is a scribal error for על.

21 Assuming that נשא נפש can be used in this manner – it is attested only with common nouns, not with infinitives. Alternatively, a different idiom altogether, such ולהמיתו אל תחפץ, or ואל תבקש המיתו (cf. Exod 4:24, Jer 26:21, or להמיתו, as at Ps 37:32) would have been used.

22 This reading is rejected by Fox on these grounds.

23 On the one hand, while the grammar of אל המיתו is highly unusual and unparalleled, the phrase could be considered technically grammatical on the assumption that הֲמִית had come to be perceived as a common noun rather an infinitive. However, the construction with אל would still be awkward for, a form derived from the infinitive. On the other hand, it is pos-

usage of a double-edged word depends to a great extent on the dexterity of the author, who is often forced to resort to rare or awkward grammatical constructions in order to retain the desired duality. We will return to this formal tool for the identification of double-edged words in our treatment of Job, the chastised son who is struck time and again, his complaint unheeded, but not killed (Job 2:6; see also Eliphaz's words in 5:17–19).

It is difficult to prove that authors were trained in a particular technique such as double-edged wording, or were even consciously aware of its availability, since there is no surviving Ancient Israelite literature comparable to Aristotle's *Poetics* or Demetrius' *On Style*. Even the most striking examples of the use of a literary technique, after all, may be a figment of the interpreter's imagination – and may provide valuable literary insight into the text but not any historical information about the scribal circles in which it was produced.

This example supplies us with two criteria that may assist in recognizing that double-edged wording was a generative technique in Israelite Wisdom circles: multiple attestation in diverse syntactic constructions, and irregular grammar. In this case, the *double entendre* upon which the double-edged word is a further elaboration is found in more than one Biblical tradition and in one non-Biblical text (the double-edged word, however, is unique to Prov 19:18). And the rough grammar of Prov. 19:18 gives the author away. One cannot expect the two criteria – multiple attestation in different languages and grammatical irregularity – to both be present very often. The likelihood of finding the same pun three times is particularly slight, and irregular grammar is likely to be found only where the author *fails* to execute the *double entendre* perfectly. In other words, the better the crime, the fewer the fingerprints.

However, even a small number of examples suffice to demonstrate that the study of double-edged wording in Israelite Wisdom literature belongs not only to the realm of reader response, but that such wording was an available technique in ancient Israelite Wisdom circles.

3 Dramatic Irony

We will now turn to the second technique mentioned above, dramatic irony. Dramatic irony arises when the reader is privy to vital information that is de-

---

sible – if somewhat strained – to read the phrase נשא נפש, usually "long for," more generally as "focus on," both here and in its other attestations, e.g., Deut 24:15.

nied to one or more of the characters, and, as a result, is able to ascribe a sharply different sense to certain of the characters' own statements.[24]

As a preliminary to our discussion of dramatic irony in the Book of Job, it is necessary to acknowledge the problem of the text-historical relation between the book's frame narrative and the dialogues. While there is some indication that the frame narrative (roughly, 1–2, 42:7–17) and the dialogues (roughly, 3–42:6) were at the very least joined intelligently and purposefully, the text-historical relation between them remains subject to scholarly debate. Moreover, the dialogue itself is almost certainly not the work of one author (the speeches of Elihu, for example, which will not be discussed here, are often considered secondary), and the text of the frame narrative may also be composite.[25] In the following discussion, it will be assumed that at least parts of the dialogue were shaped with a clear awareness of the central themes of the frame narrative. Note that the dialogue in its present form presupposes the existence of a frame narrative, though not necessarily precisely the surviving narrative.

Some poignant examples of dramatic irony are predicated primarily on plot shifts rather than grammatical twists, such as Oedipus' opening speech in Sophocles' *Oedipus Rex*,[26] and Duncan's self-assured gratefulness in *Macbeth* 1.6. The words of Eliphaz in 15:8–9 offer a pertinent example:

הבסוד אלוה תשמע ... מה ידעת ולא נדע תבין ולא עמנו הוא

Have you listened in the council of God? ... What do you know that we do not know? What do you discern that is not available to us?

Eliphaz takes Job's insistence on his own righteousness as a personal insult against his intelligence. He begins with accusing Job of choosing "crafty words" (ותבחר לשון ערומים) – a clever poetic device, since "choosing crafty words" is precisely what our poet is doing in the present verse. Sarcastically, Eliphaz asks Job whether he is older and wiser than his friends: "Are you the firstborn of the human race? Were you brought forth before the hills?" The

---

24 Baldack, Chris, *The Oxford Dictionary of Literary Terms*, 3rd *Edition*, Oxford University Press, Oxford 2008.

25 For a recent brief summary see Choon Leong Seow, *Job 1–21: Interpretation and Commentary*, William B. Eerdmans Publishing, Grand Rapids 2013, 27–29; for a concise history of the scholarship on this topic see Newsom, *The Book of Job*, 3–11.

26 The statement "Children, it were not meet that I should learn [these things] from others" (ll. 6–7) ironically encapsulates the king's condition; on the other hand, his self-portrayal as (potentially) *dysálgētos* in l. 12 may be a pun on "hard-hearted" (the sense implied to his interlocutors) and "hard-to-be-borne, painful" (the sense available to the audience). See Sophocles, *Oedipus the King*, trans. F. Storr, Fletcher and Son Ltd, Norwich 1981, 7.

answer, of course, is negative – in fact, the friends are much older than Job (15:10).[27] Eliphaz then ridicules Job for having no "insider's knowledge" of God's plans: "Do you listen in on the divine council? … What do you know and we do not? What do you understand and we do not?"

For the reader, these questions echo against Eliphaz, for neither the interrogator nor the addressee have listened in the council of God. The reader, however, has "listened at God's keyhole"[28] during two such councils (1:6–12; 2:1–7a) and specifically during sessions that bear directly upon the course of the narrative (note the strict denotation of סוֹד [15:8] as "council"). Eliphaz is thus technically correct, but for the wrong reason: Job is mistaken in accusing God of maltreating humans (4:20–23), for he has no direct access to the divine council; yet had Job eavesdropped on the divine council, his accusation would hardly have been alleviated, as Eliphaz wishes to imply – rather, it would have been greatly exacerbated.

Moreover, Eliphaz claims that Job's "windy words" (v. 3) are self-incriminating: "It is your own mouth that condemns you and not I; Your lips testify against you." (v. 6). Yet, as we have just seen, the argument he uses to demonstrate his point is unwittingly self-referential: Eliphaz has not been in on the divine council either, and so speaks useless, windy words.

Such use of irony, "crafty" as it may be, does not depend on double-edged wording. In this case, for example, the reader knows that the implied answer to the character's rhetorical question is correct. The character is not wrong about the implied answer to the question, only about the conclusions that he draws from it. We will now turn to cases in which irony is predicated on double-edged wording, where not only the characters' implied conclusions but also their very words are subject to an alternate reading.

4 Dramatic Irony and Double-Edged Words

We will examine three cardinal ironic aspects of the Book of Job: Job's alleged accountability for his suffering, the crude view of retribution as a long-term

---

27 The phrase עִמָּנוּ in 15:9 may simply mean "on our side"; see Seow, *Job 1–21*, 695, 701, 712. Note that while the plain reading of 15:10 may suggest that Job's friends are even older than his father, it is possible that the claim is made for dramatic purposes. Seow identifies the speech as ironic, but speaks of irony in the general sense (not "dramatic irony"), not noting the privileged status of the readers and the sinister reading thus available to them.
28 The image is from Stephen Mitchell, *The Book of Job*. HarperCollins Publishers, New York 1987, 41.

investment, and YHWH's "failed numinosity." In all three cases, I will claim, the author of the dialogue has, in key passages, strategically placed extensive double-edged words in the mouths of the characters, allowing for two diametrically opposed readings: one according with the point of view of the characters, the other with the point of view of the reader.

4.1 Job's alleged accountability

YHWH, the śāṭān, and the reader, of course, know that Job was meticulously blameless, and that his suffering is the result of a heavenly wager. They are thus privy to information unavailable to Job and his friends, who have not read the text and were not present in the divine councils of Chapters 1–2. As a result, throughout the dialogue Job's "friends" claim that if Job is suffering thus, it must be due to some action on his part. Job, however, knows (unlike the friends) that he has been righteous all along,[29] and so denies his friends' allegations, repeatedly claiming: "It is nothing that I have done!" At the end, God vindicates Job, claiming that the friends had spoken wrongly (42:7)[30]; but *we* know that, in a very concrete sense, Job was wrong and the friends were right on this matter, though not in the sense that they think. We know that Job was in fact suffering because of his actions; the reason he was selected is that he was indeed so meticulously blameless. If YHWH, the śāṭān, Job, and the omniscient narrator agree upon anything, it is that Job was righteous – though they may differ as to whether his righteousness is unconditional or "bought and paid for like a waiter's smirk."[31] Thus, when Job states "It is nothing that I

---

29 In 13:26b, Job mentions the possibility of apparently minor transgressions in his youth.

30 There is ongoing debate regarding the precise import of the text of this verse, and its general import, particularly as to whether YHWH's appraisal of Job refers to the broad contours of Job's standpoint throughout the dialogue, or only to his last words. See most recently Avi Shveka and Pierre Van Hecke, "The Metaphor of Criminal Charge as Paradigm for the Conflict between Job and his Friends," in: *Ephemerides Theologicae Lovanienses* 90 (2014) 99–119. The controversies have limited bearing on the general claim made here, since YHWH unambiguously accuses the comforters of speaking wrongly.

31 The phrase is employed by Nickels in Archibald MacLeish's play *J. B.*, a modern version of the Book of Job. See Archibald MacLeish, *J. B.: A Play in Verse*. Houghton Mifflin Company, Boston 1958. In the Book of Job, the narrator (1:1) and God (1:8, 2:3) claim Job to be blameless, upright, god-fearing, and avoiding wrong. The śāṭan admits that Job has "feared" God at least thus far (1:9; יָרֵא, a stative, functions not as a participle but as a finite verb here; see Samuel Rolles Driver and George Buchanan Gray, *A Critical and Exegetical Commentary on the Book of Job*. T&T Clark, Edinburgh 1921, 1.13).

have done!" he is wrong, and when his friends claim that his suffering is due to his conduct, they are right, albeit for the wrong reason.

Such a view, in which attracting the attention of God by means of excessive righteousness can be calamitous, is explicit in Qohelet. Admittedly, Qohelet is probably a significantly later composition, but there is no reason to assume that this line of thought was not available to earlier Wisdom Literature authors.[32]

This irony is most clearly reflected in Eliphaz's final speech (Chapter 22), which he opens with a series of rhetorical questions. With the progression of the dialogue throughout the Book of Job the friends' tone has become increasingly aggressive; at this point, Eliphaz not only denies the possibility that Job was righteous beyond reproach, but proceeds to accuse him of atrocities for which he is presumably being punished:[33]

1. וַיַּעַן אֱלִיפַז הַתֵּימָנִי וַיֹּאמַר
2. הַלְאֵל יִסְכָּן גָּבֶר ...
3. הַחֵפֶץ לְשַׁדַּי כִּי תִצְדָּק וְאִם בֶּצַע כִּי תַתֵּם דְּרָכֶיךָ
4. הֲמִיִּרְאָתְךָ יֹכִיחֶךָ יָבוֹא עִמְּךָ בַּמִּשְׁפָּט

(1) *Eliphaz the Temanite spoke up and said:*
(2) *Can a man be profitable to God? ...*
(3) *Does Shaddai desire that you be in the right, or is there any gain [for Him] that you act blamelessly?*
(4) *Is it due to your piety [literally: "due to your [god-]fearing"] that He reproves you, and comes to judgment against you?*

The obvious answer to each of these rhetorical questions, at least from the point of view of Eliphaz, is negative: indeed, 5a might be rendered "What, you think it's because you are so *righteous* that God reproves you?!" Eliphaz then explicates his claims with positive indicative formulations:

(6) *For you have exacted pledges of your brothers for nothing, and stripped the naked of their clothing.*
(7) *You have given no water to the weary to drink, and you have withheld bread from the hungry ...*

---

32 For example, Qoh 7:16. See J. Pedersen, *Scepticisme Israelite*, Librairie Felix Alean, Paris 1931, 29–54. For a relatively early dating of the Book of Job, see Seow, *Job 1–21*, 45.
33 Naphtali H. Tur-Sinai's privative reading of מִיִּרְאָתְךָ, and his view that the entire passage is not Eliphaz's own view but a quotation of Job's, is not followed by most commentaries and translations. See Naphtali H. Tur-Sinai, *The Book of Job: a New Commentary*, Hotza'at Yavneh, Tel Aviv 1954, 203.

It stands to reason that even Job would agree with certain premises underlying Eliphaz's rhetorical questions – for example, that it cannot be due to his righteousness that God reproves him – though he clearly rejects Eliphaz's subsequent accusations.

The reader, however, knows that the correct answer to all of Eliphaz's rhetorical questions in vv. 2–4 is actually affirmative. *Does Shaddai desire that you be in the right, or is there any gain [for him] that you act blamelessly?* Yes, for YHWH has much to gain or lose from Job's conduct – Job's conduct being the basis for YHWH's wager with the *śāṭān* – and so YHWH certainly desires that Job remain righteous, and he has quite a lot to gain if Job acts blamelessly. (4) *Is it due to your piety that He reproves you, and enters into judgment with you?* Indeed, it is precisely due to Job's piety that YHWH has chosen to target him, and to enter into judgment with him. As noted earlier, the omniscient narrator reveals in the opening scene that had Job *not* been תם ("blameless") and ירא אלהים ("god-fearing," "pious") it is likely that none of these calamities would have befallen him (1:8).[34]

Note, too, that in the words underlined above, Eliphaz alludes twice – unwittingly, of course – precisely to the words in the frame narrative that disclose the true answer that is unavailable to him. For God twice says to the *śāṭān*,

השמת לבך על/אל עבדי איוב ... איש תם וישר ירא אלהים וסר מרע

Have you taken notice of my servant Job ... blameless and upright, pious [literally: god-fearing] and avoiding wrong? (1:8, 2:3)

This usage of double-edged words becomes even more significant when we consider its critical placement in the final major speech from the three friends – this speech was perhaps, originally, the last of their speeches[35] and in a sense epitomizes the friends' claims. This point is further evidenced by the appearance of double-edged words in another clearly strategic location of the friends' argument: the opening of Eliphaz's speech. Such placement implies that double-edged wording not only appears in the Book Job, but also literally frames the entirety of Job's friends' claims, setting the tone for their speeches.

---

34 Robert Gordis terms Eliphaz's statement "bitterly ironic," but by this he means "sarcastic" – apparently not noticing the dramatic irony that it entails; see Gordis, *The Book of Job*, 245. Both elements of this dramatic irony are noted, however, in David J. A. Clines, *Job Vols. 1–3*, Word Biblical Commentary 17, 18A, 18B, Thomas Nelson Publishers, Inc., Nashville 1989–2011, 2.551, 554, respectively.

35 The brief speech of Bildad III (25:1–6), at least in the present state of the text, is little more than an echo of Eliphaz I and II (4:17, 15:14–15). On the possibility that originally the comforters' speeches ended at 22:30 (Eliphaz III) see Tur-Sinai, *The Book of Job*, 227–228.

In Eliphaz's first speech, following an initial chastisement of Job (4:2–5), he poses a rhetorical question to Job (v. 6):

הלֹא יראתך כסלתך תקוותך ותם דרכיך

The verse is often translated along the following lines:

> Is not your <u>piety</u> [literally, "[god]-fearing"] your confidence, / Your integrity your hope?[36]

This reading suits its context well. It caps vv. 2–4, referring to Job's previous security (Eliphaz has not yet come to deny that Job was a god-fearing and blameless man), and introduces 6–11, in which Eliphaz insists that the wicked, not the righteous, shall be destroyed. Thus Eliphaz rationalizes Job's previous flourishing (as being due to his piety and blamelessness) and enjoins Job to persist in his piety, lest he perish.

However, the reader, having just read Chapters 1–2, recognizes that Eliphaz's words are patently false. The reader knows that Job's extreme piety, far from vouchsafing his enduring success, is the source of his present calamities. The suspicious reader will also note two grammatical irregularities, the first being the verse's strange structure.

Since most translators and commentators agree that the verse, like the rest of the passage, is composed in *parallelismus membrorum*, one would expect the *waw* to precede the word תקוותך ("your hope"), or to be absent altogether. To most commentators and translators, in fact, this is so self-evident that the verse is simply translated as if the unusual *waw* did not exist – it is ascribed to a sloppy copyist, or interpreted away on various (legitimate) philological grounds.[37]

However, a much more straightforward reading, one that does not require interpreting away the *waw*, produces the reading "your piety, your hope and your righteousness are/were your *kislâ*." (*Kislâ* is still the natural predicate of the verse, though not the only possible one).[38] This is precisely the syntax reflected in the Septuagint and in some Medieval Jewish commentaries (such as Rashi).

The second irregularity is the unusual and ambiguous form *kislâ*. The term appears only once again in BH, in Ps 85:9 (if MT is correct), where it is usually

---

36 The word order in each hemistich in the translation is reversed to accord with conventions of subject-predicate order in English. On the verse's syntax see Hoffman, "The Use of Equivocal Words in the First Speech of Eliphaz," 118 n. 1. Translation based on JPS.

37 For example, *waw emphaticum* or pleonastic *waw* (Clines, *Job*, 1.109).

38 Once again, the subject-predicate order in the English translation accords with English style. On the verse's syntax see Hoffman, "The Use of Equivocal Words in the First Speech of Eliphaz," 118 n. 1.

translated as "folly."[39] In Job 4:6, scholars generally view it, quite justifiably, as equivalent to כֶּסֶל/כֵּסֶל. However, this form is itself ambiguous: it denotes both "security" (Prov 3:26, Ps 78:7, and twice in Job – 8:14 and 31:24) and "folly" (or "stupidity") (Qoh 7:25, Ps 49:14).[40] But which of these does Eliphaz imply?

One is tempted to claim that *kislâ* here must denote "confidence, security," since Eliphaz could not possibly have claimed that Job's piety was his folly (Eliphaz, after all, had not read the frame narrative); it is also tempting to rely on the parallelism with 4:6b, claiming that *kislâ* is roughly synonymous with תקוה ("hope") just as יראה ("piety"; literally, fear [of God]) is roughly synonymous with תֹם דְּרֶךְ ("blamelessness of way"). However, as noted, no such parallelism exists in 4:6, which reads "your piety, your hope and your righteousness are/were your *confidence/stupidity*." Eliphaz certainly did not intend to denote that it was folly on Job's part to be so righteous; the reader, however, knows that in a very concrete sense it was Job's greatest error.

The strange grammatical incongruity of the verse speaks in favor of this reading (though one must cautiously grant that the misplaced *waw* may simply be a copyist's error). Thus we see that the dramatic irony of the friends' wrong-yet-accurate accusation is reflected, by a play of double-edged meaning, not only in the storyline but also in their very accusation.

It is noteworthy that the double-edged words discussed here – taken from Eliphaz's opening and closing speeches – share a curious idiom. The term יראה ("fear") in the sense of יראת אלהים ("fear of God"/"piety") is unique to 4:6 and in 22:4, and is found nowhere else in the Hebrew Bible without God as the objective genitive (or a corresponding pronominal suffix referring to God), though the phrase יראת אלהים (roughly, "piety") is common.[41] This usage cre-

---

39 Admittedly, the text of 85:9 and its meaning are uncertain. BDB 493a emends the rest of the verse and translates כסלה as "confidence." It has been conjectured that the term is also to be restored in Pss 84:6, 143:9.

40 Ps 49:14 is difficult, but the attestation in Qohelet is unambiguous. LXX understands כסלה in Job 4:6 as "stupidity" (αςφροσυῳνη), as does Rashi (where the subversive element is lacking), and possibly the Talmudic passage in b Sanh 89b, where it is put in the mouth of Satan speaking to Abraham (and where the subversive element may be present). Gordis, despite his acute awareness of ambiguity in Wisdom Literature, and of the etymological link between the two meanings of the root כסל, does not note this double-edged wording (Gordis, *The Book of Job*, 47). Hoffman notices the ambiguity in the verse, but in a different way (rejected by Clines) than proposed here. See Hoffman, "The Use of Equivocal Words in the First Speech of Eliphaz" and Clines, *Job*, 1.109.

41 Job 15:4a (Eliphaz II) may be considered an exception, but the term אֵל is explicit in 4b. In Prov 14:16 the term ירא is not shorthand for ירא אלהים (*contra* Tur-Sinai, *The Book of Job*, 45).

ates a subtle link between the two double-edged words in Eliphaz's opening and concluding speeches, which frame the friends' speeches.

4.2 Retribution as a long-term investment

Job's friends turn out to be correct about another cardinal matter as well. Throughout the dialogue, Job complains that the wicked may flourish while the just pine away in suffering. His friends, on the other hand, assure him that, though such unfairness may occur, it is temporary. For retribution, in the long run, functions essentially like the stock market in a stable economy: there may be ups and downs along the way, but eventually good investments pay off. Therefore, the friends claim, Job's present predicament – and the apparent success of the wicked – is not indication of a general failure of the system of divine retribution, a system which is in fact fair.[42]

The argument that the apparent success of the wicked is temporary is per-haps the single most recurrent theme in the dialogue. It is repeated by each of the three friends (4:17–27; 8:4–22; 11:19–20; 15:20–35; 18:5–21; 20:5–29, *et passim*) and, though it presents a patently crude conception of YHWH as a "money-changing machine," the friends are proven right on this matter as well.[43] For in Chapter 42, Job is not only restored to his former glory but also repaid twofold.

The irony is particularly glaring in Eliphaz's closing words (22:21–30, literal and thematic allusions to the closing narrative are underlined):

אם תשוב עד שדי תבנה ... ותשא אל אלוה פניך תעתיר אליו וישמעך ונדריך תשלם ימלט
אי-נקי ונמלט בבר כפיך

If you return to Shaddai you will be <u>restored</u> ... you will <u>lift up your face to God</u>, <u>you will pray to Him</u>, and He will listen to you, and you will pay your vows ... <u>He will deliver the guilty</u>; he will be delivered through the cleanness of your hands.

As Gordis notes, "[t]here is exquisite irony in the fact that Eliphaz's confident assurance that the righteous can intercede for sinners is fulfilled to the letter in a dramatic and totally unexpected way – after the dialogue is completed, it is Job who is called upon to plead for Eliphaz and his Friends (42:7–10)."[44] Eliphaz's very wording unintentionally references actual events of the frame

---

42 Strangely, it does not accurately correspond to the central issue at hand – the righteous sufferer – but rather its mirror image – the successful wrongdoer.

43 See Miles, *God: A Biography*, 310 (though not noting the dramatic irony this entails): "Prov-erbs is confirmed in some abstract sense; its system holds up functionally if not morally."

44 Gordis *The Book of Job*, 239

narrative, such as "if you return to Shaddai" (אִם תָּשׁוּב עַד שַׁדַּי, 22:23) || "and YHWH restored Job's fortunes (literally, "returned the return" of Job)" (וה' שָׁב אֶת שְׁבִית/שְׁבוּת אִיּוֹב, 42:10), "and lift up your face to God" (וְתִשָּׂא אֶל אֱלוֹהַ פָּנֶיךָ, 22:26b) || "for to him I will show favor" (literally: "it is only his face that I will raise," כִּי אִם פָּנָיו אֶשָּׂא, 42:8b), and "you will pray to Him" תַּעְתִּיר אֵלָיו (22:27) || "pray for you" (יִתְפַּלֵּל עֲלֵיכֶם, 42:8a, see also 10).[45] The term תִּבָּנֶה (22:23), too, may carry overtones of bearing progeny, referred to in 42:13 (cf. Gen 16:2). Eliphaz is thus not only ignorant that his claims will be realized, but also that he himself is using the language that will describe their realization.

Gordis and others are well aware of the irony in Eliphaz's speech,[46] and there is in fact a sense of poetic justice in this particular aspect of the denouement of Chapter 42. However, the aspect of the irony that I wish to stress here is not that Eliphaz unwittingly predicts his own predicament and future need for Job's intercession, but rather that he is actually technically correct – to the letter – in formulating his central claim, which is false: that divine retribution is unfailing and just. The falsity of Eliphaz's general claim, despite its technical accuracy in Job's case, is established by YHWH himself, who declares, in Job 42:7, that Eliphaz's general claims are false. While YHWH's declarations do not necessarily reflect the views of the author, one would be hard pressed to claim that the reader, having progressed this far into The Book of Job, would be even minimally accepting of the traditional view of just retribution.[47]

Irony here takes a more temporary form than it did in the previous section, for in this case Eliphaz eventually discovers what is unknown to him. The irony presented resembles that of the previous section, however, in that it is strategically placed not only in Eliphaz's final speech but also in his opening speech (5:17–27):[48]

---

45 Translations based on JPS.

46 Note, too, the close link between the beginning of Eliphaz III (הֲלֹא יִסְכֹּן גָּבֶר, v. 2), the irony of which was just discussed, and the end of Eliphaz's speech discussed here (הַסְכֶּן נָא עִמּוֹ וּשְׁלָם, v. 21).

47 Note that at least one other ancient Israelite Wisdom text explicitly declares this traditional view to be false, namely Qohelet (e.g., Qoh 9:2). Northrop Frye has wryly noted that "[t]he Book of Job is technically a comedy by virtue of Job's restoration in the last few verses, but the comic conclusion seems so wrenched and arbitrary that it is hard to think of it as anything but a wantonly spoiled tragedy." See Northrop Frye, "Blake's Reading of the Book of Job," in *The Book of Job* (ed. Harold Bloom; New York: Modern Critical Interpretations, 1988) 21–35 (the quote is from p. 23).

48 For example, 8:7 (Bildad I) – where the use of רֵאשִׁיתֶךָ and אַחֲרִיתֶךָ, "your beginning || your end", is echoed by the use of the pair in the frame narrative (42:12). Note the reference to the death of Job's (first set of) sons in 8:4 (cf. 1:19).

(17) *How happy is the one whom God reproves; therefore do not despise the discipline of Shaddai.*

(18) *for He wounds, but He binds up; He strikes, but his hands heal*

(19) *He will deliver you from six troubles; in seven no evil shall touch you* (לֹא יִגַּע בְּךָ רָע) ...

(21) *You shall be hidden from the scourge of the tongue* (בְּשׁוֹט לָשׁוֹן), *and shall not fear destruction when it comes ...*

(25) *You shall know that your descendants will be many, and your offspring like the grass of the earth.*

(26) *You shall come to your grave in ripe old age ...*

In vv. 25–26 Eliphaz describes the events of Chapter 42:13, 16–17 quite accurately; in vv. 19–21 he unwittingly echoes the opening scene thematically and idiomatically,[49] as if he knew that the *śāṭān* was the source of Job's suffering (in fact Eliphaz probably knows nothing of the existence of this celestial being).

In the final verse of this opening speech (5:27), Eliphaz declares *"See, we have investigated this and it is just so – listen to it, and you – find out for yourself!"* He believes he is addressing Job and telling him to listen to his words. However, the irregular, pleonastic use of the independent pronoun *"you"* in this verse may suggest that Eliphaz is in fact offering the engaged reader an unfailing and practical empirical device for ascertaining the truth of his (false) claim: namely, *"turn to the end of the narrative, and find out for yourself!"*

4.3 Failed Numinosity

An especially notable reading of the Book of Job, and one that has markedly impacted scholarship over the past century, is Rudolph Otto's treatment of the biblical text, in the tenth chapter of his work *The Idea of the Holy*.[50] Broadly speaking, Otto highlight the irrational aspect of creation that is revealed to Job in YHWH's final speeches; this aspect – the combination of *tremendum* and *fascinans* that typifies the deity itself – is conveyed to Job *and to the reader* (note the conflation of hierarchies of knowledge at work in this interpretation) through the overwhelming descriptions of Leviathan, Behemoth, and other

---

49 For instance, the six troubles recall the several consecutive strikes (five, to be precise) inflicted by "the evil one" in Chapters 1–2. Many commentators associate שׁוֹט לָשׁוֹן with the *śāṭān*, who repetitively describes his activities by using a language of שׁוּט בָּאָרֶץ (1:7, 2:2). Lastly, the imagery of evil *touching* Job echoes the harmful touching of Job discussed in 1:11 and 2:5.

50 Otto, Rudolf, *The Idea of the Holy: An Inquiry into the Non-Rational Factor in the Idea of the Divine and its Relation to the Rational,* trans. John W. Harvey. Oxford University Press, New York, 1923.

dreadful creatures. Yʜᴡʜ's speeches are also inhabited by brainless birds who leave their eggs to be trampled by other beasts, and by rain that falls on uninhabited deserts, with no apparent design or purpose and certainly not for the benefit of humanity, which is insignificant and powerless in comparison with the crown of creation, Leviathan (41:26).[51]

Certain aspects of Otto's reading have garnered criticism, yet there is validity to his basic arguments that God in these speeches highlights irrational aspects of creation rather than focusing exclusively on its impeccable design, and that humanity is depicted as relatively insignificant within the created world. Yet this reading of the monstrosities of creation renders new kinds of monstrosities – logical incongruities that threaten to undermine Otto's reading altogether.

First, if in His speech from the whirlwind Yʜᴡʜ's wishes to convey to Job that "You think you are important enough for me to stoop to talk to you? Well, you are not" – then, aside from the general paradoxical nature of this formulation,[52] the message is starkly contradicted by the frame narrative. Yʜᴡʜ's first words to the śāṭān regarding Job are "Have you noticed my servant Job?" (twice: 1:8 and 2:3) In a sense, then, His effusive disquisition about Leviathan and Behemoth is merely a cover story for what is actually a petty game with the śāṭān. Aware of the frame narrative, the reader is therefore cognizant of the falsity of Yʜᴡʜ's claim in a way that Job is not.

More importantly, as has often been noted, Yʜᴡʜ does not provide Job satisfying answers to his questions. Certainly, He does not reveal to him that there was a wager and that he has just withstood a trial, as happens in Genesis 22 and in the story of Hariścandra discussed below. Instead, Yʜᴡʜ resorts to "cosmic bullying,"[53] and "triumphantly displays a number of trump cards that seem to belong to a different game."[54]

This behavior on the part of Yʜᴡʜ leads to what one might term "failed numinosity." Otto's reading may be insightful, but only from the point of view

---

51 The fact that parts of Yʜᴡʜ's speeches are suspected to be secondary additions (see Briggs Curtis, "On Job's Response to Yahweh") does not detract from the argument made here – indeed, there is greater likelihood that a late interpolator would have been acquainted with the frame narrative.

52 This was noticed by Frankel; see Frankel, "The Image of God in the Book of Job," 47, n. 54. A modern analogy from popular culture would be Carly Simon's famous line "You're so vain, you probably think this song is about you."

53 Alter, Robert, *Truth and Poetry in The Book of Job*." In *The Book of Job*, ed. Harold Bloom, Chelsea House Publishing, New York, 1988, 64. T. C. Ham, however, discerns a comforting tone in God's speech; see T. C. Ham, "The Gentle Voice of God in Job" in: *Journal of Biblical Literature* 132.3 (2013): 527–541.

54 Frye, Northrop, "Blake's Reading of the Book of Job" in: *The Book of Job*, ed. Bloom, 21–35.

of a character trapped within the perspective of Job and his friends. The reader of the Book of Job, having read the frame narrative, is unable to trust YHWH's self-aggrandizement and self-professed numinosity: for the reader, YHWH cannot be the sublime, disinterested, "wholly Other" that He claims to be – one who hardly takes notice of worthless human beings. The numinous effect of YHWH's speech is thus undermined by the frame narrative, for "thanks to the ingenuity of the Job-fabulist, the Lord's inscrutable ways have been made all too scrutable."[55]

These conflicting descriptions of YHWH are demonstrated in Job's final words, in 42:2–6. Considering its strategic location in the narrative, this speech has received ample attention and has been subject to much scholarly scrutiny. Job's brief response to YHWH contains several interpretive cruxes, including questions of lower and higher criticism, vocalization, verbal morphology, and the connotation of certain phrases. More generally, scholars disagree on whether the general tone of Job's reply expresses resignation, confession, defiance, sarcasm, or various combinations of these tones.[56]

Readers since antiquity have viewed the prevailing tone of Job's final remark (42:2–6) as one of repentance and recanting. However, since the 1970s it has become increasingly common to reject the ancient reading as pietistic and to instead read Job's words as being heroically defiant.[57]

Not all evidence amassed in recent literature in favor of a defiant Job (in Chapter 42) is equally convincing,[58] but enough evidence has been furnished

---

55 Miles, *God: A Biography*, 315. To be sure, that aspect of YHWH's numinous character which is refuted by the frame narrative is not the *tremendum* aspect, which is all the more present, but the *fascinans* aspect and the property of being inscrutable and "wholly other."

56 The problem is compounded by the interpretation of God's evaluation of Job's words in v. 8 (see footnote 30).

57 The shift in scholarship began in the 1970s (for example, see Dale Patrick, "The Translation of Job XLII 6," in: *Vetus Testamentum* 26 (1976): 369–371; and Briggs Curtis, "On Job's Response to Yahweh" – note that while Patrick departs from the traditional remorseful reading of Job's statement his alternative reading describes the speech as one of praise, not defiance) and was popularized in the 1980s – see Miles, *God: A Biography*; and Mitchell, *The Book of Job*. See also Frankel, "The Image of God in the Book of Job." Traditional readings still abound (see for example, John E. Hartley, *The Book of Job*, Eerdmans, Grand Rapids 1988, 537). The shift in interpretation is quite telling, since – as Newsom states – "[The Book of Job's] elusive nature allows interpreters to see mirrored in it perspectives congenial to the tenor of their own age" (see Newsom, *The Book of Job*, 3).

58 Particular stress has been placed on the intransitive use of אמאס (vocalized with MT as *qal*) without a direct object (or at the very least, an implied object), which is anomalous but not entirely unparalleled; and on the syntax of אמאס ונחמתי על עפר ואפר (v. 6), a phrase which, according to Tur-Sinai, "actually has no meaning whatsoever" (see Tur-Sinai, *The Book*

to raise serious suspicions against the exclusively repentant tone traditionally ascribed to the verses. Although a spectrum of grammatically legitimate readings of Job 42:2–6 exists, I will focus, in keeping with the argument presented thus far, on two extremes of this spectrum. Thus, I will argue that through clever deployment of double-edged wording – rhetorical questions with alternative implied answers, awkward grammar that allows for diametrically opposed readings, and equivocal use of direct speech which is itself embedded in direct speech – both readings were craftily condensed into a single phonetic (and graphic) sequence. The effect is that the verbal sequence lends itself to two diametrically opposite readings – the first has a recanting tone that one might expect from the character's point of view, whereas the second is a defiant reading that accords with the reader's perspective.

Let us begin with Job's first statement following the final speech from the whirlwind, in which the deity, rather than addressing Job's specific claims, responds with a display of omnipotence. Job begins with an acknowledgement, יַדַעְתִּי כִּי כֹל תוּכָל וְלֹא יִבָּצֵר מִמְּךָ מְזִמָּה ("I *now realize* [or: *have always known*] that you can do all things, and that no purpose of yours can be thwarted").[59]

The phrase וְלֹא יִבָּצֵר מִמְּךָ מְזִמָּה is ambiguous. The term מְזִמָּה denotes "plan" with no negative connotations, in several Biblical verses – indeed, it is often used as a stock parallel for such terms for knowledge and understanding as דַעַת and תְבוּנָה, and in Wisdom Literature it often carries positive connotations (see Prov 1:4, 2:11, 3:21, 5:2, 8:12). However, more often than not, the noun itself (even without an adjective with negative connotations), like the negatively charged verbal forms of זָמַם, carries a specific negative connotation, such as evil thoughts (Ps 10:4, Job 21:27), a plan to cause harm (Jer 23:20, 30:24, 51:11, 37:7), or more narrowly "machination" or "plot," particularly one that ought to be thwarted (Ps 10:2, 21:12, Prov 12:2, 24:8).

In our case, Job could be acknowledging that YHWH is almighty and capable of carrying out any plan, thereby expressing that he has internalized the message from YHWH's show of power (though in fact he had never denied

---

of Job, 350). The *ketib/qeri* (יָדַעְתָּ(י) (v. 2) has also been noted in this context – for a discussion see Clines, *Job 38–42*, 1207–1208.

59 This is one of many instances where Job states "I know"; in fact all instances of יָדַעְתִּי in the Book of Job (eleven in number – 9:2, 28, 10:13, 13:2, 13:18, 19:25, 21:27, 23:3 ("I wish I knew"), 29:16 ("one whom I do *not* know"), 30:23, 42:2 – are from Job. In other words, throughout the book Job insists that he knows, but in the end he learns that he knows nothing. I thank Gary Rendsburg (written communication) for this insight. Consideration of other forms of this verb complicate the statistics, but the numbers are striking. Elihu's statement לֹא יָדַעְתִּי in 32:22 is different inasmuch as it pertains to competence ("know how to") – rather than cognition ("know that").

Yhwh's omnipotence). As one scholar paraphrases, "[Job] believes that every-thing occurring on earth takes place within the framework of the divine wis-dom. No hostile force, be it earthly or heavenly, prevents God from carrying out His purpose."[60] However, given what a bully Yhwh has now proven himself to be, Job could equally well be saying, "I now realize you could be up to *anything* – I wouldn't put *any* machination past you."[61]

The specific negative overtones of the term מְזִמָּה (f. sg.) are strengthened here by the use of the preceding masculine form, יִבָּצֵר ("be too difficult," "be beyond one's reach") rather than the expected feminine, תִּבָּצֵר. While such alterations in the gender of the verb certainly occur in BH, particularly when a 3.m.sg. verb precedes the subject, it is by far the less likely choice – and may be a result of the author's allusion to Genesis 11:6.[62] The echo would not have been as strong had the author resorted to the (grammatically natural) feminine תִּבָּצֵר – hence the roughness of the grammar once again indicates that addi-tional literary forces are at work.

The second ambiguity pertains to the identification of direct speech. In Biblical literature, particularly in poetry, direct speech is often introduced with-out any verbal marker such as "he said"; thus the lack of graphic markers (for example, quotation marks) in the text in many cases renders the speaker ambiguous: the words uttered could be ascribed to a character expressing his or her own opinion, a quote within direct speech (for example, the view of his interlocutor), or simply the words of the narrator.

Verses 3a and 4 in the final speech of Job exemplify such ambiguity. Al-though these lines appear within a speech of Job, commentators usually con-sider them intrusive in the speech. Many commentators consider them a scribal error, or a direct quote of Yhwh's introductory words (38:2, 3b; 40:7b) within Job's direct speech (nearly verbatim, in 3a; by means of paraphrase, in 4), as in the left column of Table 1. Even scholars who ascribe the words to Job never-theless tend to hear in them subordination and supplication.[63] At any rate, the

---

60 Hartley, *The Book of Job*, 535–536.
61 Norman C. Habel recognized the negative connotation, with a "sidelong glance to the origi-nal 'scheme' of Yahweh to test Job" (Clines, *Job*, 1205). See Norman C. Habel, *The Book of Job: A Commentary*, Westminster Press, Philadelphia 1985, 581.
62 The intertext has been noted by many; for example, see Tur-Sinai, *The Book of Job*, 350.
63 For a representative sample of the scholarly views, see August Dillmann. *Hiob*. S. Hirzel, Leipzig 1869, 366; Heinrich Ewald, *Ewald's Commentary on the Book of Job*, trans. J. Frederick Smith, Williams and Norgate, London 1882, 311–312; Gordis, *The Book of Job*, 491, Habel, *The Book of Job*, 575–578; Marvin H. Pope, *The Anchor Bible Job*, Doubleday, New York 1965, 348; Harry Torczyner (Naphtali H. Tur-Sinai). *The Book of Job: A New Commentary*, Kiryath Sepher, Jerusalem 1957, 578–579. LXX preserves a vocative addressed to Yhwh in v. 4, clearly implying

implied answer to the rhetorical question ("me") appears so self-evident to commentators that some have gone so far as to emend the text accordingly – אני זה מעלים ("I am the one concealing ...").[64]

However, before resorting to this (admittedly legitimate) technique of supplying quotation marks on the basis of scholarly reconstruction of what one might expect Job to say, let us consider the verse as it stands – without inserting quotation marks. When this is done, Job's response is colored by a quite different tone, as in the right column of Table 1.

Table 1:

I acknowledge that you are omnipotent, and that no plan is too difficult for you.	ידעתי כי כל תוכל ולא יבצר ממך מזמה	I know you can do anything, and no _machination_ is beyond you.
You said, "Who is thus obscuring counsel without knowledge" – indeed, I spoke about things without understanding, about wondrous things without knowing.	מי זה מעלים עצה בלי דעת לכן הגדתי ולא אבין נפלאות ממני ולא אדע	Now, who is the one concealing his counsel without knowledge? Well, I really was talking without understanding, things hidden from me that I had not known about.
You said, "Listen here, so that I may speak, let me question you so that you can inform me"	שמע נא ואנכי אדבר אשאלך והודיעני	Now **you** listen to **me** speak, let **me** ask **you** and **you** tell **me**.
I had heard of You by hearsay, but now my own eye has seen You.	לשמע אזן שמעתיך ועתה עיני ראתך	I heard all about you, but now I have actually seen you.
Therefore, I despise [myself] and repent for being dust and ashes [or: upon dust and ashes].	על כן אמאס ונחמתי על עפר ואפר	Therefore, I am contemptuous and regretful, here upon dust and ashes.

Note that in this case, as in our first example from Chapter 22, the double-edged wording is based on the possibility of two alternative answers to a single rhetorical question – either "me" (Job) or "you" (YHWH). Note, moreover, that the "concealed" reading, which is technically unavailable to Job, is betrayed by Job's particular choice of words. For in 3a Job reiterates YHWH's rhetorical

---

that the words are Job's own. Note that even Miles and Mitchell do not remove the quotation marks.

64 For a summary and discussion see Clines, _Job 38–42_, 1205; see also Hartley, _The Book of Job_, 536, though he does not emend the text.

question (38:2), nearly verbatim. However, he replaces Yʜᴡʜ's term מחשיך
("darkens"/"obscures"), in the phrase מי זה מחשיך עצה ("who is it that darkens counsel [or: obscures the plan]"), with מעלים ("conceals"). Since מעלים
(unlike מחשיך) has the additional denotation of concealing information from
another person (as at 2 Kgs 4:27), the right-hand column could well be read as
Job's sardonic response – "Now, who is really the one concealing a scheme?"[65]

The argument has been made thus far without specific reference to v. 6,
which is notoriously ambiguous.[66] That the double-edged reading of Job's final
response also works for v. 6 can be evidenced by juxtaposing the "traditional-
ist" reading (left column, based on NRSV) with readings offered by several
scholars since the 1970s (right-hand column).[67] While none of the readings
suggested in the past are entirely satisfactory, a juxtaposition of two alternative
extremes on the spectrum of readings is illuminating:

Table 2:

Therefore I despise [myself]	על כן אמאס ונחמתי	*Therefore I despise [You, O Yʜᴡʜ]*
And repent in dust and ashes	על עפר ואפר	*and I am sorry for mankind*

A detailed analysis of the evidence in favor of each of the elements in these
readings would lead well beyond the scope of the present essay, but suffice it
to say that the grammar is awkward enough to render all the readings suggested thus far improbable. The lack of anything resembling scholarly consensus
about the import of these words also testifies to the absence of any satisfying
explanation.

In addition to the alternative answers that are available for Job's rhetorical
question in v. 3 and the possibility of reading Job's sentence as either a quotation of Yʜᴡʜ or a direct address to Yʜᴡʜ, other techniques for the formation
of double-edged words can now been identified in Job's final speech. For instance, the morphology of the unvocalized verb אמאס allows for a transitive
reading (אֶמְאַס "I despise") or a reflexive/medio-passive reading (אֶמָּאֵס "I despise myself"/"I am despised"), as well as other readings not discussed here.
The syntax of ונחמתי על עפר ואפר is also unclear: ונחמתי may be read as

65 See Isa 19:11, 40:13, 44:26; cf. 29:15, where לסתר עצה means hiding one's schemes (from
God).

66 See above, footnote 58.

67 See above, footnote 57.

forming a hendiadys with אֵמָאס and closing the first hemistich, in which case
על עפר ואפר likely (though not necessarily) denotes a location, the actual dust
and ashes in which Job now wallows; or it may be considered part of the idiom
[נח"מ] (niph'al) + על + indirect object] in the sense of [regret + direct object],
in which case it opens the second hemistich, which some scholars read as
describing a sense of regret about the human condition (humanity is figurative-
ly "dust and ashes", Gen. 18:27).

It is noteworthy that the Masoretes, rather than obliterating the ambiguity,
for example by vocalizing אֵמָאס as a *niph'al* (as possibly understood in the
Septuagint) or making a clear choice regarding the placement of ונחמתי in the
first or second hemistich, retained the ambiguity by leaving a transitive אֶמְאַס
dangling without an object (or even an implied object mentioned elsewhere in
the verse); and by retaining a *pataḥ* in ונחמתי (rather than a *qamets*, cf. Zec
8:14), despite the fact that one might expect it to be in pausal form, considering
its cantillation with an *etnaḥ*.[68] Thus, roughness in the grammar proves to be
a useful tool not only in the formation of double-edged words and in their
identification but also in their transmission.

5 Summary: Rhetorical Motivations of the Double-Edged Word

Thus far, we have distinguished clearly between the reader's point of view and
that of the characters in the Book of Job. We identified the author's use of
double-edged words, particularly when the readings are theologically

---

68 Regarding the status of this *etnaḥ* in אמ"ת (in a verse where an עולה ויורד is not present)
and the pausal form it would normally entail, see Ben-David, Israel. *Tsurot heḳsher ye-tsurot
hefseḳ ba-'Ivrit sheba-Miḳra : taḥbir ye-ṭa'ame ha-Miḳra.* Yerushalayim: Hotsa'at sefarim 'a. sh.
Y. L. Magnes, ha-Universiṭah ha-'Ivrit, 1995, 14 (admittedly, there are exceptions to the general
rule, and Ben-David has found ten such exceptions). Moreover, one cannot simply speak of
intentionality on the part of the masoretes in this case: on the one hand, they might have
been simply recording what they heard (in which case one might attribute the retention of the
ambiguity to the reciters, which is possible but more difficult to demonstrate); on the other
hand, they might have been recording two different contingent traditions at two different stages – without trying to conform the cantillation marks with the vowel system (see E. J. Revell,
"Pausal Forms and the Structure of Biblical Poetry," in: *Vetus Testamentum* 31 (1981): 186–199).
At any rate, the form as it stands – with a *pataḥ* on the pausal form – is not standard and
retains the ambiguity. On an additional ambiguity involved in this form, see Ben-David, *Tsurot
heḳsher*, 4 and the internal references there.

charged – offering conflicting views of the ideal of righteousness and divine retribution; and, in the last case discussed here, portraying an evil, conniving aspect of YHWH. Let us now consider the protagonist, rather than the author, as the intentional formulator of double-edged words. In other words, while the use of the technique is ultimately the author's, we must entertain the possibility that the author has endowed a character with the ability to speak with a split tongue. In the last case, in particular, one must consider the possibility that Job, at some level of consciousness, wishes to bless and "bless" YHWH at one and the same time.

For the purpose of contrast and clarification, let us examine a case of *double entendre* where the subversive, alternative reading is available to the character speaking. The Mārkaṇḍeya Purāṇa, a medieval Sanskrit narrative, tells of Hariścandra (sometimes termed, problematically, "the Indian Job"), the righteous and prosperous king of Ayodhyā, who was forced to forfeit his kingdom to the sage Viśvāmitra, to sell his wife and young son into servitude in order to pay off a debt to him, and finally to become slave to a lowly and harsh corpse-handler. One day, while the former king, in his devotion to truth, is working dutifully at the cremation grounds to serve his master, his wife suddenly arrives, carrying the corpse of their young boy in her arms. Although Hariścandra is covered in ashes from head to toe, his wife recognizes him and the two, overcome with grief, prepare to jump into the pyre together – but at this point the gods appear. Indra reveals that Hariścandra's devotion to truth has proven to be supreme; also, the lowly corpse-handler who had been Hariścandra's cruel master turns out to have been none other than Dharma, Law and Justice personified, in disguise. The boy is brought back to life and Indra announces to Hariścandra that he may now ascend to Heaven, having proven his devotion to truth.

At this point, the righteous king responds that it would be a grave crime for him to abandon his subjects in Ayodhya:

brahmahatyā gurorghāto govadhaḥ strīvadhastathā
tulyamebhirmahāpāpaṃ bhaktatyāge 'pyudāhṛtam
bhajantaṃ bhaktamatyājyamaduṣṭaṃ tyajataḥ sukham
neha nāmutra paśyāmi ... (MP 8.250–251)

Brahmin-killing, guru-slaying, woman-slaughter cattle-murder;
Evil on a par with these commits a devotee-deserter.
One deserting an underserving loyal, pious, devotee –
Nothing in this world or the next for [such a scoundrel] do I see.

Thus, Hariścandra refuses to accept the offer to ascend to heaven, suggesting instead, somewhat irreverently, that Indra ascend there himself. "If they [my subjects] go up to heaven with me," he explains, "then I, too, shall go;" but if they do not, he insists that he would rather descend to Hell than abandon them.

This speech, which echoes the words of Yudhiṣṭhira in the final passages of the seventeenth book of the *Mahābhārata*,[69] contains veiled criticism of Viś-vāmitra and the deities who were cognizant of Hariścandra's trial. The term *bhakta*, or "devotee" (ll. 251 and 252), while denoting the relation of a subject to the king (the meaning of the king's words at face value), also denotes the relation of a devotee – in this case, Hariścandra – to a deity. Hariścandra, who now recognizes that the agony he was subjected to was merely the test of his devotion to truth, is able to hurl – somewhat like Job in 42:2–6 – double-edged words at the gods, accusing them of the heinous crime of abandoning a pious and blameless devotee such as himself.

In the case of Job 42:2–6, the attribution of double-edged wording to the character is less likely, since Job never learns that his suffering was the result of a wager. However, such attribution is not impossible, since YHWH's harsh-ness is plainly evident from His response from the whirlwind even if He does not reveal the wager to His devotee. Moreover, it may be argued that YHWH, in speaking of the sea monster Leviathan – who, in the Book of Job, is no more than YHWH's rubber ducky (e.g., 40:29), but is elsewhere associated with pri-mordial antagonistic powers (Isa 27:1, Ps 74:14) – indicates that monstrous for-ces are inherent in creation – thus vaguely hinting to Job that satanic powers are involved in his present predicament.[70]

Thus, whether one may attribute the double-edged wording to Job (the character) depends on whether he is considered subliminally aware of the reading technically available only to the reader. The degree to which readers are willing to concede that the characters are subliminally aware of the irony they themselves generate stands in direct relation to the degree to which the readers are willing to forego flattering their own intelligence at the expense of the characters, and thus in reverse relation to a fundamental principle of iro-ny.[71] However, the artful craftsmanship of the Israelite Wisdom authors is evi-

---

69 Mahāprasthānika, 3.

70 See *The New Oxford Annotated Bible with the Apocryphal/Deuterocanonical Books: New Re-vised Standard Version*, eds. Michael David Coogan et al., Oxford University Press, New York 2010, 771–772. The identification of Satan and the serpentine Sea Monster, however, is the product of a later process of thought (see Elaine Pagels, "The Social History of Satan, the 'Intimate Enemy': A Preliminary Sketch," in: *The Harvard Theological Review* 84. 2 (April 1991): 105–128); it is found in the Greek Testament of Job 43:8.

71 See Baldack, *The Oxford Dictionary of Literary Terms*; and William Empson, *Seven Types of Ambiguity*, New Directions, New York 1947, 38–47.

dent in these verses either way. Examples of double-edged wording in the Book of Job could be extensively multiplied: sifting through the ancient and recent scholarship on the Book of Job reveals many more cases of the coupling of irony and double-edged wording, and a careful reading of certain chapters (e.g., Chapters 9–10) reveals other cases which were not noted in the past.

I have chosen to focus here on three strategically located speeches – the opening and closing speeches of Eliphaz, the most prominent and outspoken of the friends (quantitatively and qualitatively, see also Job 42:7); and Job's strategically located final response to Yнwн, in Chapter 42 – in order to argue that dramatic irony encapsulated in double-edged wording is an organizing principle in the Book of Job. These two techniques are employed in such a way that they converge to create two systematically opposite readings that stretch over extended passages, and, substantially, throughout the entire dialogue. While it might suffice to center on this organizing principle as a purely literary property of the text, irrespective of the literary conventions available in ancient Israelite Wisdom circles, I have aimed to demonstrate that on rare occasions – specifically when the "crime" is the least perfect – the artists' compromise on rough grammar discloses what is otherwise hidden from the reader.

The authors' choice of double-edged irony as an organizing principle in the Book of Job can be explained in more than one way. It could be viewed as an art of subversive writing in the face of intellectual persecution, or it could be viewed as reflecting the authors' fundamental doubt with regard to the nature of the divine. Alternatively, it may be viewed more generously as reflecting a religious experience that encapsulates the tension between diametrically opposite understandings of the workings of Yнwн.

Bibliography

Alter, Robert. "Truth and Poetry in The Book of Job." *The Book of Job*. Ed. Harold Bloom. New York: Chelsea House Publishing, 1988.

Baldack, Chris. *The Oxford Dictionary of Literary Terms*, 3rd edition. Oxford: Oxford University Press, 2008.

Ben-David, Israel. *Tsurot heksher ye-tsurot hefseķ ba-'Ivrit sheba-Mikra: taḥbir ye-ṭa'ame ha-Miķra*. Jerusalem: Magnes Press, ha-Universiṭah ha-'Ivrit, 1995.

Briggs Curtis, John. "On Job's Response to Yahweh." *Journal of Biblical Literature* 98.4. Atlanta: Society of Biblical Literature, 1979. 497–511.

Bronner, Yigal. *Extreme Poetry: The South Asian Movement of Simultaneous Narration*. New York: Columbia University Press, 2010.

Clines, David J. A. *Job, Vols. 1–3*, Word Biblical Commentary 17, 18A, 18B. Nashville: Thomas Nelson Publishers Inc., 1989–2011.

Conybeare, F. C. et al. *The Story of Ahikar*. London: Cambridge University Press Warehouse, 1898.

Coogan, Michael David et al. *The New Oxford Annotated Bible with the Apocryphal/ Deuterocanonical Books: New Revised Standard Version*. New York: Oxford University Press, 2007.

Crenshaw, James L. *Reading Job: A Literary and Theological Commentary*. Macon, Smyth and Helwys, 2011.

Dillmann, August. *Hiob*. Leipzig: S. Hirzel, 1869.

Driver, Samuel Rolles and Gray, George Buchanan. *A Critical and Exegetical Commentary on the Book of Job*. Edinburgh: T&T Clark, 1921.

Empson, William. *Seven Types of Ambiguity*. New York: New Directions, 1947.

Ewald, Heinrich. *Ewald's Commentary on the Book of Job*. Trans. J. Frederick Smith. London: Williams and Norgate, 1882.

Fox, Michael V. *Proverbs 10–31: A New Translation with Introduction and Commentary*. New Haven: Yale University Press, 2009.

Frankel, David. "The Image of God in the Book of Job." *Shnaton* 22. Jerusalem: Magnes Press, 2013. 27–65.

Frye, Northrop. "Blake's Reading of the Book of Job." *The Book of Job*. Ed. Harold Bloom. New York: Chelsea House Publishing, 1988, 21–35.

Gordis, Robert. *The Book of Job: Commentary, New Translation, and Special Studies*. New York: Jewish Theological Seminary of America, 1978.

Greenstein, Edward. "In Job's Face / Facing Job." *The Labour of Reading: Desire, Alienation, and Biblical Interpretation*. Eds. Fiona C., Roland Boer, and Erin Runions. Atlanta: Society of Biblical Literature, 1999. 301–317.

Habel, Norman C. *The Book of Job*: A Commentary. Philadelphia: Westminster Press, 1985.

Ham, T. C. "The Gentle Voice of God in Job." *Journal of Biblical Literature* 132.3. Atlanta: Society of Biblical Literature, 2013. 527–541.

Hartley, John E. *The Book of Job*. Grand Rapids: Eerdmans, 1988.

Herrnstein, Barbara. *Poetic Closure: A Study of How Poems End*. Chicago: University of Chicago Press, 1968.

Hoffman, Yair. *A Blemished Perfection: The Book of Job in Context*. Sheffield: Sheffield Academic Press, 1996.

Hoffman, Yair. "The Use of Equivocal Words in the First Speech of Eliphaz." *Vetus Testamentum* 30. Leiden: Brill, 1980. 114–118.

Hurowitz, Victor Avigdor. "Alliterative Allusions, Rebus Writing, and Paronomastic Punishment: Some Aspects of Word Play in Akkadian Literature." *Puns and Pundits: Word Play in the Hebrew Bible and Ancient Near Eastern Literature*. Ed. Scott B. Noegel. Bethesda: CDL Press, 2000. 63–88.

Hurowitz, Victor Avigdor. *Proverbs*. Tel Aviv and Jerusalem: Am Oved and Magnes, 2012.

Ḳil, Yehudah. *Sefer Mishlei*. Jerusalem: Mossad Harav Kook, 1983.

Kraft, Robert A. et al., eds. *The Testament of Job*. Missoula: Scholars Press for the Society of Biblical Literature, 1974.

MacLeish, Archibald. *J. B.: A Play in Verse*. Boston: Houghton Mifflin Company, 1958.

Miles, Jack. *God: A Biography*. New York: Alfred A. Knopf, 1995.

Mitchell, Stephen. *The Book of Job*. New York: Harper Collins Publishers, 1987.

Newsom, Carol A. *The Book of Job: A Contest of Moral Imaginations*. New York: Oxford University Press, 2003.

Noegel, Scott B. *Janus Parallelism in the Book of Job*. Sheffield: Sheffield Academic Press, 1996.

Noegel, Scott B., ed. *Puns and Pundits: Word Play in the Hebrew Bible and Ancient Near Eastern Literature*. Bethesda: CDL Press, 2000.

Otto, Rudolf. *The Idea of the Holy: An Inquiry into the Non-Rational Factor in the Idea of the Divine and its Relation to the Rational*. Trans. John W. Harvey. New York: Oxford University Press, 1923.

Pagels, Elaine. "The Social History of Satan, the 'Intimate Enemy': A Preliminary Sketch." *The Harvard Theological Review* 84. 2. 1991. 105–128.

Patrick, Dale. "The Translation of Job XLII 6." *Vetus Testamentum* 26. Leiden: Brill, 1976. 369–371.

Pedersen, J. *Scepticisme Israelite*. Paris: Librairie Felix Alean, 1931.

Pope, Marvin H. *The Anchor Bible Job*. New York: Doubleday, 1965.

Porten, Bezalel and Yardeni, Ada. *Textbook of Aramaic Documents from Ancient Egypt*. Jerusalem: The Hebrew University, 1993.

Revell, E. J. "Pausal Forms and the Structure of Biblical Poetry." *Vetus Testamentum* 31. Leiden: Brill, 1981. 186–199.

Seow, Choon Leong. "Orthography, Textual Criticism, and the Poetry of Job." *Journal of Biblical Literature* 130.1. Atlanta: Society of Biblical Literature, 2011. 63–85.

Seow, Choon Leong. *Job 1–21: Interpretation and Commentary*. Grand Rapids: William B. Eerdmans Publishing, 2013.

Shveka, Avi and Van Hecke, Pierre, "The Metaphor of Criminal Charge as Paradigm for the Conflict between Job and his Friends," *Ephemerides Theologicae Lovanienses* 90. 2014. 99–119.

Sophocles. *Oedipus the King*. Trans. F. Storr. Norwich: Fletcher and Son Ltd, 1981.

Torczyner, Harry (Naphtali H. Tur-Sinai). *The Book of Job: A New Commentary*. Jerusalem: Kiryath Sepher, 1957.

Tur-Sinai, Naphtali H. *The Book of Job: A New Commentary*. Tel Aviv: Hotza'at Yavneh, 1954.

Vanderkam, James C. "Ahikar/Ahiqar (Person)." *The Anchor Bible Dictionary,* Volume 1. Ed. David Noel Freedman. New York: Doubleday, 1992. 113–115.

Vanderkam, James C. "Ahiqar, Book of." *The Anchor Bible Dictionary,* Volume 1. Ed. David Noel Freedman. New York: Doubleday, 1992. 119–120.

Yosefa Raz
Reading Pain in the Book of Job[1]

> "Learn to think with pain." – Blanchot, *The Writing of the Disaster*[2]

The Book of Job has been read in both the Jewish and Christian traditions as a text that raises unsettling theological and philosophical questions. Why do the just suffer? How can God be all-powerful, just, and good at the same time? How is it possible to remain faithful to a religious system, given the great and small injustices of human life? The book troubles religious commonplaces and pieties, refusing to provide an easy answer. Even though the poem ends with a divine epiphany – a seeming response to the querulous voice of Job – the voice from the whirlwind maddeningly offers no straight-forward solutions to the religious reader. In response to processes of Enlightenment secularization, modern biblical exegesis and reception have shifted the focus away from these theological questions and towards moral, ethical, and aesthetic concerns.[3]

My reading in the following pages continues this trajectory. Specifically, I propose to consider the somatic experience as depicted in the text – that of the body in pain. In "thinking with pain" we could say that the Book of Job asks us to consider a different set of questions: How does the experience of pain change and transform personal and social life? How does pain influence the self, whether destroying or forming it? What is the relation between pain, language, and power? Finally, what value does pain have – whether religious, aesthetic or moral? I locate my reading within what has been recently called

---

1 This essay was first conceived as a paper for Ilana Pardes's seminar on Job at UC Berkeley in 2006. I am grateful to her and to Maya Barzilai, who first suggested reading the Book of Job via Elaine Scarry.
2 Blanchot, Maurice, *The Writing of the Disaster*, trans. Ann Smock, University of Nebraska Press, Lincoln 1995, 145.
3 To cite two powerful readings, Amos Funkenstein and Robert Alter each call for a shift from the abstract to the concrete, whether this is the specificity of the speech act of Job, or the poetics of a text that attempts to represent the voice of God. Funkenstein doubts the "the very assumption that the book contains a question to which God answers" (see Amos Funkenstein, *Perceptions of Jewish History*, University of California Press, Berkeley 1993, 59). Alter argues for a close literary reading, as philosophical readings "glide too easily over the fact that God's speeches at the end have, after all, a specific content, which is articulated with great care and to the details of which we are presumably meant to attend carefully" (see Robert Alter, *The Art of Biblical Poetry*, Basic Books, New York 1985, 86).

the "the corporeal turn."[4] This focus on the body entails redirection, a particular type of attention to a text which has often been read allegorically. To cite but one example, René Girard begins his masterful reading of the Book of Job by glossing over the physical: "It is true that Job complains about physical ills, but this particular complaint is easily linked to the basic cause of his lament. He is the victim of countless brutalities; the psychological pressure on him is unbearable"[5]. We must resist the tendency to elide or dismiss the somatic aspect of Job's experience as a kind of secondary affect in a greater system of signification. In *The Culture of Pain,* David B. Morris suggests that this reading might begin by placing the Book of Job in the genre or tradition of texts of physical and emotional pain.[6] I propose, then, to read the Book of Job as the record of a body in pain, and, more broadly, the relation of this pain to the formation and shattering of both language and power.

How does pain enter language? One of the basic recurring metaphors of the Book of Job is the wound. As Carol Newsom argues, the book's language about bodies is dominated by the language of wounds and wounding. The metaphors for change and transformation offered by Job's friends are borrowed from the plant world. They speak of sprouting and seeding as metaphors for healing and regeneration. Yet, for Job, "the basic truth about the body is found in the image of the wound and in the pain of the wound."[7] This language of the wound comes to represent, explain, and amplify Job's sense of suffering. At the same time, via Job's recurring use of these metaphors, the wound becomes the lens through which we see God in the text. If Job is the wounded Everyman, at many moments divinity is narrowed down to the role of Supreme Wounder. Thus, the language of wounds and wounding is basic to the notion of God in the text.

My reading builds on the groundbreaking work of Elaine Scarry, who reads the particular case of physical pain and language about pain as a basis for the formation and destruction of human subjectivity, agency, and civilization. The struggle to project the self outward into language, despite the isolation of pain and its deteriorating effect on language, is viewed by Scarry as the foremost ethical and creative of projects: "To be present when a person moves up out

---

4 For an overview of the corporeal turn in Jewish Studies, see Barbara Kirshenblatt-Gimblett, "The Corporeal Turn," in: *The Jewish Quarterly Review* 95:3 (2005): 447–461.

5 Girard, René, *Job, the Victim of His People*, trans. Yvonne Freccero, Stanford University Press, Stanford 1987, 6.

6 Morris, David B., *The Culture of Pain*, University of California Press, California 1991, 138.

7 Newsom, Carol A., *The Book of Job: A Contest of Moral Imaginations*, Oxford University Press, New York 2003, 134.

of that pre-language and projects the facts of sentience into speech is almost to have been permitted to be present at the birth of language itself."[8] Scarry's readings give a dignity and importance to the language of pain and its use in both unraveling and making the world. Scarry's understanding of the primacy (and betrayal) of physical suffering, its mimicry of the language of creation, its relation to space and skin, and its unstable language of agency are important tools for reading the specificity of Job's pain. Before proceeding to specific moments in the Book of Job, I will explain several concepts from Scarry that will be useful to my discussion.

The most basic fact about physical pain, according to Scarry, is its unshareability. As opposed to emotional pain, about which we talk easily, thereby leading to empathy and understanding, physical pain creates an "absolute split between one's sense of one's own reality and the reality of other persons."[9] Thus "intense pain is world-destroying"[10] because it severely limits the possibility of communication. In pain, language is in danger of being reduced to inarticulate cries, yet it can also be magnified, exaggerated, swollen. The language of pain can also be characterized as a hyper-verbality, an attempt to use the voice to overcome the spatial entrapment of pain and the vulnerability of the body. This hyper-verbality originates in the way physical pain seems to obliterate all other considerations, creating a sense that the body can swell "to fill the entire universe."[11] Attending to the needs of the gargantuan, monstrous body, one's horizons shrink. In this "horrible momentum of world contraction"[12] the struggle to stay alive and to extend the self beyond the boundaries of the body takes place through the projection of the voice. For characters like Shakespeare's King Lear[13] or Beckett's Winnie, as for Job, "ceaseless talk articulates [the] unspoken understanding that only in silence do the edges of the self become coterminous with the edges of the body it will die with."[14] Thus speech counters the anxiety of shrinking, of becoming only a body without a voice.

The struggle to communicate pain – to tell one's pain, or to hear the other's pain – is viewed by Scarry as a building block of civilization. In other words,

---

8 Scarry, Elaine. *The Body in Pain*, Oxford University Press, New York/Oxford, 1985, 6.
9 Scarry, *The Body in Pain*, 4.
10 Scarry, *The Body in Pain*, 29.
11 Scarry, *The Body in Pain*, 35.
12 Scarry, *The Body in Pain*, 32.
13 King Lear is himself a Joban figure, as Ruth Nevo observes (see Ruth Nevo, *Tragic Form in Shakespeare*, Princeton University Press, Princeton 1972, 260–261).
14 Scarry, *The Body in Pain*, 33.

while pain is in many ways deeply resistant to communication, we can still talk about heroic attempts of self expression, of finding ways to share the unsharable. Because pain is often isolating, metaphors of agency can function as a way to redeem language, to "coax pain into visibility."[15] Metaphors involving weapons, such as "it feels like a knife is cutting me" or "it hurts as if someone is shooting arrows at me" help others to understand the experience. At the same time, however, these metaphors of agency open the language of pain to instability and exploitation. The vague "someone" holding the weapon in the metaphor can be manipulated "because [the language of agency] permits a break in the identification of the referent and thus a misidentification of the thing to which the attributes belong."[16] Thus, dangerously, the language of pain can be appropriated to become the language of power. The intensity of the felt pain can be severed from the pain itself and conferred on an outside agent, a political construct. Scarry terms this appropriation of pain away from the suffering body and into a fictional or fraudulent political power a process of "analogical substantiation."[17]

A prime example of this "analogical substantiation" is torture: regimes of torture, according to Scarry, establish their power on the vulnerability of the human body. In torture, the power of the torturer grows in relation to the diminishment of the prisoner: "It is only the prisoner's steadily shrinking ground that wins for the torturer his swelling sense of territory."[18] The vehicle for this assertion of power is generated by forcing the prisoner ever deeper into a bodily existence, and seizing his voice, while the torturer, through his commands, interrogative questions, and taunts, gains an ever greater disembodied voice. Moreover, torture takes advantage of pain's tendency to unravel and disintegrate language. It demonstrates "the backward movement along the path by which language comes into being and which is here being reversed or uncreated or deconstructed."[19] Torture's language of "uncreation" mimics and undoes the objects and gestures of civilized life. Material objects that shelter and make humans comfortable, such as a room, chair, and bed, are inverted and used as weapons. Thus, not only does torture deny the humanity of the person being hurt, it also denies the "collective human present in the products of civilization."[20] Ultimately, by analyzing this structure of torture, it is possible to gain

---

15 Scarry, *The Body in Pain*, 13.
16 Scarry, *The Body in Pain*, 17.
17 Scarry, *The Body in Pain*, 14.
18 Scarry, *The Body in Pain*, 36.
19 Scarry, *The Body in Pain*, 20.
20 Scarry, *The Body in Pain*, 43.

insight into how the inverse of unmaking occurs: how a weapon can be transformed into a tool, how a self and a world are created.

In addition to considering an eclectic set of texts on torture, and, more broadly, texts on war – from Amnesty International reports to military-tactical instructional books – Scarry proposes to read the biblical text in the light of "analogical substation." The god of the Old Testament "does not have the power of self-substantiation."[21] As opposed to this invisible, disembodied god, the human body can "substantiate something beyond itself as well: it is able not only to make more amply evident its own existence, presence, aliveness, realness, but to make ever more amply the evident, the existence, presence, aliveness, and realness of God."[22]. Consequently, the scene of wounding, especially in Scarry's reading of the Pentateuch, "carries emphatic assurance about the 'realness' of God, but one that (for the participants inside) contains nothing that makes his 'realness' visible except the wounded human body."[23] The "Old Testament" becomes, in Scarry's readings, a text characterized by the rhythm of this scene of substantiation, that is, an epiphany of divine power enacted through the wounding of the human body.

The problem posed by the radical monotheism of the Hebrew Bible presents a different inflection when we read the Christian scriptures, for the corporeal status of the divinity now changes. "God's most intimate contact with humanity, His sensory contact with the human body, is in the Hebraic scriptures mediated by the weapon and in the Christian addition is mediated by Jesus."[24] The Old Testament is dependent on the "rhythmic invocation of scenes of hurt" occurring between the disembodied voice of God and the wounded human body to establish divine power. The Christian scripture, in contrast, which "no longer depends on a discrepancy in embodiness," is characterized by "a rhythmic return to a scene of healing."[25] In discussing the gospels, Scarry seems to be seeking a way out of the bleak theology of god-as-torturer. Indeed, her argument becomes markedly teleological as she charts a development from "the Old Testament mind" to the Christian scriptures, a point I return to later.

Scarry's influential analysis has been subject to several important critiques that have unsettled her strong claims about the uniqueness of physical pain and its social isolation. For Scarry, physical pain is a kind of primary human

---

21 Scarry, *The Body in Pain*, 200.
22 Scarry, *The Body in Pain*, 193.
23 Scarry, *The Body in Pain*, 200.
24 Scarry, *The Body in Pain*, 213.
25 Scarry, *The Body in Pain*, 184.

experience, utterly distinct from mental pain and anguish. She implies that physical pain and sensation exist before language and must be "translated" into a social context by such figures as the doctor, the witness, the human rights lawyer. In recent years, however, scholars such as Davis Morris and Talal Asad have emphasized the inseparability of physical and mental pain. In a dualistic mechanistic model of the mind/body, pain is understood as a simple bodily sensation like cold or heat. Pain has an objective reality within the individual sufferer. Yet scientists and doctors no longer regard the body as a self-sufficient machine, independent of its mind and surroundings. As Morris notes, "Families, lovers, ethnic groups, advertising campaigns, wars, scientific discoveries – all directly or (most often) indirectly influence our perception of pain."[26] As Morris explains, medicine is in the process of shifting away from regarding pain as a *sensation*, and towards considering pain as *perception*.[27]

If we regard pain as a subjective perception, conditioned by past experiences, relations with others, and cultural norms, then physical and mental pain become inseparable. Furthermore, the self that experiences pain is embedded in a social context, which influences the feelings a person will have. Asad makes a similar point about the social and cultural aspects of pain, noting that "pain is not merely a private experience but a public relationship as Wittgenstein taught long ago."[28]

In a sense, Morris and Asad's critiques recast what Scarry deems an essential universal experience into the particular. Pain is now viewed as a perception or event that occurs at the intersection between the body and the brain, the culture and the ever-shifting self.[29] My critique of Scarry, though focused on the biblical text rather than on medicine or anthropology, participates in this

---

26 Morris, David B, *The Culture of Pain*, University of California Press, Berkeley 1991, 76.

27 "This shift represents an absolute repudiation of the dominant thinking about pain that has characterized nineteenth- and twentieth century medicine ... Sensations, like heat and cold, require little more than a rudimentary, functioning nervous system ... Perceptions, by contrast, require minds and emotions as well as nerves" (see Morris, *The Culture of Pain*, 75).

28 Asad, Talal, *Formations of the Secular: Christianity, Islam, Modernity*, Stanford University Press, Stanford 2003, 81. According to Asad, Scarry's theory of pain depends on a Western, secular notion of agency that presents the person in pain as a victim, a passive object. This humanist approach posits a universal experience of pain. However, other (that is, non-Western) cultures may construct the self and its agency with regards to pain in different ways. "The progressivist model of agency diverts attention away from our trying to understand how it is done in different traditions, because of the assumption that the agent always seeks to overcome pain conceived as object and as state of passivity" (see Talal, *Formations of the Secular*, 84).

29 To anticipate my argument below, we could say that Morris and Asad call attention to the polyphonic nature of pain.

move toward the particular. In the same way that Morris and Asad argue for examining the socially constructed nature of pain and how the subject may be constructed differently in non-Western cultures, I argue for acknowledgement of the constructedness of the biblical text, for attention to the particular and peculiar text of the Book of Job. Scarry's reading of the biblical text as formative of Western culture reads the text along the grain, as an authoritative origin. Specifically, her reading of the "Old Testament mind" attributes a singular agency to the biblical text. However, in contrast to reading for an overarching biblical narrative – formed by generations of ideological redactors – we must also read the biblical text at its more ragged edges. The regulated and meaningful violence that Scarry describes as characteristic of the Old Testament is in fact disrupted by the senseless violence of the Book of Judges, the traumatic violence of Lamentations, and the polyphonic articulations of the relation between humans, God, and pain that appear together in the Book of Job. These texts allow us to read against the grain of the unifying tendencies of tradition as well as religious and cultural canonization – to read where the biblical outsiders dwell, in the sometimes effaced countertraditions of the Bible.[30]

The Book of Job challenges and problematizes Scarry's reading of the biblical text, especially her portrayal of the "Old Testament God" as a wounder and a torturer. Moreover, the contradictory and complex text of the Book of Job can aid in transforming our understanding and assumptions about the presumed firm foundations of "Western culture" and what Scarry reifies as "the structure of belief"[31]. As Newsom argues, the text of the Book of Job does not present a single ideology or philosophical approach; its variance in genre, style, and address are read, after Mikhail Bakhtin, as "polyphonic."

> Read as a polyphonic work, the purpose of the book is not to advance a particular view: neither that of the prose tale, nor that of the friends, nor that of Job, nor even that of God. Rather, its purpose is to demonstrate that the idea of piety in all its "contradictory complexity" cannot in principle "be fitted within the bounds of a single consciousness." The truth about piety can only be grasped at the point of intersection of unmerged perspectives.[32]

---

30 Job's skin disease may remind us of other biblical outsiders with skin diseases, such as Miriam, who becomes for Ilana Pardes the first example in an argument calling for "the heterogeneity of the Hebrew canon, for an appreciation of the socio-ideological horizons evident in this composite text" (see Ilana Pardes, *Countertraditions in the Bible: A Feminist Approach*, Harvard University Press, Cambridge, 1992, 3).
31 Scarry, *The Body in Pain*, 181.
32 Newsom, *The Book of Job*, 30.

As opposed to a manifestation of the singular "Old Testament mind," and by implication, the suffering body, we could speak about the Book of Job as a text that is polyphonic in its understanding of pain and its position to power. At times, pain is viewed as a pedagogical tool, part of the dreadful test God and the Adversary have devised for Job. In this sense, God does not need to inflict pain – it is required only because of his human subjects. Yet the text also contains many moments of "analogical substantiation", in which pain is understood as a means to establish God's power. In the dialogues, Job returns repeatedly to the idea of God as torturer, whose power is witnessed by the wound of the victim-believer. Finally, the speeches from the whirlwind suggest an alternative to analogical substantiation. The non-anthropomorphic perspective of these final poem-speeches constructs divine power independent of the human body. In these poems, the human gaze is displaced. The voice from the whirlwind describes unfamiliar times and places that humans cannot reach, as well as the mysterious bodies of Behemoth and Leviathan. These fantastical creatures are offered as strange, inhuman witnesses to a divinity whose creative forces are not based on diminishing and wounding the bodies of human believers.

What is pain for? I will begin with one of the most conventional answers posed by the Book of Job: Eliphaz's first speech to Job, which contains clear articulation of the reason for human pain, as well as its relation to divine power.

> Behold, happy is the man who is chastised by God –
> Do not spurn Shaddai's discipline!
> For He hurts but also binds up,
> Wounds but His hands heal (5:17–18).

This speech is part of an extended inquiry into the purpose of suffering. Eliphaz explains suffering as a pedagogical tool, a way to test and teach the righteous. God only *seems* to be acting aggressively or malevolently, masking his true benevolent nature in order to educate his "happy," or lucky, human subjects. In taking for his subject the fatherly punishments of God, Eliphaz also aspires to another pedagogical aim. He claims, characteristically of Wisdom literature, that a human lack of understanding obscures the deep symmetry between wounding and healing.

His explanation begins with the deictic marker "behold" (*hinēh*) (5:17), which befits a pedagogical speech act. However, this deictic marker may also echo a quite different speech act, from the prophetic poem at the end of Deuteronomy:

See now that I, I am He,
And there is no god beside me.
I kill and I make alive,
I wound and I heal (Deut 32:39).

This poem, like Eliphaz's speech, relies on similar images of wounding and healing. Yet the command "see now" (*rĕʾû ʿatâ*) is not so much pedagogical as a powerful self-assertion of Yahweh, who is here depicted in the role of the divine warrior, a specter of terrifying power. The call to see and witness this absolute power is predicated upon the frail, mortal human body. Rather than viewing God only as a chastising or disciplining father figure, the intertext from Deuteronomy reminds us of the relation between the human wound and the power of the divine warrior, his fiery anger and his consuming sword. We might describe Yahweh's wounding of humans as a consequence of his great power, a manifestation of his anger and jealousy. Scarry's analysis, however, reverses this description. Rather than violence to humans being an unavoidable aspect of immense power, it is precisely this violence which enables the imagination of power through analogical substantiation.

In the following pages, I endeavor to read Job's speeches in line with Scarry's understanding of pain. As opposed to the symmetry between wounding and healing in both Eliphaz's speech and the passage from Deuteronomy, the focus of Job's speeches about wounds and wounding is not balanced by an optimistic corrective. Job's depiction of pain stands against his friends' pieties, exposing the fiction of God being a benevolent pedagogue. In the language of Scarry, we can say that Job is determined to expose the fraudulent nature of analogical substantiation, despite being unable to offer another way of imagining power.

The primacy of physical suffering, and the way that it betrays all other considerations, is given voice both in the speeches and in the prologue.[33] While the prologue relates that Job loses his children, the prose and poetry emphasize

---

33 Though the prose-tale segments and the poems situated between them have different ideologies, narrative strategies, and stylistic devices, Newsom suggests a "heuristic fiction," which I will follow, in which the same author composed the prose and poetry by "juxtaposing and intercutting certain genres and distinctly stylized voices, providing sufficient interconnection among the different parts to establish the sense of the 'same' story but leaving different parts sharply marked and sometimes overly disjunctive" (Newsom, *The Book of Job*, 16). This heuristic fiction is substantiated by linguistic evidence, which dates the language of the prose tale as "unmistakably characteristic of post-exilic Hebrew," similar to the language of the poem (see Avi Hurvitz, "The Date of the Prose-Tale of Job Linguistically Reconsidered," in: *Harvard Theological Review* 67 (1974): 17–34, 17).

Job's isolation through the continual unraveling of the language of family. In this sense, Job's experience illustrates Scarry's understanding of the unsharability of pain; it is important to note, however, that the text's emphasis on family as a source of honor and social standing is particular to this cultural context. In the prologue, family relations are constructed with great attention and care. The typological wholeness of the number of sons and daughters, their frequent communal celebrations, and the care and responsibility that Job exerts on their behalf as family patriarch serve to underscore his loss.

It is surprising, then, that in the prologue Job's final misfortune is not the loss of his children, but rather the injury to his skin. Here, the Adversary challenges Job in two rounds: first, he suggests to Yahweh that he afflict, or literally touch "everything that is [Job's]."[34] Perhaps we could compare Job's loss of his children to the most difficult test posed to Abraham: the demand to sacrifice his long-awaited, beloved son. Yet in this tale, also seemingly set in the patriarchal landscape, the Adversary returns for a second round of testing, subsequent to the loss Job's children and possessions. In 2:7, Job is struck with skin disease – a "grievous burning rash,"[35] as Alter translates it. This second round of testing is introduced by a cryptic phrase, apparently a folk saying: "Skin for skin! Everything a man has he will give to save his life" (2:4). It seems that the Adversary is suggesting that Job values his own life over his family. Or perhaps the Adversary wants permission to move beyond (*bĕʿad*) Job's skin, to his innermost vulnerabilities. The prose story here shrewdly understands the undermining power of physical pain: "people can accept the loss of external goods, Satan reasons, but intense pain suffered within our own bodies in finally unacceptable and unendurable."[36]

The sense of physical pain as overwhelming all other emotions and relations is also expressed in one of Job's replies to his friends:

> His sons will be honored and he will not know,
> Brought low, and he will not understand their plight.
> But the flesh upon him will hurt,
> And his own being will mourn itself (14:20–21).

The passage appears to be based on a commonplace of Wisdom Literature: that in death, it is impossible to know the joys and sorrows of one's descendants.

---

34 Biblical translations are my own, unless otherwise indicated. My translations are based partially on those by Marvin H. Pope and Robert Alter. See Marvin H. Pope, *Job*, Doubleday, Garden City 1965; and Robert Alter, *The Wisdom Books: Job, Proverbs, and Ecclesiastes: A Translation with Commentary*, W. W. Norton & Co., New York 2010.
35 Alter, *The Wisdom Books*, 13.
36 Morris, *Job*, 139.

But the verse also seems to imply the persistent endurance of pain, almost beyond the grave. I wish to suggest that here, as in the prologue, Job's speech grieves the isolating quality of suffering, the way a person in pain may not know or even care about the destiny of his children.

In a later speech, the language of family – now parents rather than children – dramatizes Job's undoing:

> If I anticipate Sheol to be my home,
> Cushion my couch with darkness,
> I would say to the pit, "you are my father"
> "My mother and sister," to the maggot (17:13–14).

The unfamiliar experience of extreme suffering is dramatized here through the undoing of familiar objects. The house, an image for safety and protection, is now located in the underworld. The couch, meant to ease the sleeping body, is cushioned with darkness rather than with wool or linen. In the same way, in this uncomfortable, inside-out home, the protective and nurturing functions of the father, mother and sister have been replaced by images of desolation and death.[37] We will see that the language of family is once again recast and defamiliarized in the speech from the whirlwind.

In addition to unraveling the specific language of family, Job's speeches dramatize the impact pain has on language more generally. An example of pain's unraveling of language occurs in Job's first speech, when he imagines himself reduced to groans and cries: "For my groan will come before my food / And my roars pour out like water" (3:24).[38] Pain and its expression have taken primacy over other needs, such as eating and drinking. The verse is cast in poetic parallelism, in which the noun "groan" ('anḥātî) is nearly synonymous with "roars" (šaʼăgōtāy).[39] However, there is a slight difference between the two uses: "groan" signifies a general sound of distress, whereas "roars" express a more specific voicing related to animals. This minute transformation illustrates the disintegration of Job's human self. Both nouns are paired with active verbs, rendering Job the passive subject of the phrases. His cries pour

---

37 See also 30:29, where Job becomes brother to the jackal.

38 At the same time, though, it is important to note that his inarticulate language is *represented* in highly crafted biblical poetry. The tension between silence and speech, between the representation of Job's difficult, limiting circumstances and some of the most beautiful and expansive poetry of the Hebrew Bible is retained throughout the text and is part of its power.

39 My reading of what Robert Lowth termed "biblical parallelism" follows Alter's careful distinctions in *The Art of Biblical Poetry*, especially his sense that there is a dynamic of intensification or narrativity from verset to verset.

out of him without his control, as if he is unable to control his physical functions.

In addition to the passivity expressed above, images of spatial entrapment are common in Job's speech. In 16:3, for example, nameless troops of God encircle him. In 19:6, he describes being trapped and hunted: "Know, then, that God twisted me, / Encircled me in His net." Pope compares this net to the one Marduk cast over Tiamat in the Babylonian Creation Epic.[40] Since Marduk's defining act as a God was to vanquish the power of chaos in the world, this comparison emphasizes the way in which God, as a kind of divine warrior, is defined by the act of imprisoning and limiting the human.

The overall structure of the text also seems to trap Job into a small place. Each time Job speaks, he appears to be in the exact same place, and we do not know how much time passes. This lack of a spatial and temporal framework creates a sense of claustrophobia. For those who are experiencing this encircling, Scarry notes, "the voice becomes a final source of self-extension; so, as long as one is speaking, the self extends out beyond the boundaries of the body, occupies a space much larger than the body."[41] This idea of self-extension appears to explain, in part, Job's hyper-verbality – his strings of curses and tirades, his desire to answer the friends despite their acute inability to understand him, his reaching for language despite his fear or understanding that it will not achieve cessation of his pain. If I speak, he says, my pain is not lessened, (16:6) and yet he speaks, again and again. In silence, Scarry explains, "the edges of the self become coterminous with the edges of the body it will die with."[42] Job's voice becomes the only expression of his vitality, his struggle against pain, suffering, and miserable mortality. His eloquent voice resists the muffling of the net, and functions as a mirror image to the roaring, untrammeled voice of God, itself coterminous with no body.

We have seen that pain can lead to diminished language – a pre-verbal, animalistic cry – as well as a hyper-verbality. Just as the torturer described by Scarry uses commonplaces objects to "ape" creation and human civilization, the poetic language of the Book of Job expresses the reversal of commonplace meaning – the sense that ordinary life and communication have been turned inside out. This complex use of language against its commonplace meaning reflects both a psyche unraveling and an attempt to remake language itself. For example, eating and drinking are everyday actions to sustain the body and keep it alive, yet they also have emotional resonance. Feeding is nurturing, the

40 Pope, *Job*, 131, n. 6b

41 Scarry, *The Body in Pain*, 33

42 Scarry, *The Body in Pain*, 33.

primal maternal action, the way in which the external world is incorporated into the internal world. In one of the first descriptions of pain in the dialogues, (6:4) Job imagines his pain as an attack by a divine archer: "For the arrows of Shaddai are in me[43] / My spirit drinks their venom." This archaic divine epitaph also suggests breasts; this would render the scene a reversal of primal nurturing, as here the maternal God force-feeds Job venom instead of milk. The verb for drinking (shōtâ) becomes a way that the body is breached and made to harm itself.

A reversal of the nurturing act of feeding is also evident in 9:18: "He does not permit me my breath / For he sates me with bitterness." The root /śbʿ/, which connotes abundance and having one's desire satisfied, is here turned inside out. It becomes another image of force-feeding, a way in which the body's desire to be well-nourished is turned against itself. The same root occurs in reference to sleeplessness. In 7:4, Job's insomnia is described as "I was sated with sleeplessness" – a kind of oxymoron in which the body's own craving for sleep and relief is what ultimately causes it the most suffering. In each case, the verb is turned inside out, so as to mean the opposite of its regular referent.[44]

Just as the language of family, and of eating and drinking, undergoes reversal, so too is the commonplace action of clothing oneself reversed, thereby shattering and reforming the language itself. Clothing indicates social roles, and dressing marks civilization at its most basic level. In the J creation story, Adam and Eve sew themselves fig leaves; this is the first action of postlapserian civilization, and later Yahweh dresses them in skins. Job, in contrast, is stripped by God: "He stripped my glory from me / Removed the crown from my head" (19:9). Not only is Job stripped of the protection of clothing and even of skin, but the act of dressing is "aped" to achieve the opposite affect:

> My flesh was clothed in putrification
> My skin a clod of earth
> Split and ran with pus (7:5).

Clothes, which are meant to protect the skin, here become a means by which it is polluted. The subject of the verb "clothed" is not Job but rather his "flesh" – as if Job's self has been made separate from his body. Finally, the verb rāgaʿ, which I translate here as "split," though it could also mean "harden" or

---

43 For the MT "in me" or "with me" (ʿmādî), the Greek translation glosses "in my flesh".
44 With the restoration of the epilogue, the root is restored to its positive valence: Job dies at a markedly old age, "sated" with days (42:16).

"congeal", is read against its primary meaning, "to rest." Thus, language itself betrays. The expectation of returning to rest, perhaps after the pain noted in the first part of the verse, is turned into another description of wounded skin.

Indeed, besides staging the undoing of everyday actions, Job's metaphors mine the language for instabilities and double meanings. As Newsom observes, "Job picks his way through a shattered language that he can wield only in fragments ... he pries apart the words themselves, setting their different meanings against one another, as he tries to bend them to his expressive purposes.[45] Whereas Scarry emphasizes the passivity of the person in pain, Newsom's language for Job is anything but passive: he picks, wields, pries, sets and bends. If arrows, nets, and venom are God's weapons, Job's weapon is language itself, through which he fashions an active relationship with pain, functioning as what Asad calls a "[mode] of living a relationship".[46] As discussed earlier, whereas Job imagines his speech as a passive outpouring of pre-verbal groans and roars, the speeches are in fact set in highly crafted poetry, expressing a tension between passivity and the control necessary for a sophisticated craft.

We have seen how Job's speeches reverse common images and tropes of family, shelter, and clothing. Perhaps the most uncanny reversal depicted in the speeches concerns Job's skin. In a series of images, Job's marked, wounded, turned inside-out skin becomes a witness to the power of God. While many of the ailments that afflict Job relate to the neck, teeth, and internal organs (such as the bowels and kidneys), the skin is a special site of wounding. Skin is at the boundary between inner and outer, the way in which internal suffering can be projected externally. As Job states, "My skin blackens off me, / My bones are scorched by heat" (30:30). Here, the burned or diseased skin no longer functions as protective covering of the body. Furthermore, the progression in the parallelism – from skin to bones – charts the revelation of the burning bones beneath the skin, thereby reversing what is inner and what is outer. A similar reversal appears in 19:26: "After they flay my skin / From my flesh I will behold God."[47] The flesh, usually protected by the cover of the skin, beholds Yahweh, and this "beholding" is both vulnerable and terrible.

---

45 Newsom, *The Book of Job*, 131.

46 Asad, *Formations of the Secular*, 84.

47 In the Greek this verse has a radically different variant, which appears to have arisen from a series of scribal errors. In translation: "May my skin, which patiently endures these things, rise up" (see Claude E. Cox, trans., "Iob," in: *A New English Translation of the Septuagint: And the Other Greek Translations Traditionally Included Under That Title*, eds. Albert Pietersma and Benjamin G. Wright, Oxford University Press, New York 2007, 667). This variant has become part of a Christian interpretation relating to the doctrine of resurrection.

Wounds become a particular case of the text God writes upon the skin:

For you write on me bitterness,
Make me heir to the crimes of my youth,
Put my foot in fetters,
Guard all my ways,
Engrave yourself on the soles of my feet (13:26–27).[48]

Suffering, or bitterness here, is a text read upon the body. However, God's invisible ink is readable only when provided with the screen of the human body on which it can be seen, and this is almost always a painful or humiliating process. In verse 27 God marks, or engraves, Job's feet, perhaps with the markings of a slave. In this sense, the slave's body is an expression of the master's power. Paradoxically, it is only by seeing the subjugation of the slave that we can comprehend the power of the master.

While pain is explained as pedagogy by Eliphaz, or torture, by Job, the poetic text itself[49] recognizes an important relation between pain and creativity. Analogical substantiation, as Scarry describes it, is a highly unstable mechanism: it is the process by which the torturer acquires his power over the victim, yet it is also the kernel of a creative act, the ability to imagine material objects into being. In the metaphors of the text, and especially in the multivalent use of the root /ʿṣb/, we find an awareness of the intimacy of pain and creation that Scarry has made explicit. The root /ʿṣb/ seems to reflect two different etymological histories: it connotes sorrow, pain, suffering, sadness, as well as craft, design, making. From the point of view of historical linguistics, it is unclear whether the two root stems of /ʿṣb/ have one origin; however, their use in the poetic text points to a mutually intrinsic connection.

The root first appears in a negative valence in 7:15, as Job wishes for "death rather than suffering."[50] Later, Job says, "I was in terror of all my suffering [ʿaṣbōtāy]" (9:28). This negative valence may echo the curse of humans in Genesis 3:16–19, where the root /ʿṣb/ is repeated to great effect as a *leitwort*. Hu-

---

48 Verse 26 is usually translated as "write *against* me," rather than "on me." The final verb in this series of images is probably more correctly translated here as "mark" or "brand." I retain this literal, somewhat clunky translation, so as to show how the metaphorical language allows us to imagine God writing and engraving on Job, turning his skin into text.
49 Whom we might, very carefully, call "the poet of Job."
50 There is some scribal confusion between ʿaṣbōtāy ("my suffering") and ʿaṣmô tāy ("my bones"). The Masoretic Text in 7:15 reads "my bones," whereas the Greek translation preserves a version that seems to have read "my suffering." The same mistake repeats itself in 9:28 – here the MT reads "my suffering" and the Greek offers "my bones." In each reading, translation to "my suffering" produces a more coherent text.

mans are cursed with suffering in childbirth and in agriculture; however, the Genesis text also firmly ties the hurt of the human body to the two most basic creative actions, the place where human life is touched with the divine. The root appears in this creative sense in Chapter 10 of the Book of Job. This chapter contains a series of images that describe how God made Job and is now oppressing him: "Your hands shaped me [ˈiṣbûñî] and made me, / Circled round and then destroyed me" (10:8). Here, the root appears in the sense of making, crafting, or designing. However, as the second part of the verse suggests, being touched by God's hands is oftentimes a painful experience. God's hands shift from an artisan's tool to a weapon; their once careful creating touch becoming painful and chaotic.

If the first part of the poem appears under the sign of the ˈeṣeb of suffering, toil, trouble, sorrow, the second part of the poem – the speeches from the whirlwind – is under the sign of the ˈeṣeb of craft, creation, and care. In a sense, by using the same root to refer to both actions, the poet of the Book of Job has created an intimate relation between the pain of Job and the creation of the world. These contradictory valences capture Scarry's sense of the slippery intimacy between divine creative power and the human wound.

While much of the text of the Book of Job indeed suggests a connection between human pain and divine creation, in the whirlwind speech human suffering is dwarfed by the panoramic descriptions of primordial landscapes and inhuman bodies. In this segment of the poem-text, in contrast to Scarry's generalizations about the Old Testament God, divine power is no longer founded on analogical substation. The whirlwind speech attempts to imagine God's power as distinct from his power over his human subjects, almost as if it is imbuing ˈeṣeb with new meaning. For Scarry, positioning God and humanity at either end of a weapon "seems to define the structure of belief itself".[51] The whirlwind speech, however, enacts a struggle to re-imagine the this structure of belief, and thereby severs the link between suffering human bodies, on one hand, and divine power and creativity, on the other.

In some ways, a wounding or punishing god is in greater dialogue with humanity. Commentators have considered the image of God in the whirlwind to be distant and aloof to Job's suffering. Alter speaks of "the perennial puzzle"[52] of the structure of the Book of Job, in which the revelation from the whirlwind does not address Job's questions about justice, but rather harps irrelevantly if not cruelly on the act of creation. In other words, there is a sense of disjunction between Job's plaints and the divine response. Close attention

---

51 Scarry, *The Body in Pain*, 183.
52 Alter, *The Wisdom Books*, 85.

to the structure of pain helps illuminate a "responsive" element in the divine speech, in the way that pain is "answered" by a description of creation. The speech functions as a counterpoint, a different voice in the polyphonic meditation on pain, power, and meaning of the text.

The struggle to re-imagine the structure of belief involves a reshaping of the anthropocentric account of creation presented in much of the biblical text. In Scarry's understanding, the anthropocentric narrative of creation is part of the construction of divine power by analogical substantiation. The biblical text must constantly "restore the original direction of creation [which] requires the continual reminder that it is God who created everything ... *that most important, it is he who created humanity* [emphasis added]."[53] In order to re-imagine this structure of belief, the whirlwind speech provides a radically non-anthropocentric understanding of creation and of divine power. In Genesis, for comparison, both the J and P stories of creation culminate in the creation of humanity. In fact, the initial poem of Chapter 3 of the Book of Job is a sort of pathological example of this anthropocentric perspective. As Alter notes, "various elements of the larger world were introduced only as reflectors or rhetorical tokens of [Job's] suffering."[54] Thus, the cosmos and God are understood or constructed exclusively through the human experience. For Alter, the speech from the whirlwind constitutes "a brilliantly pointed reversal, in structure, image, and theme, of that initial poem of Job's."[55] Building on Alter's understanding of the speech as reversal, we could say that the speeches provide a climactic, expansive vision of the creation of the cosmos in which humans are precisely not at the center. Consequently, it provides a different way to imagine God's power: rather than predicating God's power on the wounds and marks upon the human skin, the passage forwards a catalogue of cosmological, meteorological, and zoological wonders that are almost beyond human perception.

How, then, does the whirlwind speech re-imagine 'eṣeb? Here, I wish to extend Alter's argument regarding the reversal of images from Job's speeches in the whirlwind speech. I contend that the whirlwind speech functions as a counterpoint to the torturing God by transforming images that were presented in Job's earlier speeches. For example, we have seen how in the prologue Job's loss of his children is mirrored in his poetic speeches by images of the family unmade. The disconnect between parents and children that was profoundly troubling to Job is subsequently seen in the whirlwind speech as a natural part of the animal kingdom. In this kingdom it is perfectly natural, for example,

---

53 Scarry, *The Body in Pain*, 225
54 Alter, *The Wisdom Books*, 97.
55 Alter, *The Wisdom Books*, 96.

that the ibex's children leave and never return (39:4). These images reconfigure the notion of family:

> Does the rain have a father?
> Or who begot the dew?
> From whose belly came the ice?
> And the sky-frost – who birthed it? (38:28–29).

The rain and dew did not "lose" their parents – in fact, the parents never even existed. But this loss or absence is not a source of suffering in a non-human-centered world. In this worldview, natural forces are not fashioned into the image of humans. The images are liberated from the language of torture, and are now in the realm of mysteries to be contemplated.

The final crescendo of the powerful epiphany of the voice from the whirl-wind is the description of Behemoth and Leviathan.[56] The detailed descriptions of these mythological bodies serve to underscore their invulnerability in com-parison to the vulnerability of the human body.

> Can you take him [Behemoth] with your eyes,
> Peirce his nose with barbs?
> Can you draw Leviathan with a hook,
> And press its tongue down with a cord?
> Can you put a cord through his nose,
> Pierce his cheek with a hook? (40:24–26).

The transition from the description of Behemoth to Leviathan may be consid-ered abrupt, yet it emphasizes the commonality of this invulnerability. Neither Behemoth nor Leviathan can be captured or pierced. The text continues, in more than forty lines, to describe Leviathan's body. Unlike Job, who is poi-soned, hunted, wounded, split open, and flayed, this creature is shielded with double mail with no space between, folds of flesh, and a heart of stone. Job is netted, but Leviathan's head cannot be caught in a fisherman's net (40:31).

As noted, the whirlwind speech transforms, or reconfigures, imagery from earlier in the text. Job refers to similar mythological imagery in a bitter screed: "am I *Yamm* or the Dragon, that you set a guard upon me?" (7:12) In Ugaritic texts, which appear to reflect many of the myths that came to shape Israelite culture, the weather god Baal defeats the sea god Yamm and his minion, the Dragon. Though the preserved texts are incomplete, Baal probably then re-

---

56 According to Pope, "Behemoth, like Leviathan in the Ugaritic texts, had a proto-type in pre-Israelite mythology (see Pope, *Job*, 269). Leviathan is also mentioned in the Psalms and Isaiah, and has a rich afterlife that extends to *Moby-Dick* and other modern works.

tained them forever under guard.[57] Job's dragon seems to be another version, or at least a close relative, of the sea beast Leviathan. Here, Job creates a rhetorical contrast between these great forces and his puny self, whose "days are a breath" (7:16): God should not pit himself his weak human creation, as if Job was a mythological force to be defeated. In this image, Job preserves the conventional sense of Baal, or in this case Yahweh, as divine warrior. As discussed earlier, the notion of the divine warrior is closely linked, if not predicated upon, his power to maim and wound.

The whirlwind speech takes up Leviathan differently than earlier Near Eastern and Hebrew texts, and in counterpoint to Job's speech. The battle between the sea beast and a divine warrior who imposes order on a chaotic, watery force is here muted, if not completely absent.[58] As Newsom explains, "the shock of this passage is that it runs counter to the expectations of those who think of Leviathan in terms of the *Chaoskampf*"[59]. Here, unlike in texts that present the divine warrior battling and enslaving a mythological beast, God's power lies not in harming these creatures where others could not, but rather in having created them. Furthermore, the great strength of both mythological creatures does not serve to scare or hurt humans. Instead, these creatures are offered to Job as witnesses to the primordial power of God. Behemoth is "the first of God's ways" (40:19). In their inability to be wounded, these creatures are outside the paradigm of analogical substantiation. One cannot make an agreement with Leviathan – he is outside covenant. In the same way, this section of the Book of Job suggests that the divine voice itself is outside human time and place, outside agreement and understanding, outside wounds and wounding, and outside healing.

By "thinking with pain" we can see that the prose-frame and the poetic speeches of the Book of Job are deeply concerned with bodies – their vulnerability and invulnerability, and how they inscribe power. While conventional

---

57 Generally, the powerful sea monster is described by both Ugaritic and Hebrew texts as a force to be vanquished. Isaiah 21:7 describes Yahweh's slaying of Leviathan in the eschaton, and Psalms 74:14 extols the divine warrior, slayer of Leviathan and Taninim. In the psuedoepigrapha and rabbinic literature, the slain Leviathan's flesh is food for the righteous. Jer 5:22 and Psalms 104:9 both allude to the primal guard made for of watery chaos. See Pope, *Job*, 60, 268–286. The most often cited passage from Ugarit in this context is KTU 1.5 I 1–3. For an accessible version of Ugaritic poetry see N. Wyatt, *Religious Texts from Ugarit: The Words of Ilimilku and His Colleagues*, Sheffield Academic Press, Sheffield, 1998.
58 In Alter's translation, "Who could go before me in this I'd reward, / under all the heavens he would be mine." Yet this battle remains a hypothetical impossibility conjured by the text, and thus a rhetorical flourish.
59 Newsom, *The Book of Job*, 249.

biblical rhetoric, as we have seen in the speech of Eliphaz, may provide an apologetics for the stark notion of God's malevolence, Job's plight rips away these masks and pieties. In Job's speeches, God is nakedly exposed as wounder and original tyrant. The divine warrior who fought mythological forces, thereby bringing order to the world, also pits his strength against vulnerable human bodies – indeed, this is how he gains his power. However, the language of agency is complicated, transformed, and sublated in the polyphonic text. In powerful poetry, language itself is taken apart and re-formed, and the structures of pain (described so precisely by Scarry) shift and bend into new shapes. For Scarry, the only escape from the paradigm of the wounding god is the wounded god of Christianity, who heals rather than hurts. The prose epilogue of the Book of Job also attempts to imagine a God who tests and restores, who wounds and heals. Yet the whirlwind speech constitutes an attempt to imagine a pure power, a power that is not also a power-over. In a sense, the rhythm of rhetorical questions in the whirlwind speech attempts to force a reversal of the dynamic of "analogical substantiation." The question constitute an attempt to imagine a corrective vision of how unmaking and making are related to each other, not as a perversion of power but rather as mirror images, as question and answer.

Scarry's understanding of physical pain offers a compelling model for examining pain and its relation to the construction of power, language, and the self. Nonetheless, the status of pain in the text of the Book of Job remains difficult to pin down. Rather than a structurally coherent manifestation of an "Old Testament mind," the text provides multiple perspectives on the question of pain. Even the whirlwind speech, which seems to be leaving behind the question of pain and the human body, is so finely stitched into the longer text that divine power and human pain remain inseparable. Perhaps this stitching suggests that the experience of the vast divine panorama of creation is made possible by hearing and listening to the suffering of Job. By listening closely to pain's intimate and ever-narrowing troubles and despairs, the text trains us to also hear the singing of the morning stars. One perspective, however, that is missing, or perhaps resolutely omitted, is the question of national catastrophe. Job is not an Israelite, and the Book of Job makes no reference to any suffering of war, exile, or national destruction, though it seems likely to have a post-exilic provenance. I suggest that this silent possibility also be heard in polyphony, if not as strict historical-critical evidence, then at the least as part of the long, cultural history of the Book of Job.

I have argued that the complex and contradictory positions on pain and divine power are an expression of the text's polyphony. Perhaps we might also say that this polyphony is painful because it "can only be grasped at the point of intersection of unmerged perspectives."[60] As we read the Book of Job in the twenty-first century, the voices of victims of war and torture, refugees, and prisoners, continue to "birth language itself." The Book of Job, as we read it today, is a palimpsest of attempts to afford shape and coherence to pain in the face of mortality and the catastrophe of history. Its attempt to imagine a power that is not tyrannical is a brief utopian gesture.

Bibliography

Alter, Robert. *The Art of Biblical Poetry*. New York: Basic Books, 1985.

Alter, Robert. *The Wisdom Books: Job, Proverbs, and Ecclesiastes: A Translation with Commentary*. New York: W. W. Norton & Co., 2010.

Asad, Talal. *Formations of the Secular: Christianity, Islam, Modernity*. Stanford, Calif: Stanford University Press, 2003.

Blanchot, Maurice. *The Writing of the Disaster*. Trans. Ann Smock. Lincoln: University of Nebraska Press, 1995.

Cox, Claude E. trans. "Iob" in Pietersma, Albert, and Benjamin G. Wright. *A New English Translation of the Septuagint: And the Other Greek Translations Traditionally Included Under That Title*. New York: Oxford University Press, 2007.

Funkenstein, Amos. *Perceptions of Jewish History*. Berkeley: University of California Press, 1993.

Girard, René. *Job, the Victim of His People*. Trans. Yvonne Freccero. Stanford, Calif: Stanford University Press, 1987.

Hurvitz, Avi. "The Date of the Prose-Tale of Job Linguistically Reconsidered." *Harvard Theological Review* 67 (1974): 17–34.

Kirshenblatt-Gimblett, Barbara. "The Corporeal Turn," *The Jewish Quarterly Review* 95:3 (2005): 447–461.

Morris, David B. *The Culture of Pain*. Berkeley, California: University of California Press, 1991.

Nevo, Ruth. *Tragic Form in Shakespeare*. Princeton, N. J.: Princeton University Press, 1972.

Newsom, Carol A. *The Book of Job: A Contest of Moral Imaginations*. New York: Oxford University Press, 2003.

Pardes, Ilana. *Countertraditions in the Bible: A Feminist Approach*. Cambridge, Mass: Harvard University Press, 1992.

Pope, Marvin H. *Job*. Garden City, N. Y.: Doubleday, 1965.

Scarry, Elaine. *The Body in Pain*. New York, Oxford: Oxford University Press, 1985.

Wyatt, N. *Religious Texts from Ugarit: The Words of Ilimilku and His Colleagues*. Sheffield, England: Sheffield Academic Press, 1998.

---

60 Newsom, *The Book of Job*, 30.

Ilana Pardes
Melville's Wall Street Job: The Missing Cry

"Eh! – He's asleep, aint he?" asks the grub-man upon meeting the lawyer by the prison wall, where the wasted Bartleby is seen "strangely huddled" with "his knees drawn up." "With kings and counsellors," murmurs the lawyer.[1] For anyone not haunted by the echoes of the King James Version, as the grub-man may be, the lawyer's words seem an assertion of Bartleby's royal grandeur despite his lowly death as a wretched vagrant in a New York prison. But behind the lawyer's tribute to Bartleby is a curious invocation of Job's initial, agonized outburst. "Why died I not from the womb?" cries Job in the opening note of the Dialogues, "Why did the knees prevent me? Or why the breasts that I should suck? For now should I have lain still and been quite, I should have slept: then had I been at rest, With kings and counselors of the earth" (Job 3:3–24). If Job speaks of death longingly in an attempt to convey his acute misery, Bartleby takes this death wish literally. He dies in a prison called the "Tombs," in the posture of a dead fetus or a stillborn, providing a dire realization of his biblical precursor's blasphemous craving for the restful darkness of not being.

Melville never ceases to invent and reinvent himself through his biblical characters. His grand homage to Job begins not with "Bartleby" but rather in *Moby-Dick*, where – rejecting any notion of character consistency – he splits the biblical rebel among the various crew members of the *Pequod*.[2] Each whaler – be it Ahab, Ishmael, or Fleece – marks a different potential reading of Job. This exegetical excess, however, was by no means exhaustive. In 1853, just two years after the publication of *Moby-Dick* – and, in many ways as a response to the failure of this momentous book, which he had envisioned as a Bible of sorts, to reach the reading public – Melville fashioned a new Job: this time, not a wild, renegade whaler but rather an "incurably forlorn" Wall Street copyist.

1 Melville, Herman, "Bartleby, the Scrivener: A Story of Wall-Street" in: *The Piazza Tales and Other Prose Pieces 1839–1860*, eds. Harrison Hayford et al., Northwestern University Press and Newberry Library, Evanston and Chicago 1987, 45.
2 Melville's treatment of Job in *Moby-Dick* has received considerable attention. See Nathalia Wright, *Melville's Use of the Bible*, Duke University Press, Durham 1949; as well as Nathalia Wright, "Moby Dick: Jonah's or Job's Whale?" in: *American Literature* 37.2 (May 1965): 190–195; Lawrence Thompson, *Melville's Quarrel with God*, Princeton University Press, Princeton 1952; Hugh Holman, "The Reconciliation of Ishmael: *Moby-Dick* and the Book of Job," in: *South Atlantic Quarterly* 57 (1958): 478–490; Janis Stout, "Melville's Use of the Book of Job," in: *Nineteenth-Century Fiction* 25.1 (1970): 69–83.

Melville's Wall Street Job, I believe, is bleaker than the *Pequod* Jobs – even more than tragic Ahab. Yet this dark rendition of the plight of the biblical rebel does not lack a peculiar sense of stubborn vitality, a vitality that owes much to the audacity with which Melville probes new aesthetic possibilities, never hesitating to test the limits of his own exegetical imagination.

My reading of "Bartleby" sets out to trace the aesthetic-hermeneutic shift in Melville's configuration of Job as he moves from *Moby-Dick* to his Wall Street story. In each work, I argue, Melville's preoccupation with Job is not only a token of his admiration for the biblical rebel but also a metacommentary, a response to the intricate exegetical history of this biblical text.[3] Though intrigued by all commentaries on Job, Melville had a special fascination with the privileged position of the text as an aesthetic touchstone in the writings of the continental advocates of the literary Bible within the context of European Enlightenment and Romanticism.

1 The Rise of Job as an Aesthetic Touchstone

The Bible, Jonathan Sheehan reminds us, was not always venerated as a founding text of Western literature.[4] The literary Bible emerged in the eighteenth century both in England and in Germany as the invention of scholars and literati who sought to rejuvenate the Bible by transforming it from a book justified by theology to one justified by culture. The aim of this post-theological project was not quite to secularize the Bible – though it was now construed as the product of human imagination – but rather to reconstitute its authority in aesthetic terms. The Book of Job held a vital role in enhancing this transformation. Sheehan goes so far as to trace what he calls a "Job revival" within the context of English and German Enlightenment, a revival that included numerous new translations and scholarly studies of the text. Among the leading scholars of this trend was Robert Lowth, one of the prominent forerunners of the literary approach to the Bible, whose book on biblical poetry, *De Sacra Poesi Hebræorum* (*On the Sacred Poetry of the Hebrews*, 1753) – known primarily for its groundbreaking study of biblical parallelism – includes a substantive compari-

---

3 I provide an extensive reading of Melville's *Pequod* Jobs in relation to the aesthetic turn in biblical exegesis in the first chapter of *Melville's Bibles*. See Ilana Pardes, *Melville's Bibles*, University of California Press, Berkeley 2008, Chapter 1.

4 Sheehan, Jonathan, *The Enlightenment Bible: Translation, Scholarship, Culture*, Princeton University Press, Princeton 2005.

son of the poetic form of Job with that of Greek tragedy.[5] Indeed, the Book of Job acquired so prominent a position as an aesthetic touchstone that Edmund Burke, in his *A Philosophical Enquiry into the Origin of Our Ideas of the Sublime and Beautiful* (1757), evoked it as an exemplary text for the exploration of the sublime experience in its relation to power and terror.[6]

But the aesthetic revival of Job continued beyond the age of Enlightenment. It became even more prominent in Romantic thought and literature, though its poetic grandeur was now colored by Romantic aesthetic ideals. J. G. Herder, another important forerunner of the literary approach to the Bible, devotes a whole section of his renowned *The Spirit of Hebrew Poetry* (1782–1783; translated into English by 1843) to Job. Setting his work against the dry technical study of Lowth, Herder transfers Job into the realms of the heart, of vision, and of vivid Oriental imagination.[7] God's whirlwind poem is the poetic epitome of Job, for like the Oriental descriptions of nature "it awakens a love, an interest, and a sympathy for all that lives."

> What wretch, in the greatest tumult of his passions, in walking under a starry heaven, would not experience imperceptibly and even against his will a soothing influence from the elevating contemplation of its silent, unchangeable, and everlasting splendors. Suppose at such a moment there occurs to his thoughts the simple language of God, "Canst thou bind together the bands of the Pleiades," etc. – is it not as if God Himself addressed the words to him from the starry firmament? Such an effect has the true poetry of nature, the fair interpreter of the nature of God. A hint, a single word, in the spirit of such poetry often suggests to the mind extended scenes; nor does it merely bring their quiet pictures before the eye in their outward lineaments, but brings them home to the sympathies of the heart.[8]

For Herder, God's rhetorical questions, the aesthetic hallmark of the divine response from the whirlwind – "Canst thou bind together the bands of the

---

5 For a discussion of Robert Lowth's contribution to the rise of the literary Bible, see David Norton, *A History of the Bible as Literature: From 1700 to the Present Day*, Cambridge University Press, Cambridge 1993, 59–73. On the interrelations between the literary and historical approaches to the Bible, see Ron Hendel, "Either/Or: The Literary and the Historical in Biblical Studies" (forthcoming).

6 For more on the question of Joban sublimity in English Enlightenment, see Jonathan Lamb, *The Rhetoric of Suffering: Reading the Book of Job in the Eighteenth Century*, Oxford University Press, New York 1995.

7 For more on Herder and the Bible, see Hans W. Frei, *The Eclipse of Biblical Narrative: A Study in Eighteenth and Nineteenth Century Hermeneutics*, Yale University Press, New Haven 1974.

8 Herder, J. G., "God and Nature in the Book of Job" (from *The Spirit of Hebrew Poetry*), in: *The Dimensions of Job: A Study and Selected Readings*, ed. Nahum N. Glatzer, Schocken Books, New York 1969, 154.

Pleiades?" (Job 38:31) – hold the power of an irresistible address which no one can ignore. He marvels at the sublimity of God's depiction of nature, at the power of the "simple language of God," with its minute hints, to interpret the starry firmament so that it becomes tangible to the observing eye. The experience of this vision is even richer: the external natural sights do not remain animate only "in their outward lineaments" but rather seep inward, bringing heavenly scenes into the inmost spheres, to the "sympathies of the heart." "It is as *effect*," writes Sheehan, "that theodicy is redeemed. Not through knowledge of, nor through insight into the workings of God, but rather in the *power* that these workings exert over our imaginations."[9]

The impact of Herder's reading is evident in Thomas Carlyle choice to evoke the Oriental sublimity of Job's visionary rendition of natural sights in his discussion of Islamic culture in *On Heroes, Hero-Worship, and the Heroic in History* (1840). Carlyle may not have been a prominent advocate of the literary Bible, but his brief comment on the Book of Job (he too focuses on the divine rhetorical questions) succinctly captures the Romantic adoration for the book as a text of exceptional literary merit, one whose descriptions of nature exert unparalleled impact on the eye and the heart. Job, he declares,

> is a noble Book [...] our first oldest statement of the never-ending Problem, – man's Destiny, and God's ways with him here in this earth. And all with such free flowing outlines; grand in its sincerity, in its simplicity; in its epic melody, and repose of reconcilement. There is the seeing eye, the mildly understanding heart. So *true* everyway; true eyesight and vision for all things; material things no less than spiritual: the Horse, – 'hast thou clothed his neck with *thunder*? – he *laughs* at the shaking of the spear!' Such living likenesses were never since drawn. Sublime sorrow, sublime reconciliation; oldest choral melody as of the heart of mankind; – so soft, and great; as the summer midnight, as the world with its seas and stars! There is nothing written I think, in the Bible or out of it, of equal literary merit.[10]

English and German Romantic literary/artistic exegesis followed suit. Blake and Goethe carved out their respective Jobs (Blake's *Illustrations of the Book of Job* [1825] and Goethe's *Faust* [1832]); yet, in contradistinction to the scholarly studies of Lowth, Burke, and Herder, they defined the book's sublimity as inseparable from its predominant anti-theodician character. To modern readers, Job's protest against the arbitrariness of divine conduct is the thrust of the book, but until the Romantic period the predominant interpretive tendency

9 Sheehan, Jonathan, "The Poetics and Politics of Theodicy," in: *Prooftexts* 27.2 (Spring 2008): 211–232.
10 Carlyle, Thomas, *On Heroes, Hero-Worship, and the Heroic in History*, ed. Carl Niemeyer, University of Nebraska Press, Lincoln 1966, 49.

was to read the Book of Job as theodicy and to prefer the patient, pious Job of the folkloric Prologue to the rebellious Job of the poetic Dialogues.[11] Romantic writers and artists were, in fact, the first to put forth the radical possibility of reading both God and Job as imperfect.[12] Instead of seeing the book as a confirmation of normative faith, they treated it as an inspiring point of departure for a critique of institutional modes of religion.

In Blake's *Illustrations*, the patient Job of the Prologue lives in a mode of error under the auspices of institutional churches. His erroneous mode of being is poignantly conveyed by the first illustration, where different musical instruments hang, unused, on the tree under which Job sits, all too drowsy, with his family. It takes a crisis to free him from clinging to the false God of conventional faith and to find the way to the true God of imagination, the mirror-image of his poetic self. In shaping the contours of Job's spiritual transformation, Blake relies on Burke, but his notion of "fearful symmetry" modifies Burke's definition of sublime experience by combining horror with wonder, mystery, and the infinite power of imagination.[13]

Goethe, who was the first to superimpose a Joban dimension upon the drama of Faust, offers yet another version of an imperfect Job and an imperfect God.[14] Faust is not a righteous Job who knows no evil. He roams about with Mephistopheles, taking advantage of the latter's devilish powers. Similarly, the Lord's ways are rather dubious. The wager between God and the Adversary in the Prologue is in *Faust* turned into a parody of divine vigilance. Indifferent to the potential suffering which may be inflicted upon Faust, the Lord readily

---

11 The Book of Job opens with a folkloric prose Prologue (Chapters 1–2) and ends with a stylistically similar prose Epilogue (Chapter 42). The bulk of the text includes the poetic Dialogues between Job and his friends/comforters (Chapters 3–37). God's whirlwind poem comes after the Dialogues and before the Epilogue (38–41). For an extensive account of the structure of the Book of Job, see Marvin Pope, *Job*, Doubleday, Garden City 1973.

12 The one notable precursor of this exegetical move is Shakespeare's *King Lear*. For a reading of the anti-theodician Joban qualities of Lear, see Ruth Nevo, *Tragic Form in Shakespeare*, Princeton University Press, Princeton 1972.

13 On "The Tyger" and Job, see Harold Fisch, *The Biblical Presence in Shakespeare, Milton, and Blake: A Comparative Study*, Clarendon Press, Oxford 1999, 318–325.

14 Readers in the nineteenth century were well aware of the Joban character of *Faust*. In an essay on Goethe published in *The Dial*, in 1841, Margaret Fuller suggests that "The Jewish demon assailed the man of Uz with physical ills, the Lucifer of the middle ages tempted his passions, but the Mephistopheles of the eighteenth century bade the finite strive to compass the infinite, and the intellect attempt to solve all the problems of the soul"; see Johann Wolfgang von Goethe, *Faust: A Tragedy: Interpretive Notes, Contexts, Modern Criticism*, trans. Walter Arndt, ed. Cyrus Hamlin, Norton Critical Editions, W. W. Norton, New York 2001, 565.

allows Mephistopheles (a court jester of sorts) to lure the doctor without restricting his moves.

In contradistinction to the central position of Job in European Romanticism, the biblical book had but little resonance within the American Romantic milieu. Job did not quite lend itself to the optimism of leading literary figures such as Emerson or Whitman. But even Hawthorne and Dickinson – whose biblical poetics were of a darker hue – offered only dim echoes of Job rather than elaborate interpretations of the text. *Moby-Dick* filled in this lacuna in American literary biblicism with a splash. While joining the above distinguished genealogy of continental advocates of Job, Melville carved out a Job no European could have imagined.

2 Dead-Wall Reveries

If Melville were asked to single out the most sublime moment in Job while writing *Moby-Dick,* he would have undoubtedly pointed to God's response from the storm, as do Burke, Herder, and Carlyle. The ultimate source of inspiration for Melville in 1851 is located in the climactic closing lines of the divine poem, where Leviathan is presented as the inscrutable, ungraspable epitome of creation (Job 41). Melville's distinct exegetical brilliance, however, does not lie in foregrounding Leviathan's natural sublimity (a distinct poetic feat in itself) but rather in the unexpected projection of this poem onto the world of American whaling. Leviathan in *Moby-Dick* is at once a natural awesome wonder, an imaginary demonic-divine phantom – "the overwhelming idea of the great whale" – and a common commodity – caught, dissected, and sold in one of America's largest industries. With unique Romantic irony and humor, Melville situates Joban sublimity between the metaphysical and the physical in ways that offer a decisive departure from his continental precursors. If Job can be regarded as "aesthetically noble," claims Ishmael, in "The Advocate," so can the supposedly "unpoetic" business of whaling with its infamous butchering.[15] The refreshing redefinition of the boundaries between sacred writing and literature – a redefinition brought about by the aesthetic turn in biblical exegesis – should, Melville proposes in *Moby-Dick*, lead to an even more radical opening of concepts such as "aesthetic" and "sublime."

---

15 Melville, Herman, *Moby-Dick; or, The Whale*, eds., Harrison Hayford, et al., Northwestern University Press and the Newberry Library, Evanston and Chicago (1851) 2001, 111.

In "Bartleby," Melville takes this sacrilegious aesthetic inquiry a step further. In leaving the *Pequod* for another quintessential American workplace – Wall Street – he ventures to bolster the moments of mock aesthetic and mock sublime in *Moby-Dick*, and goes so far as to question the very value and validity of any quest for sublimity in Job or beyond. Instead of playing with physical and metaphysical leviathans, instead of juxtaposing Job's sorrows with the dazzling sights of Creation, Melville positions Chapter 3 – where the "kings and counsellors" appear – at the center of his canvas, regarding it as the most suitable Joban scene for the representation of human suffering in a city devoid of divine vigilance.

Job's opening cry is one of the most resonant biblical poems. The innocent sufferer, no longer willing to bear his pain with equanimity, "opens his mouth" and curses.

Let the day perish wherein I was born,
And the night in which it was said,
There is a man child conceived.
Let that day be darkness;
Let not God regard it from above,
Neither let the light shine upon it;
Let darkness and the shadow of death stain it;
Let a cloud dwell upon it;
Let the blackness of the day terrify it. [...]
Lo, let that night be solitary,
Let no joyful voice come therein.
Let them curse it that curse the day. [...]
Let the stars of the twilight thereof be dark;
Let it look for light but have none;
Neither let it see the dawning of the day:
Because it shut not up the doors of my mother's womb,
Nor hid sorrow from mine eyes.
Why died I not from the womb?
Why did I not give up the ghost when I came out of the belly?
Why did the knees prevent me?
Or why the breasts that I should suck?
For now should I have lain still and been quiet,
I should have slept:
Then had I been at rest,
With kings and counsellors of the earth,
Which built desolate places for themselves;
Or with princes that had gold,
Who filled their houses with silver:
Or as an hidden untimely birth I had not been;
As infants which never saw light.
There the wicked cease from troubling;

And there the weary be at rest.
There the prisoners rest together;
They hear not the voice of the oppressor.
The small and the great are there;
And the servant is free from his master.
Wherefore is light given to him that is in misery,
And life unto the bitter in soul;
Which long for death, but it cometh not;
And dig for it more than for hid treasures;
Which rejoice exceedingly, and are glad, when they can find the grave?
Why is light given to a man whose way is hid,
And whom God hath hedged in?
For my sighing cometh before I eat,
And my roarings are poured out like the waters. (3:3–24)

Job probes the very limits of language and of life. The punishment for cursing God, according to biblical law, is death. Job does not actually curse God, as the Adversary had predicted he would, though he comes tantalizingly close to this abyss in imprecating the day of his birth, the divinely ordained gift of life. His blasphemy does not end here. It sweeps up a whole array of biblical configurations of creation, inverting the cosmic deeds of the Creator. In a bold act of de-creation (with its mythical echoes of Mesopotamian cosmogonic battles), Job summons darkness, blackness, and clouds to hide the light of that cursed day, even its first twilight stars, and wishes that his cursing be reinforced by magicians with the power to blot days from the calendar.[16] His cursing is a powerful cry of pain and rage, an exercise in not-being, in self erasure. If only the womb were a tomb, if only no breasts had welcomed him into the world. Death, the ultimate rest, is his only consolation. He abhors the thought of living in a world in which sorrows, sighs, and catastrophes pile up ceaselessly, in a world whose Creator is not a benevolent, just Judge but rather a grand Torturer who provides light and life only to "hedge in" mortals.

It is precisely this "hedged in," grave-like setting that Melville reproduces through Wall Street. To be more precise, he literalizes the name of the district – in turning Wall Street into a site of walls – and superimposes onto this nineteenth-century urban setting a Joban inscape. Consider the lawyer's expository remarks concerning his chambers:

My chambers were up stairs at No. – Wall-street. At one end they looked upon the white wall of the interior of a spacious sky-light shaft, penetrating the building from top to bottom. This view might have been considered rather tame than otherwise, deficient in

---

16 See Robert Alter, *The Art of Biblical Poetry*, Basic Books, New York 1985, 76–84.

what landscape painters call "life." But if so, the view from the other end of my chambers offered, at least, a contrast, if nothing more. In that direction my windows commanded an unobstructed view of a lofty brick wall, black by age and everlasting shade; which wall required no spy-glass to bring out its lurking beauties, but for the benefit of all near-sighted spectators, was pushed up to within ten feet of my window panes. Owing to the great height of the surrounding buildings, and my chambers being on the second floor, the interval between this wall and mine not a little resembled a huge square cistern.[17]

This is among the tale's most amusing mock aesthetic moments. The lawyer's glorifying description of his chambers discloses the absurdities of a stifled office blocked by walls from all sides. Ironically, the only "unobstructed view" is the spectacle of two supposedly contrasting walls – the white wall of the shaft "deficient in what landscape painters call 'life'" and the "aged" black brick wall. For all those who were ever eager to find natural sublimity in Job – Melville included, of course – these walls seem to offer a sobering sight: the greatest aesthetic advantage they hold lies in their capacity to "push up" their "lurking beauties" close to their spectators while forming an airless cistern around them.

The lawyer, in many ways, is Wall Street's counterpart to Job's so-called friends. Like them, he finds the normative both justifiable and pleasurable. He sees neither the oppressive dimension of the architectural aesthetics of Wall Street nor the violence embedded in normative management practices. He insists on the beauty of his office chambers, much as he regards himself as a benevolent boss. (His counterpart in the Coen brothers' Joban film "A Serious Man" is Rabbi Scott, the junior rabbi who perseveres in admiring the parking lot visible from his office window.)

As the primary Joban character in the tale, Bartleby introduces an anti-theodician perspective into these blocked vistas. Job, as one recalls, cherishes lightless graves and locked wombs as the most sought-for treasure of all. Bartleby follows suit in taking his dire condition ad absurdum, venerating the walls in which he is trapped as if they were the only objects worthy of reverie. "Looking out, at his pale window behind the screen," he immerses in long, immobile "dead-wall reveries."[18]

3 "I Would Prefer Not to": The Joban Cry

There is, however, one striking omission in the scrivener's anti-theodician stance: the disappearance of the Joban cry. This lacuna is undoubtedly one of

---

17 Melville, "Bartleby, the Scrivener," 14.
18 Melville, "Bartleby, the Scrivener," 28.

"Bartleby"'s most dramatic exegetical departures from *Moby-Dick*. Ahab, as one recalls, never hesitates to cry against his dismemberer as he "chases with curses a Job's whale round the world": "Aye, aye! It was that accursed white whale that razeed me; made a poor pegging lubber of me for ever and a day! [...] Aye, aye! And I'll chase him round Good Hope, and round the Horn [...] and round perdition's flames before I give him up [...] How can the prisoner reach outside except by thrusting through the wall? To me, the white whale is that wall, shoved near to me. [...] He tasks me; he heaps me; I see in him outrageous strength, with an inscrutable malice sinewing it."[19]

Setting out to "strike through the mask," Ahab seeks to lay bare the arbitrary malevolence which lies behind the impenetrable overbearing wall of the deity – be it Moby Dick or God. Blasphemy seems closer to the bleak Truth and serves as a means to unmask the false presuppositions of theodician claims.

Bartleby, in stark contrast, hardly even utters a word let alone cries. The only formula he stubbornly reiterates whenever he is asked to copy a document is brief, plain, and monotonous: "I would prefer not to." Nothing seems farther from the poetic grandeur of the "roarings" that "pour out" of Job's mouth "like waters" in an unending stream of painful sighs bearing the volume and force of a lion's growl. Nothing seems farther than the poetic power of Ahab's ever flowing, blunt, blasphemous cries.

"Though I wrote the Gospels in this century, I should die in the gutter," writes Melville to Hawthorne in June 1851, as he was putting the final touches on his "Whale."[20] That Melville could anticipate the failure of his grand, all-encompassing Bible did not make the lack of recognition that followed the publication of *Moby-Dick* any easier. In his 1853 Wall Street tale, Melville seems to prefer not to invent another grand poetically-inspired Job; he also appears to prefer not to be a scribe (his privileging of the term "scrivener" over "copyist" underscores such theological connotations) in a world in which a writer's vocation is treated like a low Wall Street clerical job: rarely acknowledged and poorly paid.

But the wonder at the base of "Bartleby" is Melville's paradoxical insistence, in spite of himself almost, to draw from dead letters and dead walls a new Joban figure and a new mock aesthetic that could serve, at the same time, as a different kind of aesthetic. A closer translation of Job into modern times, Melville ventures to suggest, would entail the invention of a sufferer whose fate is so bleak that he is not even granted the privilege of expressing his grief,

---

19 Melville, *Moby-Dick*, 163–164.
20 Melville, Herman, *Correspondence*, ed. Lynn Horth, Northwestern University Press and the Newberry Library, Evanston and Chicago 1993, 192.

misery, and protest in grand poetic form. Melville opts to probe the potential for a minimalist language and mute gestures to serve as the most effective modern equivalent to Job's cry.

In *The Writing of the Disaster*, Maurice Blanchot, the first in a long genealogy of continental thinkers fascinated by the tale, regards Bartleby's formula as exemplary of the language of disaster.

> Bartleby gives up (not that he ever pronounces, or clarifies this renunciation) ever saying anything; he gives up the authority to speak. This is abnegation understood as the abandonment of the self, a relinquishment of identity, refusal which does not cleave to refusal but opens to failure, to the loss of being, to thought. "I will not do it" would still have signified an energetic determination, calling forth an equally energetic contradiction. "I would prefer not to ..." belongs to the infiniteness of patience; no dialectical intervention can take hold of such passivity. We have fallen out of being, outside where, immobile, proceeding with a slow even step, destroyed men come and go.[21]

Blanchot's observations shed light on the contours of Melville's redefinition of Joban aesthetics in "Bartleby." The scrivener follows Job in the trail of "destroyed men" but carves out a somewhat different space. Whereas the biblical rebel immerses in dark, detailed imaginings of self-erasure and de-birthing, Bartleby's minimalist formula offers an even more radical "abandonment of the self" and "falling out of being." In Melville's Wall Street tale, the melancholy Job of Chapter 3 adopts, as it were, the patience of Job of the Prologue, only to create the kind of passivity that is so extreme in its "infiniteness of patience," in its lack of will, and lack of language that it becomes utterly unsettling.[22]

The power of this irreverent formula to do precisely what Job's blasphemous cries do – to probe the very limit of faith, language, and life itself – becomes all the more apparent in light of Gilles Deleuze's renowned elaboration of Blanchot's brief comments. At each occurrence of the formula, writes Deleuze, in "Bartleby; or The Formula,"

> there is a stupor surrounding Bartleby, as if one heard the Unspeakable or the Unstoppable [...] Without a doubt the formula is ravaging, devastating, and leaves nothing standing

---

21 Blanchot, Maurice, *The Writing of the Disaster*, trans. Ann Smock, University of Nebraska Press, Lincoln 1995, 17.
22 In *The Gift of Death*, Jacques Derrida mentions the affinity between Bartleby and the Job who "dreams of not being born" but does not develop this observation. See Jacques Derrida, *The Gift of Death*, trans. David Wills, University of Chicago Press, Chicago 1995, 74. For a recent, extensive treatment of "Bartleby" and the question of passivity, see Branka Arsić, *Passive Constitutions, or, 7 1/2 Times Bartleby*, Stanford University Press, Stanford 2007.

at its wake [...] Bartleby has won the right to survive, that is, to remain immobile and upright before a blind wall. Pure patient passivity, as Blanchot would say. [...] He is urged to say yes or no. But if he said no (to collating, running errands ...) or if he said yes (to copying), he would quickly be defeated and judged useless and would not survive. He can survive only by whirling in a suspense that keeps everyone at a distance."[23]

Deleuze goes so far as to see in Bartleby's formula a continuation of the "language of the Whale" that Melville had fashioned in *Moby-Dick*, a language that "runs beneath English and carries it off," a language capable of sweeping up "language in its entirety, sending it into flight, pushing it to its very limit in order to discover its Outside, silence or music."[24]

If Job questions the ways of the divine Judge, the scrivener's "I would prefer not to" interrupts the normative hierarchies and procedures of earthly lawyers. Nothing remains the same once the scrivener introduces this formula into everyday life at the lawyer's office. The copying of legal documents is suspended and with it the belief in their inherent value. A new minimalist language emerges in the midst of this Wall Street void, sending the Joban cry "into flight, pushing it to its very limit," laying bare the unspeakable that lurks behind.

4 The Starved Body: The Food of Melancholy

Pain in the Book of Job often undermines the distinction between body and soul.[25] Job's corporeal suffering (he is struck with boils) inflames his rage towards God, and conversely the horror of losing hope for benevolent divine intervention seeps into the wounds of the flesh. When Job cries, "For my sighing cometh before I eat / And my roarings are poured out like the waters" (3:24), it is not clear whether actual eating and drinking have become physical-

---

23 Deleuze, Gilles, "Bartleby; or The Formula," in: *Essays Critical and Clinical*, trans. Daniel W. Smith and Michael A. Greco, University of Minnesota Press, Minneapolis 1997, 70–71.
24 Deleuze, "Bartleby; or The Formula," 72.
25 Elaine Scarry reminds us that God's presence in the Bible is made visible via the wounded, ill body of humanity. Not unlike the torturer and the prisoner, God and the human being, she claims, are differentiated by the "immunity of the one and the woundability of the other." See Elaine Scarry, *The Body in Pain: The Making and Unmaking of the World*. Oxford University Press, New York 1985, 183. However insightful, Scarry's account of bodily pain overlooks Job's protest against such modes of divine substantiation (the Book of Job is curiously missing from her discussion) much as it relegates to the margins the ways in which pain, in the biblical text and elsewhere, tends to undermine the distinction between body and soul. For more on Scarry and the Book of Job, see Yosefa Raz's article in this volume.

ly unbearable for him, or whether his agony lies in the realization that God is so busy stuffing sighs and overflowing "roarings" into the mouths of his human creatures that he does not even make possible the consumption of the most elementary nurturing products – bread and water.

Bartleby's body, I would suggest, is as inseparable from the Joban cry as the scrivener's formula. Both the scrivener's starved body and his starved language bear witness to Job's deprivation, while attesting to the collapse of grand poetic language in the face of misery and pain. In the domain of the flesh, I would add, the formula's turning of passivity into a radical "falling out of being" and an "abandonment of the self" becomes a tangible "abandonment of the body."

Ginger nuts are apparently the only food which Bartleby consumes, and this in meager quantities. Melville's choice of ginger leads Branca Arsić to Burton's *Anatomy of Melancholy*, where ginger (along with cinnamon and cloves) is defined as a spice that enhances melancholy. Bartleby, according to Arsić, "is a melancholic who eats what induces melancholy only in order to be eaten up by it."[26] Something similar could be said of Job: he supposedly eats the sighs that precede – or even replace – bread, only to be eaten up by them. In "Bartleby," however, starvation is not temporary (the Book of Job ends with a feast) but rather a mode of bodily self-effacement that culminates in the scrivener's complete rejection of eating in prison.

5 Fluid Typologies: "Ah Bartleby! Ah humanity!"

Melville's search for a different Joban cry that would be attuned to modern sensibilities is inseparable from a new experiment with fluid typologies. The key to understanding Melville's ongoing fascination with the splitting and merging of his biblical characters lies in Chapter 14 of *The Confidence-Man*. In a self-reflexive moment, the narrator protests against the common expectation of readers to find consistent characters in the novels they read: "Upon the whole, it might rather be thought, that he, who, in view of its inconsistencies, says of human nature the same that, in view of its contrasts, is said of the divine nature, that it is past finding out, thereby evinces a better appreciation of it than he who, by always representing it in a clear light, leaves it to be inferred that he clearly knows all about it."[27] To represent human character as

---

26 Arsić, *Passive Constitutions*, 49.
27 Melville, *The Confidence-Man: His Masquerade*, ed. Hershel Parker, Norton Critical Edition, W. W. Norton, New York 1971, 59.

consistent means to smooth out the incomprehensibility of human nature, the prevalent lack of coherence that characterizes human life. In a playful iconoclastic move, Melville demands that the same attention given to divine inconsistencies (all the more so since the rise of biblical criticism) should also be given to human ones.[28]

In his Wall Street tale, Melville fashions one of his most intriguing exegetical inconsistencies as he undermines a boundary he had never previously questioned: that between Job and his friends.[29] His strategy is an unusual one. He follows the supposedly normative perspective of a prudent Wall Street lawyer (his narrators are typically more immediate spokesmen of their author) and probes the biblical dichotomy between Job and his comforters through the splits and inconsistencies of this peculiar narrative voice.[30]

Against his better judgment, the lawyer, who should have been the discursive authority of his office, finds himself overwhelmed and infected by the scrivener's words. "Somehow, of late," he notes, "I had got into the way of involuntarily using the word 'prefer' upon all sorts of not exactly suitable occasions."[31] Bartleby's formula turns out to be a contagious formula with the maddening power to seep into others' mouths and debilitate any sense of stable subjectivity or mastery.

The linguistic merging of the two characters underscores an emotional merging whereby the lawyer gradually identifies with Bartleby to the extent of losing, at times, any sense of distinction. One Sunday morning, instead of visiting Trinity Church (an emblem of institutional religion and the site of a major scandal regarding the use and abuse of church wealth in the late 1840s), the lawyer goes to his office only to find that Bartleby is inside, preferring not "to admit" him at that moment. Perplexed, he wanders the empty streets of New York's financial district and is suddenly struck by the same kind of melancholy he attributes to Bartleby:[32]

---

28 On typologies in *The Confidence-Man*, see Shira Wolosky, "Melville's Unreading of the Bible: *Redburn* and the *Confidence Man*," in: *Letterature D'America*, 21: 88–89 (2001): 31–52.
29 The multiple *Pequod* Jobs live within an ambit of their own, rarely having any interaction with the ship's principal owners, Captains Peleg and Bildad, the latter of whom is named after one of Job's comforters. Allan Silver was among the first to call for a more nuanced reading of the lawyer; see Allan Silver, "The Lawyer and the Scrivener," in: *Partisan Review*, 48.3 (1981): 409–424.
30 On the unique position of the narrator in "Bartleby," see Michael T. Gilmore, "'Bartleby, the Scrivener' and the Transformation of the Economy," in: *American Romanticism in the Marketplace*, The University of Chicago Press, Chicago 1985, 145.
31 Melville, "Bartleby, the Scrivener," 31.
32 For more on the history of Trinity Church, its ties with John Astor, and the pertinent real estate scandals, see Barbara Foley, "From Wall Street to Astor Place: Historicizing Melville's 'Bartleby,'" in: *American Literature*, 72.1 (2000): 87–116.

For the first time in my life a feeling of overpowering stinging melancholy seized me. Before, I had never experienced aught but a not-unpleasing sadness. The bond of a common humanity now drew me irresistibly to gloom. A fraternal melancholy! For both I and Bartleby were sons of Adam. I remembered the bright silks and sparkling faces I had seen that day, in gala trim, swan-like sailing down the Mississippi of Broadway; and I contrasted them with the pallid copyist, and thought to myself, Ah, happiness courts the light, so we deem the world is gay; but misery hides aloof, so we deem that misery there is none."[33]

He speaks of himself and Bartleby as the "sons of Adam" but the "stinging melancholy" he experiences makes their "common humanity" more Joban than Adamic in character. Although the lawyer was initially locked in the position of Job's friends (admiring his chambers on Wall Street, never experiencing but a "not-unpleasing sadness"), his tantalizing encounter with Bartleby leads to a dramatic transformation: he becomes more Joban in character. He now questions the availability of American pursuits of happiness and discovers behind "the bright silks and sparkling faces" of Broadway the hidden misery that courts no light.

Later, visiting the prison of the Tombs, on viewing the dead scrivener (his wasted body huddled by the wall) the lawyer expresses a similar critique. This time he chooses to use Job's own words, defining Bartleby as one who "sleeps with kings and counsellors." The quotation, with which I opened, is part of a longer provocative presentation in which Job renders death as the most compelling equalizer of all: "There the prisoners rest together / They hear not the voice of the oppressor / The small and the great are there / And the servant is free from his master" (Job 3:18–20). In addition to the kings and councilors, one finds in the tombs all the wretched of the earth, among them prisoners, the most relevant to this final episode in the scrivener's life. Much as Job, with bitter irony, speaks of the realm of the dead as the only realm in which justice reigns, where no oppression is heard of, the lawyer now intuits that, even in a nation that defines itself as the epitome of all democracies, death remains the most effective equalizer of all.[34]

The lawyer uses Bartleby's words and Job's words but he cannot fully relinquish the theodician, Christian rhetoric that for so many years had defined his prudent, protected world. He is ultimately torn between being one of Job's friends and being a Job of sorts. The clash between the two roles becomes

---

33 Melville, "Bartleby, the Scrivener," 28.

34 For a succinct analysis of "Bartleby"'s dismantling of cherished American ideals, see Michael Rogin, *Subversive Genealogy: The Politics and Art of Herman Melville*, University of California Press, Berkeley 1979.

particularly humorous (in characteristically dark shades) when, crazed by Bartleby's inescapable "wondrous ascendancy" and haunting presence, he justifies his choice to furnish the scrivener with "office room" as a mission "billeted upon" him "for some mysterious purpose of an all-wise Providence."[35]

The closest the lawyer comes to the scrivener and his formula, as surprising as it may first seem, is at the story's end, in his final cry: "Ah Bartleby! Ah humanity!"[36] No one in his right mind would have dared to end a story with words so vague and banal. In Melville's hands, however, they become the most moving words in the lawyer's narrative. It is here, more than ever before, that the lawyer leaves Prudence and Providence behind and, like the scrivener, ventures to approach the very limit of language, touching on the silences of a minimalist utterance that in itself holds no poetic grandeur. For once, "hardly can [he] express the emotions which seize [him]"[37] – be they his acute longings and compassion for Bartleby, or his mourning over the scrivener's unjustifiable death, or his sense of guilt at being implicated in this death, or his sense of loss on discovering that the Wall Street he believed in had collapsed, or the despair vis-à-vis the incommunicability that prevails in an irredeemable world in which letters and people fail to reach their destination, or his growing fear as a narrator that his own tale may meet the fate of the dead letters he describes in his concluding note, or any other unutterable emotion. The lawyer had his exclamatory moments earlier in the tale – "Ah, happiness courts the light"[38] – but in this final line, his apostrophic words are bare and starved, set apart and isolated, without accompanying explanation or poetic metaphor (his figurative language having elsewhere been quite remarkable).

But something else can be heard in the collapse of the lawyer's language in the final note that goes with Bartleby beyond Bartleby. I would go so far as to define the final apostrophe – "Ah humanity!" – as the lawyer's unwitting delivery of the Joban cry over humanity which Bartleby never releases. In its minimalism, in its departure from canonical aesthetic language, the lawyer's final words are akin to Bartleby's formula, but insofar as it is a cry and a sigh it underscores the Joban roaring that until now had been utterly repressed, blocked by the walls of Wall Street and within the scrivener's incommunicable world.[39]

---

35 Melville, "Bartleby, the Scrivener," 31.
36 Melville, "Bartleby, the Scrivener," 45.
37 Melville, "Bartleby, the Scrivener," 45.
38 Melville, "Bartleby, the Scrivener," 28.
39 Eyal Perez defines *Moby-Dick* as the "teacher of the cry" through its preoccupation with the "whale" and the "wail." See Eyal Perez, *Literature, Disaster, and the Enigma of Power,*

6 Wall Street's Sublime

So far we have focused on Melville's radical rendering of a mock aesthetic language through Job in "Bartleby," but to what extent does he also experiment with the sublime? Even if natural sublimity is eliminated from Wall Street, can the sublime be traced elsewhere? In *Moby-Dick*, Melville alters Burke's notion of the sublime as associated with terror, power and obscurity by adding a Romantic touch to the blend. His monstrous, inscrutable Leviathan, much like that of Blake, is at the same time the embodiment of great wonder and wild imagination. But Melville goes beyond the characteristic Romantic modification of Burke, for he finds sublimity in the mundane activities of whalers, even the most materialistic of them: the spermaceti-squeezing procedures by which Leviathan is turned into a commodity. It is, as Ishmael playfully asserts in "A Squeeze of the Hand," the earthly, even pragmatic aspects of objects – be they spermaceti, tables, beds, or countries – that may (far more than the intellect or the fancy) end up leading to heavenly sights and insights.

Melville's Wall Street is more suspicious of the sublime than the world of whaling, but does not entirely lack it. Here, too, Melville seeks a new sublime via a mock sublime, though he is far more eager to highlight the obstacles that lie in the path of any modern search for the transcendent. To begin with, he altogether avoids acceptable objects and figures of the sublime. If anyone in the lawyer's office approaches the position of the grand White Whale it is none other than the pallid scrivener. Within Melville's ever perplexing, breathtaking juggling of typological possibilities, the scrivener is not only a Job but also, if to a lesser degree, a cross between Leviathan and God (the two are intertwined in *Moby-Dick* as well). Like the White Whale, Bartleby is construed as inscrutable, as a haunting, wondrous enigma, as an apparition or ghost that cannot be laid to rest or captured. Like God, he remains impenetrable and unaccountable. "Bartleby was one of those beings of whom nothing is ascertainable, except from original sources, and in his case those are very small."[40]

Various critics have tried to provide specific accounts of Bartleby's divine role. Bruce Franklin calls attention to the scrivener's Christ-like qualities, made more palpable by echoes of Mathew 25 and Peter's denials.[41] Deleuze ends his essay on "Bartleby" with the assertion that the scrivener is "not the patient,

Stanford University Press, Stanford 2003. Bartleby turns out to be, if differently, another "teacher of the cry."

40 Melville, "Bartleby, the Scrivener," 13.
41 Franklin, Bruce H., *The Wake of the Gods: Melville's Mythology*, Stanford University Press, Stanford 1963, 126–136.

but the doctor of a sick America ... the new Christ or the brother to us all" and Agamben modifies this assertion, claiming that "If Bartleby is a new Messiah, he comes not, like Jesus, to redeem what was, but to save what was not."[42] What has not been taken into account is Bartleby's particular affinity with Job's God. God's circumvention of Job's moral questions in his sublime whirlwind poem (he speaks of the wonders of creation instead of justifying his ways) is whimsically mimicked in Bartleby's uncommunicative response to the lawyer's inquiries and quest for contact. "At present," says the scrivener, "I prefer to give no answer."[43]

In "The Silhouette of Content," Nancy Ruttenburg succinctly defines Bartleby as a "limit figure," as the "limit-case of all character," akin to the *Muselmann,* in his apathy, profound isolation, "absolute indifference to others and to the life around them generally," his "extraordinary absence of physical vitality, and level of experience to which no one has anything remotely approaching adequate access."[44] Among the scenes that Ruttenburg highlights is the lawyer's return to his office on the Sunday afternoon when he had first felt their common melancholy. Bartleby, who earlier in the day would not unlock the office door for the lawyer, has vanished in the interim, albeit not without leaving material traces: "the faint imprint of a lean, reclining form" on the old sofa, a tin basin, a ragged towel, "a few crumbs of ginger-nuts and a morsel of cheese."[45] "Yet this irreducible residue," claims Ruttenburg, "is sufficient to compel the lawyer to confront the irreducibility of Bartleby's humanity, a confrontation to which the ongoing struggle with his conscience attests and which allows him to construe this eccentric man as, precisely in his exceptionality, the most representative of men."[46]

Let me suggest that Bartleby's position as a limit figure becomes all the more pronounced in light of his peculiar position on the border between the human and the divine. This is the very nexus Melville raises in *The Confidence-*

---

42 Deleuze, "Bartleby; or The Formula," 90; Giorgio Agamben, *Potentialities: Collected Essays in Philosophy,* trans. Daniel Heller-Roazen, Stanford University Press, Stanford 1999, 270. See also Richard J. Zlogar, "Body Politics in 'Bartleby': Leprosy, Healing, and Christ-ness in Melville's 'story of Wall-Street,'" in: *Nineteenth-Century Literature* 53.4 (March 1999): 505–529.
43 Melville, "Bartleby, the Scrivener," 30.
44 Ruttenburg, Nancy, "'The Silhouette of a Content': 'Bartleby' and American Literary Specificity," in: *Melville and Aesthetics,* eds. Samuel Otter and Geoffrey Sanborn, Palgrave Macmillan, New York 2011, 137–156. Ruttenberg relies on Agamben's observations in *Remnants of Auschwitz,* pointing to ways in which this later work may illuminate Agamben's reading of "Bartleby" in *Potentialities.*
45 Melville, "Bartleby, the Scrivener," 27.
46 Ruttenburg, "The Silhouette of a Content," 145.

Man, highlighting the affinities between human and divine inconsistencies and inscrutabilities. The kinds of assumptions, surmises, and uncertainties that Bartleby generates render him an exemplary case not only for the study of human character but also for probing the inexplicability of divine conduct. Even in this most material moment of "Bartleby," we are faced with the marks of an utterly absent body. From the lawyer's perspective, these traces are, in a sense, all too human and all too inhuman at once, which is why he regards them with a mixture of compassion vis-à-vis human misery and an eagerness to witness a sublimity he cannot grasp. That divine imprints are more commonly looked for in the Holy Land leaves Melville all the more determined to seek them on a "rickety old sofa" in a Wall Street office.

7 Petra and the Pyramids

"Bartleby" offers two minor exceptions to Melville's turning away from traditional objects of the aesthetic and the sublime: the brief evocations of Petra and the pyramids. Both sites, one should bear in mind, were considered pinnacles of oriental sublimity in the prospering Holy Land literature and art of nineteenth-century America. In *Clarel*, Melville's "Poem and Pilgrimage in the Holy Land" of 1873, the one work in which Melville chooses a traditional sacred geography – but proceeds to dismantle it – Petra is depicted as an oriental, sublime blend of Nature's terror and an Art on the abyss: "and Petra's there, / Down in her cleft. Mid such a scene / Of Nature's terror, how serene, / That ordered form. Nor less 'tis cut / Out of that terror – does abut / Thereon: there's Art" (2.30.39–43).[47] Yet, the Orient, here as elsewhere in *Clarel*, turns out to be a luring realm that is evasive and unreliable, and the aesthetic pilgrimage in the Holy Land a "hunt without one clue."[48]

In "Bartleby," the privileged aesthetic position of the Orient is equally undermined as "deserted Petra" and is used as a foil to highlight the Sunday dreariness of Wall Street. This strange link between the two distant and distinct cities is more appropriate than it may first seem. In its time, Petra was both a

---

47 Melville, Herman, *Clarel: A Poem and Pilgrimage in the Holy Land*, eds., Harrison Hayford, et al., Northwestern University Press and the Newberry Library, Evanston and Chicago 2008, 236.
48 For a detailed analysis of Melville's response to the aesthetics of the Orient, see Ilana Pardes, "Melville's Song of Songs: *Clarel* as Aesthetic Pilgrimage," in: *Melville and Aesthetics*, 213–233.

prospering financial center for the global market of the Nabataeans (the perfume trade in particular) and a city of marvelous tombs, carved into the red rock, the most famous being those of the renowned "Treasury." Bartleby's Wall Street is thus Petra's modern equivalent: a financial district that is "dead empty all the time."[49]

The pyramids appear in the lawyer's response to the Egyptian style of the prison's architecture. "The Egyptian character of the masonry weighed upon me with its gloom. But a soft imprisoned turf grew under foot. The heart of the eternal pyramids, it seemed, wherein, by some strange magic, through the clefts, grass-seed, dropped by the birds, had sprung."[50] In marveling at the "soft imprisoned" "grass-seed" at the heart of the pyramid-like prison, the lawyer, characteristically, seeks something "not unpleasing" in a gloomy setting – in this case, continuing in particular a line he had pursued in a comment to Bartleby during his previous visit: "And see, it is not so sad a place as one might think. Look, there is the sky, and here is the grass."[51] The lawyer's thoughts on the Egyptian character of the Tombs lead to the subsequent sight of the wasted Bartleby "huddled up" by the wall in the yard. They hint at a desire for a scene of resurrection whereby the scrivener "by some kind of magic" would "spring" "through the clefts." But the only wish realized here is Job's death wish. The entire prison, whose name now proves prophetic, becomes not quite a pyramid promising "eternal" life but rather a grand, Joban tomb ensuring the stillness of death in a womb that remains shut.

Situating himself against the admiration for the oriental hue of the Book of Job – promoted in the writings of the advocates of the literary Bible and in popularized form in Holy Land travel literature – Melville points to the bankruptcy of the cherished art of the Orient. Yet given that he never truly relinquishes the quest for the aesthetic and the sublime, Melville seems, above all, to question normative aesthetic norms and hierarchies.

Jacques Rancière's reading of Bartleby's formula highlights the originality of this move.

> "To prefer not to" can be paraphrased and interpreted in different ways, one of which is "to renounce preferring," "to want not to prefer." In this version, it becomes formally equivalent to one of the canonic formulas that regulate the will of literature – I mean the famous Flaubertian principle: there are no beautiful or ugly subjects, no reason to prefer Constantinople – the splendors of the Orient and of History – to Yvetot – the dampness

---

49 Arsić, *Passive Constitutions*, 47.
50 Melville, "Bartleby, the Scrivener," 44.
51 Melville, "Bartleby, the Scrivener," 43.

and history-less dullness of the French hinterland. There aren't any because style is an absolute way of seeing things.[52]

While engaging in various parodies of continental notions of the transcendent aspects in Job, Melville's Wall Street story points to the obstructed potentialities of a godless, supposedly "ugly," urban modernity to produce, against itself, new modes of the aesthetic and the sublime even in the most unlikely figures and objects. But it is not just any modernity; it is an American modernity that in its alleged distance from the canonical geographies of the sublime – the Orient in particular – can paradoxically pave the road to new configurations of Job.

8 Bartleby as Precursor

The Book of Job, interestingly enough, maintained its prime position as an aesthetic touchstone in twentieth-century literature. Indeed, it has been used as a key text for exploring the melancholies of modern times by writers and artists as different as Franz Kafka, S.Y. Agnon, and Joel and Ethan Coen.

"Bartleby" is primarily Kafka's precursor. In transferring the biblical sufferer into a modern work setting and allowing him to die without being granted either a divine response from the whirlwind or a happy end, both *Moby-Dick* and "Bartleby" lead to *The Trial*; Bartleby's Wall Street, however, with its lawyers and copyists and its vivid dramatization of Job's legal metaphors, is even closer to the Kafkaesque Job.[53] Thomas Mann's comment on *The Trial* highlights the affinity between the two texts and their respective irreverent opening of the concept of "sublime." Mann characterizes Kafka as a religious humorist who depicts the transcendent world "as an Austrian 'department'; as a magnification of a petty, obstinate, inaccessible, unaccountable bureaucracy; a mammoth establishment of documents and procedures, headed by some darkly responsible official hierarchy."[54]

---

52 Rancière, Jacques, *The Flesh of Words: The Politics of Writing*, trans. Charlotte Mandell, Stanford University Press, Stanford 2004, 147.

53 For more on *The Trial* as a rereading of Job, see Harold Fisch, *New Stories for Old: Biblical Patterns in the Novel*, St. Martin's Press, New York 1998, 81–99; Susan E. Schreiner, *Where Shall Wisdom Be Found? Calvin's Exegesis of Job from Medieval and Modern Perspectives*, University of Chicago Press, Chicago 1994. The affinity between "Bartleby" and Kafka has been noted earlier but not in relation to Job. See Deleuze, "Bartleby; or The Formula," 68. Agamben offers a similar observation; see Agamben, *Potentialities*, 243.

54 See Schreiner, *Where Shall Wisdom Be Found*, 181.

Kafka's *America*, though less pronouncedly Joban than *The Trial*, sheds light on how we might imagine a Kafkaesque Job within an American context. Like Bartleby's Wall Street, Kafka's *America* lays bare the imprisonments of the American workplace and the absurdities of its rhetoric of redemptive happiness: "The great theatre of Oklahoma calls you! Today only and never again! If you miss your chance now you miss it for ever! If you think of your future you are one of us! Everyone is welcome!"[55] The Coen Brothers' film "A Serious Man" makes the American Kafkaesque Job all the more vivid in flaunting the absurdities of various Jewish institutions in suburban America of the early sixties. Larry Gopnik goes from one rabbi to another in search of an explanation for the sudden calamities that have beset him but waits in vain before the office door of the great Rabbi Marshak, having been blocked by the stern secretary from approaching the Law.

But perhaps, above all, Melville anticipates Kafka in foregrounding hermeneutic questions in the course of reinventing Job. Jacques Derrida's renowned essay "Devant la Loi" positions the parable in the Cathedral as an exemplary text in its insistence on the impossibility of interpretation.[56] What emerges from the discussion between Joseph K. and the priest on the meaning of the parable is that all readings are necessarily misreadings. We shall never comprehend with certainty what lies behind the succession of guarded doors which divide us from the Law. Following Derrida, Harold Fisch wonders whether the parable in the Cathedral is specifically meant to question the very possibility of interpreting the Book of Job with its inexplicable trial.

Melville, I suspect, is not concerned with misreadings. The profusion of potential readings, as far as he is concerned, does not imply that any are necessarily erroneous. That such a study of biblical texts and characters is always on the verge of admitting – through its unparalleled exegetical excess – that hermeneutic enigmas are "past finding out" does not make it less alluring. Somehow, it is the impossibility of fathoming divine and human character and the vanity of all knowledge that seems to propel Melville with an ever growing drive to prefer "not to be a little reasonable."[57]

---

55 Kafka, Franz, *America*, trans. Willa and Edwin Muir, Vintage, London 2005, 234.
56 Derrida, Jacques "Devant la Loi," trans. Avital Ronell, in: *Kafka and the Contemporary Critical Performance*, ed. Alan Udoff, Indiana University Press, Bloomington 1987, 128–149.
57 Melville, "Bartleby, the Scrivener," 30.

Bibliography

Agamben, Giorgio. *Potentialities: Collected Essays in Philosophy*. Trans. Daniel Heller-Roazen. Stanford: Stanford University Press, 1999.

Alter, Robert. *The Art of Biblical Poetry*. New York: Basic Books, 1985.

Arsić, Branka. *Passive Constitutions, or, 7 1/2 Times Bartleby*. Stanford: Stanford University Press, 2007.

Blanchot, Maurice. *The Writing of the Disaster*. Trans. Ann Smock. Lincoln: University of Nebraska Press, 1995.

Carlyle, Thomas. *On Heroes, Hero-Worship, and the Heroic in History*. Ed. Carl Niemeyer, Lincoln: University of Nebraska Press, 1966.

Deleuze, Gilles. *Essays Critical and Clinical*. Trans. Daniel W. Smith and Michael A. Greco. Minneapolis: University of Minnesota Press, 1997. 68–90.

Derrida, Jacques. "Devant la Loi." *Kafka and the Contemporary Critical Performance*. Ed. Alan Udoff. Trans. Avital Ronell, Bloomington: Indiana University Press, 1987. 128–149.

Derrida, Jacques. *The Gift of Death*. Trans. David Wills. Chicago: University of Chicago Press, 1995.

Fisch, Harold. *New Stories for Old: Biblical Patterns in the Novel*. New York: St. Martin's Press, 1998.

Fisch, Harold. *The Biblical Presence in Shakespeare, Milton, and Blake: A Comparative Study*. Oxford: Clarendon Press, 1999.

Foley, Barbara. "From Wall Street to Astor Place: Historicizing Melville's 'Bartleby'." *American Literature*, 72.1. (2000): 87–116.

Franklin, Bruce H. *The Wake of the Gods: Melville's Mythology*. Stanford: Stanford University Press, 1963.

Frei, Hans W. *The Eclipse of Biblical Narrative: A Study in Eighteenth and Nineteenth Century Hermeneutics*. New Haven: Yale University Press, 1974.

Gilmore, Michael T. *American Romanticism in the Marketplace*. Chicago: The University of Chicago Press, 1985.

Goethe, Johann Wolfgang (von). *Faust: A Tragedy: Interpretive Notes, Contexts, Modern Criticism*. Ed. Cyrus Hamlin. Trans. Walter Arndt. Norton Critical Editions. New York: W. W. Norton, 2001.

Herder, J. G. "God and Nature in the Book of Job." *The Dimensions of Job: A Study and Selected Readings*. Ed. Nahum N. Glatzer. New York: Schocken Books, 1969. 141–156.

Holman, Hugh. "The Reconciliation of Ishmael: *Moby-Dick* and the Book of Job." *South Atlantic Quarterly* 57 (1958): 478–490.

Kafka, Franz. *America*. Trans. Willa and Edwin Muir. London: Vintage, 2005.

Lamb, Jonathan. *The Rhetoric of Suffering: Reading the Book of Job in the Eighteenth Century*. New York: Oxford University Press, 1995.

Melville, Herman. *The Piazza Tales and Other Prose Pieces 1839–1860*. Eds. Harrison Hayford et al. Evanston and Chicago: Northwestern University Press and Newberry Library, 1987.

Melville, Herman. *Clarel: A Poem and Pilgrimage in the Holy Land*. Eds. Harrison Hayford et al. Evanston and Chicago: Northwestern University Press and the Newberry Library, 2008.

Melville, Herman. *Correspondence*. Ed. Lynn Horth. Evanston and Chicago: Northwestern University Press and the Newberry Library, 1993.

Melville, Herman. *Moby-Dick; or, The Whale*. Eds. Harrison Hayford et al. Evanston and Chicago: Northwestern University Press and the Newberry Library, 2001.

Melville, Herman. *The Confidence-Man: His Masquerade*. Ed. Hershel Parker. New York: W. W. Norton, Norton Critical Edition, 1971.

Nevo, Ruth. *Tragic Form in Shakespeare*. Princeton: Princeton University Press, 1972.

Norton, David. *A History of the Bible as Literature: From 1700 to the Present Day*. Cambridge: Cambridge University Press, 1993.

Pardes, Ilana. "Melville's Song of Songs: *Clarel* as Aesthetic Pilgrimage." *Melville and Aesthetics*. Eds. Samuel Otter and Geoffrey Sanborn. New York: Palgrave Macmillan, 2011. 213–233.

Pardes, Ilana. *Melville's Bibles*. Berkeley: University of California Press, 2008.

Perez, Eyal. *Literature, Disaster, and the Enigma of Power*. Stanford: Stanford University Press, 2003.

Pope, Marvin. *Job*. Garden City: Doubleday, 1973.

Rancière, Jacques. *The Flesh of Words: The Politics of Writing*. Trans. Charlotte Mandell. Stanford: Stanford University Press, 2004.

Rogin, Michael. *Subversive Genealogy: The Politics and Art of Herman Melville*. Berkeley: University of California Press, 1979.

Ruttenburg, Nancy. "'The Silhouette of a Content': 'Bartleby' and American Literary Specificity."*Melville and Aesthetics*. Eds. Samuel Otter and Geoffrey Sanborn. New York: Palgrave Macmillan, 2011. 137–156.

Scarry, Elaine. *The Body in Pain: The Making and Unmaking of the World*. New York: Oxford University Press, 1985.

Schreiner, Susan E. *Where Shall Wisdom Be Found? Calvin's Exegesis of Job from Medieval and Modern Perspectives*. Chicago: University of Chicago Press, 1994.

Silver, Allan. "The Lawyer and the Scrivener." *Partisan Review*, 48.3 (1981): 409–424.

Sheehan, Jonathan. *The Enlightenment Bible: Translation, Scholarship, Culture*. Princeton: Princeton University Press, 2005.

Sheehan, Jonathan. "The Poetics and Politics of Theodicy." *Prooftexts* 27.2, (Spring 2008): 211–232.

Stout, Janis. "Melville's Use of the Book of Job." *Nineteenth-Century Fiction* 25.1 (1970): 69–83.

Thompson, Lawrence. *Melville's Quarrel with God*. Princeton: Princeton University Press, 1952.

Wolosky, Shira. "Melville's Unreading of the Bible: *Redburn* and the *Confidence Man*." *Letterature D'America*, 21.88–89 (2001): 31–52.

Wright, Nathalia. *Melville's Use of the Bible*. Durham: Duke University Press, 1949.

Wright, Nathalia. "Moby Dick: Jonah's or Job's Whale?." *American Literature* 37.2 (May 1965): 190–195.

Zlogar, Richard J. "Body Politics in 'Bartleby': Leprosy, Healing, and Christ-ness in Melville's 'story of Wall Street.'" *Nineteenth-Century Literature* 53.4 (March 1999): 505–529.

Vivian Liska
Kafka's Other Job

Kafka's work, although it never mentions Job by name, has repeatedly been read in terms of this biblical figure who challenges the claim of divine justice in the face of human suffering. In recent decades, critics have pointed out fairly convincing, concrete and detailed similarities between Kafka's work and the Book of Job. Most notably, Northrop Frye, in *The Great Code*, regards the writings of Kafka "as a series of commentaries on the Book of Job" and terms Kafka's most famous novel, *The Trial,* "a kind of *Midrash*" on this biblical book.[1] Other critics consider this novel "a conscious parallel of the Book of Job,"[2] if not its "true" and even "indispensable translation,"[3] argue that "in this novel Kafka pushes the perceptual dilemma of Job's story to its unrelenting and catastrophic limit"[4] and state that "the court in *The Trial* affirms the same set of moral values found in the Book of Job."[5] Indeed, Harold Fisch, who sees Kafka's writings as "a profound and sustained attempt to render Job for modern men," has noted that "the analogy with Job" has become "a commonplace of Kafka criticism."[6]

The most radical and daring, but also contentious parallels between Job and Kafka, however, were drawn in the late 1920s and 1930s by a group of German-Jewish thinkers who drew on the Jewish textual tradition in their reflections on the fundamental predicaments of modern existence. These figures engaged and contested each other's work, often echoing one other. Margarete Susman, in her 1929 essay "The Job Problem in Franz Kafka," contended that no other modern work "carries as purely and deeply the traits of the age-old confrontation of Job with his God."[7] Likewise, Max Brod, both in his 1931 essay

---

1 Frye, Northrope, *The Great Code. The Bible and Literature*, Routledge & Kegan Paul, London 1982, 195.
2 Kartiganer, Donald M., "Job and Joseph K: Myth in Kafka's *The Trial*," in: *Modern Fiction Studies* 8 (1962): 31–43, 31.
3 Fisch, Harold, *New Stories for Old. Biblical Patterns in the Novel*, Macmillan Press, Houndmills/Basingstoke/Hampshire/London 1998, 98.
4 Schreiner, Susan E., *Where Shall Wisdom Be Found? Calvin's Exegesis of Job from Medieval and Modern Perspectives*, University of Chicago Press, Chicago 1994, 181.
5 Lasine, Stuart, "The Trials of Job and Kafka's Josef K," in: *The German Quarterly* 63.2 (1990): 187–198, 187.
6 Fisch, *New Stories for Old*, 87, 89.
7 Susman, Margarete, "Das Hiob-Problem bei Kafka," in: *Das Nah- und Fernsein des Fremden. Essays und Briefe*, ed. Ingeborg Nordmann, Suhrkamp, Frankfurt/M. 1992, 183–203, 203. Following references to this essay are quoted as (JP, page number).

"Franz Kafka's Fundamental Experience" and in his biography of Kafka (published in 1937), suggested that "the old question of Job"[8] lies at the core of Kafka's life and work. In a letter dated 1 August 1931 to Walter Benjamin, Gershom Scholem wrote: "I advise you to begin any inquiry into Kafka with the Book of Job."[9] Martin Buber considered "Kafka's work to be the most important Jobean commentary of our time."[10] In 1934 Günther Anders asserted – albeit without presenting concrete evidence – that the Book of Job accompanied Kafka throughout his life.[11]

These German-Jewish thinkers, among Kafka's earliest and most prominent interpreters, considered him the author who, like no other, captures the human condition in modern times. They analyzed Kafka in the course of their respective endeavors to conceptualize modernity in light of Jewish scriptures, rethink the foundations of Judaism in the face of the rupture with tradition, and, more generally, reflect on the possibilities of a divine order after the "death of God." In doing so, each invoked central features of the Book of Job. In the figure of Job, a character who wrangles with God, they recognized not only a human voice addressing God against all odds, but also a precursor of modern man's doubts about divine justice. The Book of Job's multi-perspectival mode, narrative inconsistencies and myriad plot incongruities lent themselves particularly well to these thinkers' desire to reconcile the Jewish biblical tradition with the modern world rendered so keenly in Kafka's modernist prose.

The Book of Job's hermeneutic difficulties and above all its deeply paradoxical nature contribute to making it a privileged companion to Kafka's work. Like Kafka's writings, the Book of Job yields no clear moral or message. Moreover, its paradoxes and incongruities are manifold. First and foremost the Job question can, in itself, be regarded as a paradox: How, if there is no justice in the world – since the righteous and the sinners suffer alike – can it be claimed

---

8 Brod, Max, *Über Franz Kafka*. Fischer, Frankfurt/M. 1974, 182–188. Following references to this essay are quoted as (FK, page number).
9 Scholem, Gershom, Letter to Walter Benjamin, dated August 1, 1931, in: Benjamin, Walter, *Benjamin über Kafka. Texte, Briefzeugnisse, Aufzeichnungen*, ed. Hermann Schweppenhäuser, Suhrkamp, Frankfurt/M. 1981, 63–93, 64. Following references to this book are quoted as (BK, page number).
10 Buber, Martin, *Darko shel mikra*, Mosad Bilaik, Jerusalem 1964, 357; cited by Nahum Glatzer in: *The Dimensions of Job. A Study and Selected Readings*, Schocken Books, New York 1969, 48.
11 Anders, Günther, *Kafka Pro et Contra*, C. H. Beck, München 1951, 91. Although there is no explicit evidence that Kafka actually read the Book of Job, he was doubtlessly aware of it, not least through his reading of Kierkegaard's *The Repetition*, as documented in his correspondence with Max Brod, and through plays by Yiddish theater troops that Kafka attended and which referred to Job.

that God is almighty? Yet there are other, more specific paradoxes inherent here. Job, unlike his friends and supposed comforters who justify to him the ways of God and variously explain the existence of evil as punishment, didactic ordeal, or trial, rebels against God and accuses him of injustice, indifference, and withdrawal from human reach. Job does so, however, in a most direct and intimate address that confirms God's closeness. A related paradox is God's surprising response: despite Job's rebelliousness, God praises Job's attitude and rejects the friends' words as empty flattery. Finally, the resolution of the dialogue between God and Job remains puzzling. God, in his speech from the whirlwind, gives a most indirect, if not unsatisfactory, reply to Job's accusations, yet Job nevertheless eventually submits to God "in dust and ashes" (Job 42.6).

Likewise, paradoxes and unsolvable hermeneutic puzzles form the very texture of Kafka's work. There is no doubt that the paradoxes in Kafka's work can be read in light of motifs from the Book of Job. Indeed, Job's central question – about the justice of God who "destroyeth the perfect and the wicked" (Job 9.22) alike – is almost literally echoed by Kafka: a diary entry from 1915 notes, in reference to the respective heroes of *America* and *The Trial*, that "the innocent and the guilty [are] both executed without distinction in the end."[12] However, the guilt or innocence of Josef K. in *The Trial* is far from clear and has inspired endless discussions. The paradox of enacting closeness while claiming inapproachability is evident in many of Kafka's texts, among them "Letter to the Father" and "Before the Law." It is also discernible in certain lesser-known stories, such as "A Little Woman" and "Community," where the narrators display proximity, even intimacy, with an adversary without ever resolving the incongruity. Likewise, the paradox of Job's treacherously virtuous friends who seek to bring him back to the right path can be likened to Kafka's "Little Fable." This brief text begins with a lamentation – "ach" – and then relates the story of a mouse who, upon following a cat's advice to literally "turn around," is promptly eaten by her.[13] However, nothing in Kafka's story indicates who the mouse and cat actually are and whether the anecdote is a political allegory or a religious parable. The paradox of Job submitting himself to God after witnessing a display of God's might can be compared to the perplexing – and unresolved – ending of Kafka's *The Judgment*, in which the son

---

12 Kafka, Franz, *Tagebücher*, Fischer, Frankfurt/M. 2002, 757 (30 September 1915). I would like to thank Stanley Corngold for making me aware of this parallel.
13 Kafka, Franz, "A Little Fable," in: *The Complete Stories*, ed. Nahum Glatzer, transs. Willa Muir and Edwin Muir, Schocken Books, New York 1971, 445.

submits himself to his father's demonstration of power and, following the father's verdict, drowns himself in the river.

These and myriad other parallels can be discerned between Kafka's work and the Book of Job; however, these parallels are not unique to Kafka and do not capture the specific formal features of his prose, most notably a recurrent stylistic element manifested in his seemingly infinite "buts," "yets" and "howevers". This particular quality – variously termed "infinite regress,"[14] "chiastic recourse,"[15] "oscillating negation,"[16] and "rotating dialectic"[17] – entails rescinding every statement just made, only to immediately take it up again with a barely perceptible shift, and then, often, to retract it yet again within the same sentence. Readings that fail to account for this dearth of resolution, one of the most singular aspects of Kafka's work, tend to resolve the writings' undecidability and become misreadings which, although often quite interesting, convey more about the interpreters than about Kafka's work.

The early German-Jewish thinkers who referred to the Book of Job in commenting on Kafka's writings all addressed the paradoxes in his work in which they found delineations of an author for whom modernity was a godless world, but for whom, as Günther Anders noted, the experience was a "religious fact."[18] These interpretations invariably, albeit in different ways, offer selective readings of the Book of Job that resolve its paradoxes and project the resulting "solutions" onto Kafka's work. This results in both the Book of Job and Kafka's writings being divested of their resistance to closure – arguably their most singular and potentially disturbing feature – and becoming illustrations of larger theological constructs. This is particularly striking in how Susman and Brod portray Kafka, and, in a more complex way, in how Scholem presents him. Each of these critics refers to the Book of Job in their respective analyses of Kafka, yet they derive from the parallels between the biblical figure and his modern counterpart radically different visions of Kafka and, more generally, of the relation between God and man in modernity.

---

14 Baker, Jason, Introduction, in: Kafka, Franz, *The Metamorphosis and Other Stories*, Barnes & Noble Classics, New York 2003, xvi.

15 Corngold, Stanley, *Lambent Traces: Franz Kafka*, Princeton University Press, Princeton 2004, 125.

16 Glazova, Anna, "Franz Kafka: Oszillierende Negationen," 2008, http://www.kafka.org/index.php/icqlist/index.php?id=194,229,0,0,1,0 (May 30, 2014).

17 Walser, Martin, *Beschreibung einer Form. Versuch über Kafka*, Suhrkamp, Frankfurt/M. 1999, 84.

18 Anders, *Kafka Pro et Contra*, 82.

1 Saving Suffering: Margarete Susman's Judeo-Christian Theodicy

Susman's essay "The Job Problem in Kafka," published in 1929, is among the earliest German studies of Kafka.[19] It offers a philosophical portrait of the Prague author within an interpretation of Job and a Joban understanding of the fate and mission of the Jewish people. Kafka, for Susman, is the ultimate representative of the Joban experience in modernity. Moreover, in Kafka's time, Job's plight – his suffering, his desperate hope to be heard by God, his search for divine justice – had become more acute, such that any understanding of the connection between guilt and suffering, so starkly problematized in the Book of Job, was now entirely inaccessible to the grasp of modern man. Life had become empty of any direction, weight, or meaning. Kafka's artistic achievement, in Susman's words, was in having found "the form of this nothing itself" (JP, 192). And yet, for Susman, his work intimates that a hidden, almighty law permeates every aspect of life, even if this law has become so absolutely unreachable that we can no longer perceive it and are left with nothing but chaos and confusion. In short, "Kafka's work envisions a world that is truly abandoned by God – and yet – and this is its great mystery (*Mysterium*) – although He has forsaken it, everything in it is His revelation" (JP, 201).

Susman's argument is based upon a dialectic reversal of opposites by which she resolves the incongruities and contradictions that arise both from her readings of the Book of Job and Kafka's work and from her comparison of the two. In this essay, her mode of argumentation relies upon the pronounced repetition of a particular figure of thought, namely, the striking reiteration of "buts" and "howevers" throughout her text. These conjunctive adverbs introduce logical reversals, and – at least in their appearance and frequency – appear to be similar to Kafka's own recurrent use of this stylistic feature. Yet the rhetorical form in fact serves an opposite function and effect for the two authors. In Kafka's writings, it indicates an infinite oscillation between different possibilities, an oscillation that never reaches a conclusion. Susman, however, uses it uniformly, so as to reverse the negativity she diagnoses in Kafka's vision into a positive affirmation, rendering it a suitable tool for an accomplished theodicy.

---

19 For a recent, very different discussion of Susman's association of Job with Kafka see Mark Larrimore, *The Book of "Job": A Biography*, Princeton University Press, Princeton 2013, 236–239. Larrimore states that "if we recognize Job and Kafka as prophets, there is still hope in human life" (238). This hope, messianic in nature, comes at the price – more Christian than Jewish – of an affirmation of suffering.

In fact, Susman's explicit intention is to resolve the paradoxes of the Book of Job and the complexities of Kafka's work into a theodicy. For her, the Book of Job and the writings in its tradition – primarily those of the Jews in exile, and foremost among them Kafka's work – are a justification of the divine order. Susman describes Jewish thought as a result of their predicament as victims: "The very fact that [the Jews] suffer, and suffer for reasons unknown [...] imposes on them again and again the attempt to justify God and to explain suffering and guilt and their connection. There is not one great achievement of Judaism that at the bottom is not a theodicy" (JP, 188). To this end, and via means of a paradigmatic dialectic reversal, she explains away the Book of Job's central paradox, the suffering of the innocent. Furthermore, she renders Job as the one who, though he "continuously searches for his own guilt" (JP, 185), is incapable of finding it, because he does not understand, until the end, that this guilt lies not with him personally but in human sinfulness. For Susman, it is precisely because of Job's innocence that his suffering gains meaning and becomes a revelation of God's radical Otherness: the suffering of the guilty would be a mere causality and thus could be integrated into human measures. Similarly, and with even greater emphasis, she finds in Kafka a representative and spokesman for the poor and suffering. Indeed, her Kafka is even more righteous than Job, for, unlike Job, Kafka "does not beg for himself but for his world" (JP, 195). It is in the abysmal suffering of such figures as Kafka's ailing hunger artist, the sickly circus rider, and the failing acrobat that the reversal occurs, the revelation of the hidden, divine power to which we ought to subject our lives.

In accordance with this view derived from a dialectic reconciliation of opposites, Susman's interpretation of Kafka likewise amplifies and resolves the other central paradoxes present in the Book of Job. Hence, Job's intimate lament to a distant God becomes Kafka's extended monologue addressed solely to Him who, in modern times, has withdrawn completely. Similarly, the paradox of God's acceptance of Job, the blasphemous accuser, and His rejection of Job's friends who had sought to justify the divine order, become, in Susman's essay, a vision of Kafka as ultimate representative of the Jews, elected by God in spite of – or rather precisely because of – his rendering of a world from which justice has vanished. For Susman, the paradox of Job's submission to God after His inadequate response from the whirlwind – His demonstration of the grandeur of His creation, which in no way answers Job's questioning of God's claim to justice – constitutes the very epiphany of Job's experience of divine revelation. It is precisely God's withdrawal from human understanding that turns Job's submission into a full expression of faith. As such, it is not Job the rebel but Job the martyr who becomes the emblematic figure of the Jewish people and the model for Susman's *homo religiosus*.

Susman starkly underscores this point by noting Kafka's abstention from protest in the face of a God who remains inscrutably silent: "*Kafka klagt nicht,*" she observes (JP, 200). He does not even lament or protest, she explains, because in his world the distance to God has become so great. So absolute is his withdrawal that there is no longer anyone to listen, let alone answer. That Kafka does not lament is, for Susman, an expression of pure piety. In the most radical reversal of opposites, she hails the reaction of the victim (whom Susman labels "*der Gerichtete,*" or the one who is judged), when, like Job and Kafka even more so, he accepts his fate. "Totally questionless submission," she writes, "appears as the only force that at least temporarily shows a way out of total doom" (JP, 199). Kafka, like Job, and by extension the Jewish people, in taking the suffering of humanity upon himself, paradoxically becomes a kind of Christ figure, suffering for – and thereby saving – the whole of humanity.

Susman's interpretation is bolstered by a mix of Jewish and Christian theologumena. For her, Job's questioning of divine justice, his daring accusations against God, are directly linked to the legal aspect of Judaism: in this view, the Jews, more so than any other people, presume – and are entitled to expect – divine justice. Yet Susman's idea of Judaism has unmistakable Christian undertones. In contrast with the Talmudic view, in which the chosenness of the Jews is based upon their acceptance of the Torah and its laws, for Susman Jewish election is a direct correlate of suffering. It is in their subjection to the suffering inflicted on them that the election of the Jewish people manifests itself.

In this consideration of the Jews' redemptive suffering, Susman envisions their dismal fate as divine retribution for their wrongdoings. Hence, her vision of the Jew in modernity echoes the speeches of Job's friends, who justify his suffering as punishment for his sins. Yet Susman, in disregarding the fact that God, in his final address from the whirlwind, rejects the friends' false comforting, echoes their attitude, for she considers the greater distance from God that has emerged in modern times to be punishment for the modern Jews' godlessness and assimilation to modernity. Indeed, this punishment is, as with Job, precisely the sign of Jewish election. Susman would take this analysis a step further in her book *Job and the Jewish people*.[20] Here she argues (though referring only sporadically to Kafka) that the suffering of the Jews is not only a manifestation of the privilege God has bestowed upon his people, but that it is their very mission in the world, one which they would fail to fulfill if their condition as an exilic, homeless people and scapegoat of the world's nations were to become less daunting. This particular work, written in the aftermath

---

20 Susman, Margarete, *Das Buch Hiob und das Schicksal des jüdischen Volkes*, Steinberg Verlag, Zürich 1946.

of the Holocaust, not only displays various problematic implications discernible in Susman's earlier Joban interpretation of Kafka; it also comes close to a disconcerting justification of the ultimate Jewish suffering in history.

2 Bridging the Gap: Max Brod's Positive Jewish Theology

Susman's writings on Kafka and Job circulated widely among her contemporaries, including Felix Weltsch, Hans-Joachim Schoeps, Gershom Scholem and Max Brod, all of whom referred to her work on the subject. Although Brod's writings on Kafka were not overtly directed against Susman, they nonetheless amount to an attack on her readings of the author. In these writings Brod repeatedly invokes the "Job question" and, in his biography of Kafka, quotes extended passages from Job's laments and protests. These references partially overlap with Susman's; Brod, however, implicitly negates the parallel Susman posits in her reading of Kafka at its most salient points. He rejects the idea of "representative suffering" and regards human sinfulness as mere "accidental" weakness. In this respect, doubts about God result from a misunderstanding of divine justice. Brod, in his only explicit reference to Susman's reading of the relationship between Kafka and Job, contests her historical explanation of the differences between the two. For Brod, these differences derive not from the growing abyss between God and man in modernity; rather, they lie in Job's arrogant certainty about his own integrity and innocence. Kafka, unlike Job, recognized himself as flawed. Susman considers this humility as a submission to God's glory. For Brod, however, it was merely a lack of life force, one which – counter to Susman's glorification of exile – he diagnosed in Zionist terms: "As a member of a people without a land, one lacks the strength to live right."[21]

Brod's aim here was not to resolve paradoxes through dialectic reversals of extremes, but rather to harmonize such oppositions by allowing them to exist alongside each other. As with Susman, each of Brod's references to Job is followed by "but." Yet these are in fact "but also's" and merely introduce the contiguity of seemingly incompatible positions. This occurs paradigmatically in one of Brod's key sentences aligning Job's suffering with the despair pervading Kafka's world: "The majority of Kafka's sentences that disempower man certainly overwhelm the reader. But freedom and hope are *also there!*" (FK, 181; emphasis Brod). For Brod, Kafka's fiction, like the Book of Job, por-

---

21 "Als Glied eines Volkes ohne Land kann man nicht richtig leben" (FK, 184).

trays a cruel, immoral God; however, this is true only when based on the human perspective offered in each work and does not preclude Kafka's belief in a benevolent divine power. In Brod's reading, Kafka asks *"die alte Hiobsfrage"* (FK, 181; emphasis mine). Unlike Susman, Brod does not resolve the paradox of Job submitting to God despite receiving no adequate answer. Instead, he affirms both Job's and – even more so – Kafka's respective rebellions, *simultaneously* leaving God's justice intact by introducing evil powers that intervene between God and man. For Brod (FK, 195), it is not God but "intermediary figures full of guile and poison" (*Zwischeninstanzen voll Tücke und Gift*) who are responsible for the world's injustice and cruelty. Moreover, he explains that, for Kafka, God is infinitely good, regardless and independent of any image of him that may transpire through the confusion. However, the infinity Brod assigns here to the goodness of Kafka's God may be misplaced, for though Kafka's writings indeed present an idea of infinity, it is of an altogether other kind. It manifests itself in the form of his writing, with its infinity of "buts" and "yets," as an endlessness of hesitation that never becomes a final judgment. Brod, although he does not deny Kafka's skepticism, specifically repudiates any possibility of it extending to infinity: "An infinite doubt? No," Brod avers, "there was a limit, a very distant limit" (FK, 184).

Brod, in referencing the Book of Job, addresses the same problem that Susman does: namely, the incommensurability between the human and the divine realm. Yet it is in confronting this issue that the most fundamental difference between their views becomes apparent. Whereas Susman, both for the Book of Job and for Kafka, regards the impossibility of bringing these spheres together as the very locus of divine revelation, Brod disputes not only her identification of Job and Kafka but also her understanding of Kafka's theological beliefs. Although he indeed finds in the Book of Job the illustration of an unbridgeable gap between God and man, Brod sees in Kafka the affirmation of a common ground between them. He finds in Kafka a mere "lack of clarity" (*Undeutlichkeit*) (FK, 183) about the relationship between the two spheres; moreover, he reconciles Kafka's views to the traditional Jewish belief that ethical commandments function as the area of encounter between God and man. For Brod, Kafka's belief in the "mysterious bond between man and the transcendental kingdom of God" (FK, 186) is the very foundation of human existence, and he considers this point to be directly expressed in Kafka's letters, aphorisms and diaries. In contrast, the pessimism in Kafka's fictional writings is an expression of the punishment suffered by those who have lost their trust in the unity of the divine. Indeed, Brod, even more so than Susman, echoes Job's friends who cling to their belief in the causality between suffering and guilt. In this, he seals his modern theodicy.

3 Revealing Nothing: Gershom Scholem's Negative Theology

Gershom Scholem rejected the premises both of Susman's Christological reading and of Brod's positive Jewish theology, and explicitly turned against all
attempts at a theodicy. Yet, he too was not always immune to the temptations
of closure. Scholem referred to Job at various points in his life, most notably
around 1918 in his work on Jewish laments and dirges and, during the 1930s,
in his epistolary exchange with Benjamin (BK, 63–93). The differences in how
Scholem engaged the story of Job at these two moments in his thinking are
striking. His later references, which occur primarily in relation to Kafka, rest on
the biblical book's content and yield a fixed, determined meaning. His earlier
reflections on Job, however, preceded his reading of Kafka and deal with Job
in terms of lament as a genre. Surprisingly, these earlier engagements bear
greater affinity to Kafka's own "infinite" mode of writing.

Scholem's associations of Kafka with the Book of Job are sparser and more
enigmatic than either Susman's or Brod's, yet he too develops a theological
interpretation of Kafka in which references to Job play a significant role. These
interpretations, however, serve primarily to support Scholem's own views of a
God who has withdrawn and left man in a state of inconsolable despair. In his
correspondence with Benjamin, Scholem (BK, 64)[22] advises him that to better
understand Kafka's work he should begin with the Book of Job, explaining that
this would allow him to perceive "the possibility to deal in a poetic work with
the question of divine judgment," which Scholem regarded as "the only topic
of Kafka's production." In a letter to Benjamin written in 1931, Scholem describes Kafka's writings as an attempt at "a paraphrase of divine judgment
[*Gottesurteil*] in [*human*] *language*" (BK, 65; emphasis mine). But Scholem's
idea of divine judgment differs radically from both Susman's and Brod's. He
implicitly discards Susman's dialectic of suffering and election and explicitly
rejects Brod's idea of a flawed human perception of divine justice as an illusory
theodicy. Scholem is similarly skeptical of Susman's apocalyptic messianism
and of Brod's more straightforward note of hope; moreover, in his references
to the link between Job and Kafka, he develops a melancholic vision that carries traits of a negative theology with a Gnostic bent. This tendency manifests

---

22 For an outstanding discussion of the correspondence between Scholem and Benjamin concerning Kafka see Robert Alter, *Necessary Angels. Tradition and Modernity in Kafka, Benjamin
and Scholem*, Harvard University Press, Cambridge 1991, 3–23.

itself in accusations against a God who is absent yet is also the origin of the world's injustice and suffering.

In a certain sense, Scholem extends Susman's dialectical logic of opposites even further, but never resolves it into a positive synthesis. Instead, he opens up a perspective onto an infinite and desperate quest that remains unfulfilled. In a letter to Benjamin from 1931, Scholem notes that "Kafka's world is the world of revelation, but of revelation seen from the perspective in which it is returned to its own nothingness" (BK, 74). This may initially seem to echo Susman's idea of Kafka's world as the "nothing" that permeates modernity, yet it is in fact a far more pessimistic vision and one which stops short of Susman's dialectical reversal into salvation. For Scholem, nothing in the present state of the world indicates such a possibility. In his view, Kafka depicts a world in which "redemption cannot be anticipated," to which he mockingly adds, "Explain this to the Goyim!" (BK, 65), that is, to those who believe salvation has already occurred. For Scholem, Kafka's world must be seen in a theological light, albeit one permeated by darkness. "So mercilessly," Scholem writes, "the light of revelation never burnt before" (BK, 65). Scholem, in an interpretation that seems compatible with Brod's "Jewish" reading, states that "Kafka incessantly compares human existence with the ideal of absolute justice, which the Jewish tradition symbolizes in the image of divine judgment."[23] Unlike Brod, however, Scholem believes that this comparison precludes both a possible common ground and an encounter between God and man in revealed law.

Apart from his advice to Benjamin, which inaugurated an intense discussion about Kafka that was marked by various disagreements between the two, Scholem's most explicit reference to the relationship between Job and Kafka is found in a poem he sent to Benjamin along with a copy of Kafka's *The Trial*. Scholem's poem is a melancholic meditation inspired by his reading of Kafka's novel. Its fourteen stanzas lament the fate of revelation in a period when God has withdrawn completely and "the great deceit of the world / is now consummated" (SM, 153). The sixth stanza reads:

> Our position has been measured
> On Job's scales with great precision.
> We are known through and through
> As despairing as on the youngest day. (SM, 153)

Scholem's reference to "Job's scales" alludes to a metaphor that occurs twice in the Book of Job. The first image appears in Job's reply to Eliphaz, when he

---

23 Mosès, Stéphane, *The Angel of History. Rosenzweig, Benjamin, Scholem*, trans. Barbara Harshav, Stanford University Press, Stanford 2009, 151. Following references to this book are quoted as (SM, page number).

wishes that his "anguish but be weighed, / and my disaster on the scales be borne. / For now it would be heavier than the sand of the sea. / Thus my words are choked back" (Job 6.3). Job refers to the scales as a metaphor of justice that has become disjointed and buried under the weight of his misery. The metaphor reappears towards the end of the book, when Job asks God to be judged fairly, to be "weighed on fair scales" (Job 31.6). In Scholem's poem this request remains unheard, and his reference to the scales draws a parallel between Job's suffering and the weight of desolation he finds in Kafka. The metaphor also suggests the reign of a divine power responsible for this hopeless state. The "precision" and passive form of the subsequent verses indeed indicate that a higher power is performing the measuring and weighing, but that it is neither humanly graspable nor just. This "absent presence" and its finality are confirmed by the transparency suggested in the line "We are known through and through" (SM, 153): man has been fully exposed to God's omniscience, yet what ensues is sheer despair. More importantly, the very form of Scholem's poem repeats and radicalizes the central gestures of the Book of Job, namely, Job's lament about the state of a godforsaken world, his protest against the lack of justice, and his explicit declaration of God's silence, each of which is formulated in a direct address to God. This paradox is sustained throughout Scholem's poem and climaxes in an explicit anti-theodicy:

> Your trial began on earth.
> Does it end before your throne?
> You cannot be defended,
> As no illusion holds true here. (SM, 154)

The question posed in the first verses of this stanza could refer both to Job's trial that followed God's wager with Satan and to the inversion of this trial in Job's subsequent accusations against God. Scholem's response to these questions clearly rejects any defense or justification of the divine order. This point is also formulated in another stanza:

> From the center of destruction
> A ray breaks through at times
> But none shows the direction
> The Law ordered us to take. (SM, 154)

This central complaint acknowledges momentary revelation amidst the darkness – undoubtedly a reference to the radiance that shines through the door to the law in Kafka's "Before the Law" – but, in pointing to the essence of Jewish teachings (*Lehre*), the law that it has brought us provides neither sense nor orientation. Scholem, in another letter to Benjamin commenting on Kafka, calls revealed law the "absolutely concrete, which is absolutely impracticable" (BK, 66). Such law has imposed orders upon man that he cannot possibly fulfill. In a lucid interpretation of Scholem's enigmatic expression, Stéphane Mosès underscores this characterization of the law and Scholem's view of Kafka's mode of writing: "Jewish law, which is defined by its extreme concreteness, the minute precision with which it codifies the slightest aspects of daily conduct … reminded Scholem of the endless deliberations of Kafka's characters, their hesitations at the slightest concrete decision" (SM, 159). In this poem, Scholem considers the "great precision" of the scales upon which God weighs man's deeds on Judgment Day, but he does so in the negative light of a legal system that has retained its oppressive force even as it has lost its function as an existential orientation.

In the Book of Job, the most merciless aspect of God's judgment is that His verdict remains hidden and Job's questions are left without resolution. Nevertheless, for Scholem, this openness – in contrast to his earlier references to Job and to Kafka's understanding of his own "endless" writing – comes to an end. It is resolved in a negativity associated with the bleakness of divine judgment, which, in Scholem's poem, has the final word: "Oh, we must live all the same / Until your court will judge us" (SM, 154). Yet Scholem, in the finality suggested in his poem, fails to capture key formal features of Kafka's prose; foremost among these is the impossibility of arriving at any conclusion, an impossibility conveyed primarily through a recurring stylistic element that Kafka himself termed "*stehender Sturmlauf*" (immobile assault).[24] Scholem – at least insofar as concerns his interpretation of Kafka – does not account for this absence of resolution, itself one of the most singular aspects of Kafka's writings. Indeed, he tends to resolve this undecidability in a way that says more about himself at the time he authored the poem – in particular his wariness about the rise of fascism in Europe and his disappointment with Zionism – than about Kafka's writings.

Walter Benjamin, in the magisterial essays[25] on Kafka he wrote in conjunction with his correspondence with Scholem, offers another explanation for the infinite recurrence in Kafka's writings and the non-closure that characterizes so many of Kafka's texts. Benjamin similarly refers to Jewish Scriptures, yet not to the Book of Job. In a letter responding to Scholem's poem he writes that

---

24 Kafka, *Tagebücher*, 259–260.
25 Benjamin, Walter, "Franz Kafka. On the Tenth Anniversary of His Death," in: *Selected Writings, 1927–1934* (Vol. 2 part 2), eds. Michael Jennings et al., Harvard University Press, Cambridge 1999, 794–818 and Benjamin, "Franz Kafka. Beim Bau der Chinesischen Mauer," in: *Selected Writings*, 495–500.

he can fully agree with all the stanzas starting with the seventh; however, this is the stanza *following* the verses referring to Job (BK, 76). One can only surmise that Benjamin disagreed with Scholem's association of Kafka with the bleak despair Scholem derived from his Joban references. This reading is supported by Benjamin's own careful messianic hopes, in particular his search for redemption in the hidden, reverse side of Kafka's work, as is evident in his response to Scholem's verse "Only your nothingness is the experience / [this time] is entitled to have of you" (BK, 77). Benjamin, in his essay "Franz Kafka. Beim Bau der Chinesischen Mauer," compares Kafka's writing to "the Haggadic parts of the Talmud."[26] Like these Talmudic narratives, Benjamin writes, "[Kafka's] books are a Haggadah that constantly pauses, luxuriating in the most detailed descriptions, in the simultaneous *hope and fear* that it might encounter the Halachic order, the doctrine itself, en route."[27] He terms this ambivalence between hope and fear of encountering the law, of ending up in a solution or a final morality, "*Verzögerung*," or "deferral."[28] Benjamin distinguishes his understanding of this postponement from Brod's interpretation of Kafka's "strange, and so often strikingly meticulous attentiveness to detail" as "a search for perfection" and "the right path." Indeed, he considers this form of writing to be simultaneously a redeeming gesture of hope and an expression of Kafka's "fear of the end."[29] Whether this end implies death, a verdict or (as is most likely) the conflation of the two is not made explicit. This last possibility is the most plausible: Kafka's *The Trial* ends with Josef K. being brutally executed by two anonymous men who, as the novel's penultimate sentence notes, observe "*die Entscheidung*," the decision: their watching the man they have just killed implies that the decision refers to death. Deferring the end entails postponement of the execution, both in the literal sense suggested in this scene and in a more general sense of a verdict, the implementation of a judgment, the completion of a procedure or, in an even wider sense, the arrival at a conclusive message or meaning altogether.

---

26 Benjamin, "Franz Kafka. Beim Bau der Chinesischen Mauer," 496.

27 Benjamin,"Franz Kafka. Beim Bau der Chinesischen Mauer," 496 (emphasis mine).

28 The English translation in Jennings et al. (eds.), *Selected Writings* chooses "procrastination." "Verzögerung," however, has a more general meaning and is closer to deferral or postponement.

29 "But what Kafka enjoys about these interminable reflections is the very fear that they might come to an end." Benjamin, "Franz Kafka. Beim Bau der Chinesischen Mauer," 496–497. However, Benjamin in fact wrote: "Was sich aber bei Kafka in dieser Endlosigkeit gefällt, ist eben doch *die Angst vor dem Ende*" (But what Kafka enjoys about these interminable reflections is after all the fear of the end) (BK, 42; emphasis mine).

4 Another Scholem: The Language of Lament

In his reflections on Job and Kafka, Scholem formulates a vision of modernity that is as bleak as it is definitive: it is a world in which "the great deceit" has now been "consummated" (SM, 153). However, the very form of Scholem's poem not only undermines such finality but repeats and radicalizes the central paradox of the Book of Job: his description of a godforsaken world, his protest against the lack of justice, and his explicit declaration of God's silence are formulated as a direct address to God. This address is permeated with unanswered and unanswerable questions, and, counter to its conclusive, and conclusively negative, content, presents traces of what Scholem, in his earlier writings, had described as the idea and nature of lament. These traces are found in the poem's daunting string of questions, which, in the final verse – "Can such a question be raised?" (SM, 154) – culminates in the *mise en abîme* of questioning the act of questioning. This single yet highly significant sentence in this particular exchange with Benjamin hints at texts written in Scholem's youth, albeit without mentioning lament as such. These earlier reflections on Job and lament not only prefigure Benjamin's thinking about Kafka; they are also closer to Kafka's actual prose than Scholem's later writings. His subsequent theological interpretation of Kafka insists on a negativity that becomes a kind of closure; these early texts, however, are concerned with a language of deferral that shares key characteristics with Kafka's prose, which not only postpones accomplishment, resists change and progression, and thwarts any message or conclusion, but also, ultimately, refuses meaning altogether, even as it correlates this deferral with a logic of ethics, care and justice.

Immediately following his advice that Benjamin should take Job as a point of departure in reading Kafka, Scholem notes "the thoughts I formulated many years ago in my theses on justice which you know and which, in their relation to language, would be the leading thread of my reflections on Kafka" (BK, 64). Scholem refers here to his "Twelve Theses on the Order of Justice," a text he wrote in 1918, more than two decades before he composed his commentaries on Kafka.[30] These theses are derived directly from, and sometimes quote, Scholem's "On Jonah and the Concept of Justice," written earlier the same year. In the latter text, he compares the biblical prophet Jonah with Job and argues that Job, unlike Jonah, has "an inner relation to lament" (SD, 525) because Job

---

[30] Scholem read these theses, probably written in 1918, to Benjamin and his wife during a stay in Switzerland in October of the same year. Scholem, Gershom, *Tagebücher 1917–1923*, Suhrkamp, Frankfurt/M. 2000, 533–535. Following references to this book are quoted as (SD, page number).

asks questions man is not entitled to pose, primarily the question of divine justice. These questions are not only unanswerable but also subvert the established order and the very language subtending the system of communication.

In a similar context, Job also figures prominently in several of Scholem's diary entries from the same period, a time when he was exchanging lengthy letters with Benjamin about his work on Hebrew Scriptures.[31] In one such entry Scholem sketches the outline for an argument that seems to have been intended for a future and more thorough analysis of the Book of Job (SD, 376–378). For Scholem, the book contains an ironic, inverted message yet does not make this doctrine explicit; instead, it is conveyed *ex negativo*, for it concerns the legitimacy of questioning divine justice. Job initially seems guilty of asking this question, but, as his question proves neither answerable nor refutable, he is shown to be in the right ("*Hiob ist im Recht*" (SD, 377)). The very form of the book – its endlessly circular dialogues – conveys the sense that the search for divine justice is not a legitimate concern: God does not reply to Job's ethical question and instead shows him the magnificence of His creation. In refusing any answer, God invalidates Job's question (and questioning) and extracts himself from the human idea of justice. What remains for man to do in the face of this withdrawal is to lament – indeed, it is his only appropriate response. "And so [Job] legitimately laments," Scholem writes, "and this lament is infinite in all its dimensions, it is of a higher infinity than life itself" (SD, 378). His conclusion comes strikingly close to one of Kafka's central themes, especially when Scholem compares the Book of Job with a "court in front of which an accusation is continuously being repeated ... without the judge ever appearing" (SD, 378).

Scholem's references to Job in his early writings culminate in a short text amended to his translation of the third chapter of the Book of Job. This text, likely written in late 1918, is part of a series of comments to his German translations of Hebrew laments and dirges as well as the more general, theoretical text "On Lament and Dirges" (SD, 544–547). In these texts Scholem reflects on the nature and language of lament and regards Job's monologues as a paradigmatic instance of the genre. In the comment to his translation of Job's monologue – in which Job curses the day he was born – Scholem distinguishes lament from accusation: accusation always targets a particular addressee, whereas lament "accuses language itself" as a carrier of meaning, as goal-oriented mode of communication that transports a message (SD, 545). Scholem defines the characteristic of lament, and Job's lamentation in particular, as "an

---

31 See Walter Benjamin, *Sämtliche Briefe* Band I, Suhrkamp, Frankfurt/M. 2000, 422.

infinite and cyclical annihilation" (SD, 546) that occurs not from the outside (as a meaning bestowed upon its construction), but rather from within the language of lament. What occurs in this language, Scholem writes, "is an extraordinary internal liquefaction of the poem, inextricably interconnected with the law of recurrence, which shows this to be the lamentation. In the proper meaning of the poem, the question 'why does He give light to the sufferer?' is not given in order to receive a response ... rather, there is no response to this infinite plaintively recurring question. Everything in this song recurs" (SD, 546). And the recurrence, in fact, is endless.

This ongoing questioning – which expects no answer and is intrinsically infinite – can, as Scholem notes about Job's lament, "never turn into a final verdict" (SD, 546) or even into a conclusive indictment of God, as his later Kafka poem suggests. Its nature, situated at the limits between language and silence, is deferral itself. In a brief note Scholem writes: "Deferral in the word, the linguistic principle of lament" (*Verstummen: Aufschub im Worte, das sprachliche Prinzip der Klage*) (SD, 365). It is precisely because lament is an endless and infinite expression, or rather a gesture (*eine Gebärde*), that it annihilates its object in a monotonous repetition – as Scholem notes, "all monotonous things have relation to lament" (SD, 148) – and that it absorbs impending destruction into language itself. In referring to the question of suicide – which, in the Book of Job, is raised by Job's wife – Scholem writes: "Lamenting over one's birth signifies the desire for death, but not the act of bringing it about. But Judaism doesn't know more than the lament about being born. If it knew more, suicide would have a legitimate place in it. In lament, however, suicide is eliminated through a medium (*Mittleres*), the suicide of language can be reached (and may even be a source of reconciliation?)" (SD, 564). Yet it is not just suicide that is deferred by lament. As Scholem notes in his "Twelve Theses on the Order of Justice": "Acting in deferral saves from death" (*Im Aufschub handeln erettet vom Tod*) (SD, 534). Scholem's idea that lament postpones the execution of suicide and defers death is structured similar to his more general idea about justice. He calls lament, rather enigmatically, "the language that is just in its very principle" (SD, 362). This statement becomes more transparent when considered in the context of the relation he establishes between justice and deferral. Scholem's most succinct statement about justice is found in his "Twelve Theses": "Justice means: that one may judge, but that the executive power must remain radically independent of it ... The actual legal order (*Rechtsordnung*) is sublated in the deferral of the executive" (SD, 533). Scholem illustrates this definition of justice with a verse from the Book of Jonah: "And he reflected upon the judgment that he announced that he would execute upon them, and executed it not." Scholem's (SD, 528) very definition of justice in action, to which he adds the Hebrew *z'dakah* (justice), lies in the gesture of deferral: "Deferral turned into deed is justice in action" (*Der zur Handlung gewordene Aufschub ist Gerechtigkeit als Tat*). That this deferral is achieved in language, a language of endless recurrence, entails that it cannot be transformed or translated into another language. It is precisely the language of lament that achieves this deferral of the end (SD, 128).

Nothing could be closer to Kafka's "*stehender Sturmlauf*," this intense movement that does not progress and stays itself and leaves everything unchanged, than Scholem's description of the language of lament that, "as far as it is lament, remains always the same" (SD, 129). Indeed, it is in Scholem's understanding of the language of lament, rather than in his interpretation of Kafka, that his greatest affinity to Kafka's writing, and to Benjamin's idea of deferral (*Aufschub*), is found. Unlike his interpretation of Kafka that dates from the 1930's, and in which the infinity of questions that remain without answers resonates with a negative theology, these early comments on Job prefigure Benjamin's interpretation of Kafka's "infinite" writing as an avoidance of closure. The aptness of Benjamin's insight into Kafka and Scholem's comments on Job's lament can be illustrated and specified through a reading of a particular short text by Kafka, one that allows the reader to imagine how Kafka would have read the Book of Job.

5 Kafka's Other Job

"I can imagine another Abraham."[32] This first sentence of a text included in a letter Kafka wrote to Robert Klopstock in June 1921[33] is an implicit response to Kafka's reading of Kierkegaard's reflections, in *Fear and Trembling*, on Abraham and the binding of Isaac. Kierkegaard praises Abraham's obedience to God's call as an "infinite resignation that is the last stage before faith"[34] and, in a similar spirit, terms Job a "knight of faith," hailing his surrender to God after His speech from the whirlwind. Kafka never mentions Job, but his conjecture of "another Abraham" may be the closest one can come to imagining how he would have read Job.

---

32 Kafka, Franz, Letter to Robert Klopstock, Matliary, June 1921, in: Kafka, Franz, *Letters to Friends, Family and Editors*, trans. Richard Winston and Clara Winston, Schocken Books, New York 1977, 284–286, 285. Following references to this book are quoted as (LK, page number).
33 For a pioneer analysis of this text see Alter, *Necessary Angels*, 73–74.
34 Kierkegaard, Søren, *Fear and Trembling*, Penguin Classics, London 1986, 46.

Kafka imagines another Abraham, one who would not go to Mount Moriah to sacrifice his beloved son. This Abraham, Kafka (LK, 285) writes, "to be sure, would not make it all the way to patriarch, not even to old-clothes dealer." Like the biblical patriarch, Kafka's "other Abraham" is a pious man and would be ready to execute the order for his son's sacrifice with the promptness of a waiter" (LK, 285); contrary to the biblical Abraham, however, Kafka's Abraham "would still never be able to perform the sacrifice" (LK, 285). Kafka then describes two distinct scenes that enact different reasons for preventing Abraham from fulfilling the divine order. In the first, Abraham, in an imaginary reply to God, argues that "he cannot get away from home, he is indispensable; the household needs him, there is always something that must be attended to, the house isn't finished" (LK, 285). Later, Kafka continues this phantasmagoria and elaborates on Abraham's excuses for procrastinating rather than obeying God's order. His "other Abraham" now stands in the plural, for he has become a type, or even more so, an existential attitude. The "other Abrahams: They stand on their building sites and suddenly had to go up on Mount Moriah" (LK, 285). These Abrahams, as imagined by Kafka, are called by God whilst they are attending to their lives: the divine injunction reaches them when they are in the midst of their home, their house, their world-building, and they are thereupon ordered to abandon all this in order to serve God. As much as Kafka's "other Abrahams" would otherwise have been willing to oblige, they are too immersed in the care of their "building site" (*Bauplatz*) and will not heed this call of God.

Two years after this letter Kafka penned the story "Der Bau,"[35] the ultimate "infinite" narrative. It consists of a long monologue by a mole-like animal obsessively attending to his burrow. The animal constantly makes observations and decisions and confirms facts, only to instantly dismiss these with a "but" or a "however" and turn to a variety of alternatives which quickly experience the same fate. The incessant reflections and calculations give expression to an excessive attention to detail and a continuous frustration about never grasping the whole, all of which suggest an endless task. The burrow, which can neither be repaired nor completed, yet also neither abandoned nor truly inhabited, is the perfect image and embodiment of Kafka's writing, which likewise continuously cancels itself and in the process becomes an infinite process beyond any purpose and result. On the final pages of the story, the animal, both fearing and hoping for an interruption, hears a noise and imagines that "someone may

---

35 Kafka, Franz, "The Burrow," in: *Kafka's Selected Stories*, ed. and trans. Stanley Corngold, W. W. Norton & Company, New York 2007, 162–189.

be calling it to itself" with an "invitation [I] will not be able to resist."[36] The animal conjectures that the noise he hears in the burrow stems not from many little animals, but "from one single, large one."[37] The creature continues to go about its business, however, and the story, after sixteen closely written manuscript pages and yet another "but," breaks off in mid-sentence, suggesting that it would go on forever.

The final sentence of Kafka's first scene in his imagining of an "other Abraham" provides an explanation for this endlessness, an endlessness that prefigures Benjamin's idea of procrastination precisely in the face of the possible call from a unique and ominous "someone." Referring to his "other Abrahams," who resist the invitation of the call to sacrifice because they must attend to their house, Kafka speculates: "All we can do is suspect that these men are *deliberately not finishing their houses* ... so as not to have to lift their eyes and see the mountain that stands in the distance" (LK, 285; emphasis mine). The mountain is Mount Moriah, where Abraham's sacrifice of his son was to take place, yet it could also be Mount Sinai, where the voice of God called out and the Law was revealed.

If one were to imagine Kafka's "other Job" being inspired by his "other Abraham," it would certainly not be the Job who, after God's speech from the whirlwind, takes his suffering upon himself and submits himself to God in "dust and ashes" (Job 42.6). Nor would it be Job the accuser, who indicts God. Instead, this "other Job," like Kafka's "other Abraham," would know of this mountain in the distance yet would not lift his eyes to see it. Rather, he would turn his lament – an insistent mourning that is the last possible way of caring for his house – into the very means by which to keep the mountain at a distance. This Job would expect no answer from God; moreover, he would make of his lament the poetry that, in the Book of Job, it actually is – an ongoing, unanswerable expression, in what Scholem, in his reflections on lament, would call a language wrested from silence. Job's lament points in this direction when he speaks of his misery that is "heavier than the sand of the sea. / Thus my words are choked back" (Job 6.3). These words speak their own impossibility and are as infinite as the silence they emerge from. They would constitute the ongoing lament of Kafka's "other Job," just as their endlessness would avert the verdict and the end. Likewise, since there is always something, one more thing, "that must be attended to" (LK, 285), since the infinite details of any situation cannot be exhausted, any final judgment would amount to

---

36 Kafka, "The Burrow," 169.
37 Kafka, "The Burrow," 185.

injustice[38]; in short, the attention and care of the world requires the relinquishing of any claim to finality. Yet Kafka does not end even there.

"But take another Abraham" (LK, 285). These first words of Kafka's second Abraham scene – a school class with a teacher who punishes and rewards – introduce yet another argument for Abraham to refuse – or resist – the divine call. This Abraham too is a pious man, "who certainly wants to carry out the sacrifice properly and in general correctly senses what the whole thing is about, but cannot imagine that he was the one meant ... He does not lack the true faith, for he has this faith; he wants to sacrifice in the proper manner if only he could believe he was the one meant" (LK, 285). This Abraham, uncertain that he is indeed the elect, the one who has been called, fears making himself ridiculous; he envisages "that the world would laugh itself sick over him ... An Abraham who comes unsummoned! ... It is as if at the end of the year, when the best student was solemnly about to receive a prize, the worst student rose in the expectant stillness and came forward from his dirty back bench because he has misheard, and the whole class burst out laughing" (LK, 286). Just as Kafka's "other Abraham" hides in the last row of the class, his "other Job" would forego the privilege: In the biblical book Job asks God to avert his attention from him: "Am I the Sea, or the Dragon, that you set a watch over me?" (Job 7.12) and "Will You not look away from me for a while?" (Job, 7.19). No longer being singled out by God, no longer being the elect: this would save him from sacrifice and suffering. Kafka's Job would be the other of Susman's: namely, the Job, the Kafka, the Jewish people elected in and through suffering. Indeed, Kafka imagines even this possibility. In the final lines of his Abraham text, a commenting narrator, perhaps Kafka himself, focuses on the teacher who distributes the rewards and punishments. The narrator's words raise the possibility that Abraham has made no mistake, that "he has not heard wrong, for his name was actually spoken, because it is the teacher's intention that the reward of the best is to be accompanied by the punishment for the worst" (LK, 286). This possibility brings even Kafka's ongoing ruminations to a chilling halt: he offers only one, final comment about this authority who assigns suffering – the punishment of sinful humanity – as a reward for the elect: "Terrible things – enough" (LK, 286).

---

38 I would like to thank Paula Schwebel for this important insight.

Bibliography

Alter, Robert. *Necessary Angels. Tradition and Modernity in Kafka, Benjamin and Scholem.* Cambridge: Harvard University Press, 1991. 3–23.

Anders, Günther. *Kafka Pro et Contra.* München: C. H. Beck, 1951. 91.

Baker, Jason. "Introduction." Kafka, Franz, *The Metamorphosis and Other Stories.* New York: Barnes & Noble Classics, 2003. xvi.

Brod, Max. *Über Franz Kafka.* Frankfurt/M.: Fischer, 1974. 182–188.

Buber, Martin. *Darko shel mikra*, Mosad Bilaik, Jerusalem 1964. 357 in: Nahum Glatzer. *The Dimensions of Job. A Study and Selected Readings.* New York: Schocken Books, 1969. 48.

Corngold, Stanley. *Lambent Traces: Franz Kafka.* Princeton: Princeton University Press 2004. 125.

Fisch, Harold. *New Stories for Old. Biblical Patterns in the Novel.* Houndmills/Basingstoke/Hampshire/London: Macmillan Press, 1998, 98.

Frye, Northrope. *The Great Code. The Bible and Literature.* London: Routledge & Kegan Paul, 1982. 195.

Glazova, Anna. "Franz Kafka: Oszillierende Negationen," 2008. http://www.kafka.org/index.php/icqlist/index.php?id=194,229,0,0,1,0.

Kafka, Franz. "A Little Fable." *The Complete Stories.* Trans. Willa Muir and Edwin Muir, ed. Nahum Glatzer. New York: Schocken Books, 1971. 445.

Kafka, Franz. "Letter to Robert Klopstock, Matliary, June 1921." Kafka, Franz. *Letters to Friends, Family and Editors.* Trans. Richard Winston and Clara Winston. New York: Schocken Books, 1977. 284–286.

Kafka, Franz. *Tagebücher.* 1915. Frankfurt/M.: Fischer, 2002, 757.

Kafka, Franz. "The Burrow." *Kafka's Selected Stories.* Ed. and trans. Stanley Corngold. New York: W. W. Norton & Company, 2007. 162–189.

Kartiganer, Donald M. "Job and Joseph K: Myth in Kafka's *The Trial.*" *Modern Fiction Studies* 8. Baltimore: Johns Hopkins University Press, 1962. 31–43.

Kierkegaard, Søren. *Fear and Trembling.* London, Penguin Classics, 1986, 46.

Larrimore, Mark. *The Book of "Job": A Biography.* Princeton: Princeton University Press 2013. 236–239.

Lasine, Stuart. "The Trials of Job and Kafka's Josef K." *The German Quarterly* 63.2. Notre Dame: University of Notre Dame 1990. 187–198.

Mosès, Stéphane. *The Angel of History. Rosenzweig, Benjamin, Scholem.* Trans. Barbara Harshav. Stanford: Stanford University Press, 2009. 151.

Scholem, Gershom. "Letter to Walter Benjamin, dated August 1, 1931." *Benjamin über Kafka. Texte, Briefzeugnisse, Aufzeichnungen.* Ed. Hermann Schweppenhäuser. Frankfurt/M.: Suhrkamp, 1981. 63–93.

Scholem, Gershom. *Tagebücher 1917–1923.* Frankfurt/M.: Suhrkamp, 2000. 533–535.

Schreiner, Susan E, *Where Shall Wisdom Be Found? Calvin's Exegesis of Job from Medieval and Modern Perspectives*, Chicago: University of Chicago Press, 1994. 181.

Susman, Margarete. *Das Buch Hiob und das Schicksal des jüdischen Volkes.* Zürich: Steinberg Verlag, 1946.

Susman, Margarete. "Das Hiob-Problem bei Kafka." *Das Nah- und Fernsein des Fremden. Essays und Briefe.* Ed. Ingeborg Nordmann. Frankfurt/M.: Suhrkamp, 1992. 183–203.

Walser, Martin. *Beschreibung einer Form. Versuch über Kafka.* Frankfurt/M.: Suhrkamp, 1999. 84.

Walter, Benjamin. "Franz Kafka. Beim Bau der Chinesischen Mauer." *Selected Writings, 1927–1934*, vol. 2 part. 2. Eds. Michael Jennings et al. Cambridge: Harvard University Press, 1999. 495–500.

Walter, Benjamin. "Franz Kafka. On the Tenth Anniversary of His Death." *Selected Writings, 1927–1934*, vol. 2 part. 2. Eds. Michael Jennings et al. Cambridge: Harvard University Press, 1999. 794–818.

Walter, Benjamin. *Sämtliche Briefe*. Band I. Frankfurt/M.: Suhrkamp, 2000. 422.

Galit Hasan-Rokem
Joban Transformations of the Wandering Jew in Joseph Roth's *Hiob* and *Der Leviathan*[1]

This essay addresses the encounter of a traditionally acquired biblical image of Job with the painfully accumulated experience of modernity in the work of Joseph Roth, which repeatedly enlists and creatively transforms the figure of Job and other elements from the Book of Job. A personal attitude towards biblical figures marks the authorship of many modern authors, both those who were initiated into Scripture in early childhood and those who learned about such figures later. The backlighting of fictional figures by the aura of biblical individuals endows their individual fates with an extra portion of the surplus of meaning that has been identified as the hermeneutic potential of all literature, in particular of the Holy Writ and of texts engendered under its inspiration.[2]

Joseph Roth was born in Brody, in the Austro-Hungarian province of Galicia, in 1894; he died in 1939, at the age of 44, in Paris, barely three months before the German assault on Poland. His death was technically due to overconsumption of alcohol. An East European Jew who wrote in German, his work accommodates the complexity of West and East; modernity and tradition; religion, secularity and even profanation; Jewish, German, European. In certain works Roth's incorporation of Job into his fictional world strongly alludes to a later literary figure, of European rather than ancient Near Eastern provenance,

1 Much of the research for the present essay was conducted under the generous auspices of Williams College, where I was fortunate to spend the fall of 2012 as the Croghan Bicentennial Visiting Professor. Special thanks to Alexandra Garbarini, Edan Dekel and Sarah Hammerschlag for their friendship and inspiration. The final stages of thinking and writing took place in the spring of 2014, when I had the great pleasure to serve as Bildner Visiting Professor at the Bildner Center for Jewish Life at Rutgers University. I am grateful to Yael Zerubavel for her invitation, the intellectual esprit with which she led our research group on "Contested Memories", and our friendship of many years. Numerous friends and colleagues have commented, added and critiqued. Very special thanks to Ilana Pardes for her advice and to her and Leora Batnizky for their patience.
2 See for example Paul Ricoeur, *Interpretation Theory: Discourse and the Surplus of Meaning*, Texas Christian University Press, Fort Worth 1976; and Paul Ricoeur, "Philosophical Hermeneutics and Biblical Hermeneutics," in: *From Text to Action: Essays in Hermeneutics* II, transs. Kathleen Blarney and John B. Thompson, Northwestern University Press, Evanston 1991, 89–101, 97.

namely the Wandering Jew. The interpretative association of the Wandering Jew with Roth's Joban figures, though rather clearly substantiated by the author's own linguistic and thematic associations interwoven in the texts, has garnered little attention in the relevant scholarship. I shall investigate Roth's communicating of bold imbrications of historical and metaphysical levels of experience in his work by focusing on the nexus of Job and the Wandering Jew, roughly correlating to the generic modes of myth and legend in folk literary scholarship.[3] This particular nexus in Roth's texts draws attention to an oscillation between the universal and the particularly Jewish aspects of suffering and revelation – the two primary themes of the Book of Job. The emphatic bridging of the particularly Jewish and the universal in Roth's work in general is probably what has led some scholars to emphasize his literature as "European" rather than belonging to a particular nation.[4]

Whereas Job is explicitly accounted for in the title of one of Roth's major novels – namely *Hiob*, from 1930[5] – the Wandering Jew needs to be teased out from his texts, although this usually requires no great effort. Michael Hofmann's translation of Roth's *Juden auf Wanderschaft*[6] as *The Wandering Jews: The Classic Portrait of a Vanished People*[7] – the same phrasing appears in Jonathan Nierad's Hebrew translation[8]. – has at least in name spelled out the presence of this figure in Roth's work.[9] In the present essay the considerable inter-

---

3 See Galit Hasan-Rokem, *Web of Life: Folklore and Midrash in Rabbinic Literature*, Stanford University Press, Stanford 2000, 146–149.

4 Schönborn, Sibylle, "Zwischen Lemberg und Marseille: Joseph Roths Europa als 'Dritter Raum,'" in: *Rivista di letteratura e cultura tedesca* 7 (2007): 49–56.

5 Roth, Joseph, *Hiob. Roman eines einfachen Mannes*, Marixverlag, Wiesbaden 2010 (originally published in 1930). English translations include Roth, Joseph, *Job. The Story of a Simple Man*, trans. Dorothy Thompson, The Overlook Press, Woodstock 1982; and Roth, Joseph, *Job. The Story of a Simple Man*. trans. Ross Benjamin, Archipelago Books, Brooklyn 2010. My quotes are as a rule from the later translation.

6 Roth, Joseph, *Juden auf Wanderschaft,* Kiepenheuer & Witsch, Köln 2000 (originally published in 1927; second edition, with new preface, 1937).

7 Roth, Joseph, *The Wandering Jews: The Classic Portrait of a Vanished People*, trans. Michael Hofmann, W. W. Norton & Co., New York 2011.

8 יוזף רות, **יהודים נודדים** תרגם מגרמנית והוסיף העָרות: יונתן נירָאד; עורך ראשי: אוריאל קון; עריכת תרגום: דיטה גוט, ירושלים: סמטאות, 2011.

9 Victoria Lunzer-Talos has drawn attention to an essay in which Roth directly addressed the Wandering Jew under the sobriquet most often applied to him both in the written and the oral tradition in the German language, the Eternal Jew; see Victoria Lunzer-Talos, "Der Segen des ewigen Juden: Assimilation und Exil," in: *Joseph Roth: Ein europäisch-jüdischer Schriftsteller und österreichischer Universalist.* Conditio Judaica 82, eds. Johann Georg Lughofer and Mira Miladinović Zalaznik, De Gruyter, Berlin 2011, 23–38. This particular essay by Roth, entitled "The Blessing of the Wandering Jew," was published in *Die Wahrheit*, in 1935, and reflects on

pretive potential of the linking, shadowing and echoing of these two figures, Job and the Wandering Jew in Roth's work is emphasized. The relevance of this potential is heightened by the fact that much of Roth's work wrestles with the timeless Joban question of the meaning of human suffering, albeit in the historically specific context of the author, who was constantly both pushed away from and pulled back to his East European Jewish – yet not only Jewish – native culture as he strove to forge for himself a universal (understood by Roth to be German) identity.

1 Job, the Biblical Sufferer

I shall first introduce each of the two figures in some of their earlier contexts, with special reference to aspects most relevant for the present discussion. The inclusion of Job in the biblical canon may be surprising, since however much we wish to sympathize with Job's behavior as a natural reaction to his immense suffering we are confronted with a substantial text that reproduces the discourse of a character who is often angry and who rants irreverently and rebelliously; moreover, over the course of the eponymous book's 42 chapters he speaks more than half of the time. Perhaps even more surprising is that Job's identity as an Israelite is more or less denied and that he apparently lives rather far from the Holy Land, Canaan, Israel or Palestine – namely in the wonderful land of Oz, *Erets Uts*. Despite all this, he inhabits a separate book in the Hebrew Bible (*TANAKH*), which is mainly devoted to the history of one people, Israel, and which is viewed as a sacred history. Job's foreign identity may even be reflected in some of the unusual language of the Book of Job. Uts as an ethnos – e.g. in the genealogical lists of Genesis – is presented by the biblical authors as belonging to the offspring of Shem and thus as closely related to the Israelites, albeit with emphasis on the lineage not from Jacob but rather from Esau. Hence Job's identity remains significantly ambiguous.[10] The

---

the rise to power of the Nazis; see Joseph Roth, "Der Segen des ewigen Juden: Assimilation und Exil," in: *Werke in sechs Banden* volume 3, Kiepenhauer & Witsch, Köln 1989, 527–532; originally published in *Die Wahrheit* 13.30 (1935), 4–5. See also Mark H. Gelber, "Zur deutsch-zionistischer Rezeptionsgeschichte: Joseph Roth und die Jüdische Rundschau," in: *Von Franzos zu Canetti: Jüdische Autoren aus Österreich. Neue Studien*, eds. Mark H. Gelber, Hans Otto Horch, and Sigurd Paul Scheichl, Max Niemeyer Verlag, Tübingen 1996, 201–209, 203, n. 5.

10 Genesis 10:23 "The descendants of Aram: Uz, Hul, Gether, and Mash." Unless otherwise indicated all Bible quotes are from the New Revised Standard Version (NRSV); cf. also Jeremiah 25:20: "all the kings of the land of Uz."

rabbis of late antiquity who created the Talmudic-midrashic corpus, usually termed Rabbinic literature, treated Esau mostly as the typological personification of Rome and Christianity.[11] They also debated the status of Job's book, expressing divergent views that ranged from the claim that Job was one of three wise men of the ancient Near East (the others being Noah and Daniel)[12] to the assertion that "Job did not exist at all – he was a mere parable."[13] While we cannot really know whether Job's non-Hebrew identity in the Bible was intended to express the undeniable universality of the Hebrew God, it is clearly the effect of the book and it was so also for the rabbis. God's personal communication with Job in this sense diminishes the Israelites' unique position as a nation elected for revelation.

The rabbis of late antiquity did not produce a separate compilation under Job's name – unlike compilations for many other separate books, such as Genesis Rabbah, Leviticus Rabbah, Ruth Rabbah, and Lamentations Rabbah, for reasons I have discussed elsewhere[14] – but instead explicated the verses of the book extremely atomistically, even according to their own norms by which their exegetical practice tended to relate to verses one by one rather than passage by passage.[15] And perhaps precisely because the mythical imagery of the Book of Job was so utterly detached from the national success or demise, dreams or nightmares of the Israelites and the Judahites, it provided Judeo-Christian imagery with some of its boldest mythical visions, including the creatures Behemoth and Leviathan.[16]

---

11 Bakhos, Carol, "Figuring (out) Esau: The Rabbis and Their Others," in: *Journal of Jewish Studies* 58.2 (2007): 250–262.

12 Midrash Tanhuma, Warsaw edition, Chapter on Noah, paragraph 5.

13 Babylonian Talmud, Bava Bathra 15a.

14 Hasan-Rokem, Galit, "To Be or Not to Be – Job in Aggadic Literature?" in: *Mehqerei Talmud: Memorial Volume for Ephraim E. Urbach*, eds. Yaakov Sussman and David Rosenthal, Magnes Press, Jerusalem 2005, 385–402 (Hebrew).

15 Cf. Mark Larrimore, *The Book of* Job: *A Biography*, Princeton University Press, Princeton 2013, 51, 62.

16 See Jefim [Hayim] Schirmann, "The Battle between Behemoth and Leviathan according to an Ancient Hebrew Piyyut," in: *Proceedings of Israel Academy of Sciences and Humanities* 4.13 (1970): 327–369; Galit Hasan-Rokem, "Carl Schmitt and Ahasver: The Idea of the State and the Wandering Jew," in: *Behemoth, A Journal on Civilization* 2 (2008): 4–25; and Andreas Lehnardt, "Leviathan und Behemoth: mythische Urwesen in der mittelalterlichen jüdischen Tradition," in; *Tiere und Fabelwesen im Mittelalter*; ed. Sabine Obermaier, De Gruyter, Berlin 2009, 105–129.

2 Ahasver, the Wandering Jew

An instability and ambiguousness of identity – of hovering between Israel and
the nations – similar to that which the authors of antiquity and late antiquity
attached to Job, has also characterized the evolving figure of the Wandering
Jew. This figure is probably the paramount emblematic idiom referring to Jews
in European culture. His imaginary fate is rooted in a legend telling that he
refused to allow Jesus (exhausted from carrying the cross) to rest against the
wall of his house, leading Jesus to curse him to eternal wandering. The first
edition, as far as known, of what has since become the most important written
source for the European legend of the Wandering Jew was first printed in either
northern Germany, not far from Luther's Wittenberg, or Basel, in 1602.[17] In this
chapbook, which purports to report a meeting with an actual historical figure
in Hamburg in 1542, the Wandering Jew is characterized as a Jerusalemite cobbler with the odd name Ahasver.[18] His pious behavior in and out of church –
almsgiving, prayer, sorrowful penitence – bear the signs of impending fulfillment of the Christian messianic expectation of the Second Coming, embodied
in the conversion of the Jews heralding it. Historical research into the theme
of the Wandering Jew has shown that the figure was not an invention of Refor-
mation advocates, although his supposed existence served their theological
purposes. Some of its earlier sources, such as the Gospel narratives of the Roman soldier Malchus, who slapped Jesus while he was carrying the cross, and
the beloved disciple John, who was sent to sleep in Ephesus until the return
of his master, harbor a strongly polarized emotional ambivalence between
physical violence and great devotion towards the figure of Jesus. This tense
ambivalence of the early medieval material contributed to the characterization
of the Wandering Jew figure as full of internal contradictions, rendering the
figure a highly functional sign for the ambivalent relationship of Christian Europeans to Jews, and later of the European Jews towards themselves. The major
Jewish figure who may have inspired parallel narratives among Jews is the
prophet Elijah, whom post-biblical Jewish tradition transformed into an immortal, popular and itinerant helper.[19] Historical, as opposed to mythical, Jew-

---

17 Neubaur, Leonhard, *Die Sage vom Ewigen Juden*, Hinrichs, Leipzig 1893; Anderson, George
K., *The Legend of the Wandering Jew*, Brown University Press, Providence 1965.
18 Daube, David "Ahasver," in: *Jewish Quarterly Review* 45.3 (1955): 243–244; Hasan-Rokem,
Galit "Ahasver – The Enigma of a Name," in: *Jewish Quarterly Review* 100.4 (2010): 544–550.
19 Harel-Fisch, Harold, "Elijah and the Wandering Jew," in: *Rabbi Joseph Lookstein Memorial
Volume*, ed. L. Landman, Ktav Publishing, New York 1980, 125–135; Fisch, Harold, *A Remembered Future: A Study in Literary Mythology*, Indiana University Press, Bloomington 1984, 44–
45, 61–80. See also Agostino Augustimovic, *'El-khadr' and the Prophet Elijah*, trans. Eugen

ish travelers, especially those – such as Benjamin of Tudela and Petahya of Regensburg – who reported in writing about their travels to the Holy Land also contributed to the construction of the legendary figure.[20] Many of the characteristics of the imaginary cobbler Ahasver, such as his quickly learning the languages of new places, were informed by observing the actual process of Jews moving from place to place, usually, but not only, as a result of expulsions and harassments.

Some of the social and theological perceptions that European Christians held about Jews and that were projected onto the Wandering Jew stemmed directly from revered ancient authorities, perhaps the most influential being Augustine's – and before him Ambrose's and Jerome's – identification of the Jews with the primordial, mythical cursed wanderer, Cain, an association that reinforced the linkage between eternal existence and endless exilic peregrination.[21] According to the medievalist Gerhard Ladner, the wanderer, or *homo viator* in his words, emphatically expresses the tension between the human being's alienness in a world of constantly widening horizons and between the restrictions and structures of social order.[22] The period of the consolidation of the Ahasver legend was certainly a time of widening geographical scope, during which not only "discoverers" but also European merchants and soldiers began to navigate the globe, establishing the great colonial powers that would later define to a large extent European identity in the world.[23] The Jew as a traveler thus became a personification of a certain aspect of Europeanness.[24]

Hoade, Franciscan Printing Press, Jerusalem 1972; and Aharon Wiener, *The Prophet Elijah in the Development of Judaism: a Depth-psychological Study*, Routledge & Kegan Paul, London 1978.

20 Hasan-Rokem, Galit, "Homo viator et narrans – Medieval Jewish Voices in the European Narrative of the Wandering Jew," in: *Europäische Ethnologie und Folklore im internationalen Kontext, Festschrift für Leander Petzoldt*, ed. Ingo Schneider, Peter Lang, Frankfurt am Main 1999, 93–102.

21 Jerome, On Psalms, Homily 35; Augustine, Contra Faustum, Book XII; Ambrose De Cain et Abel 2.9.34–37; cf. Fredriksen, Paula. *Augustine and the Jews: A Christian Defense of Jews and Judaism*. New York: Doubleday, 2008: 320–324.

22 Ladner, Gerhart B., "Homo Viator: Mediaeval Ideas on Alienation and Order," in: *Speculum* 42.2 (1967): 233–259.

23 Greenblatt, Stephen, *Marvelous Possessions: The Wonder of the New World*, University of Chicago Press, Chicago 1992.

24 Hasan-Rokem, Galit, "*Ex Oriente Fluxus:* The Wandering Jew – Oriental Crossings of the Paths of Europe," in: *L'orient dans l'histoire religieuse de l'Europe: L'invention des origines*, eds. Mohammad Ali Amir-Moezzi and John Scheid, EPHE & Brepols, Turnhout 2000, 153–164; Hasan-Rokem, Galit, "L'Image du juif errant et la construction de l'identité européenne," in: *Le juif errant: un témoin du temps*, eds. Laurence Sigal-Klagsblad and Richard I. Cohen, Adam Biro & Musée d'art et d'histoire du Judaisme, Paris 2001, 45–54.

The tale of the Wandering Jew spread rapidly in central and northern Europe. Having been an emblem of Christian piety in a Jewish body, the Wandering Jew was from the Romantic period onwards hailed as the personification of the ideals of Enlightenment and secularization, individualism and rebellion and critique of the religious establishment (among other establishments).[25] At the same time, the psychological and philosophical depth of the figure developed through correlation with spiritual associations of themes of travel which had accrued over centuries. These associations, which included the homelessness of the soul in the material world and shamanic and angelical flights, produced the emphatically symbolical and universal character of the figure in the literature of high modernity. In James Joyce's masterpiece *Ulysses* (first published in 1922, in Paris; serialized since 1918)[26] the Wandering Jew is ingeniously coupled with Odysseus, the representative of the other major European wandering tradition.[27]

During the nineteenth century the theme of the Wandering Jew crossed extensively from the popular chapbook genre and from oral tradition and into the more canonical cultural sphere. While it maintained its legendary features in oral traditions and in the persisting popular printed modes, its introduction into canonical literary genres, including the novel, short story and drama, was marked by an enveloping of the figure in the symbolical values accrued from its adoption by the Romantics (both in English and in German).[28] The articulations of the Wandering Jew figure in the cultural milieu of modernity evidence the extreme versatility that the theme had developed, one could say in direct correlation with the capacity of the allegorical reference – European Jews – to adapt to changing times, in addition to their well-known geographic mobility.

25 Anderson, *The Legend of the Wandering Jew*; Hasan-Rokem, Galit "The Wandering Jew and the European Imagination: Self-Image and the Image of the Other in Lion Feuchtwanger's *Jud Süss*," in: *Icons and History for Richard I. Cohen*, ed. Ezra Mendelsohn, Merkaz Shazar, Jerusalem (forthcoming; Hebrew).

26 Joyce, James, *Ulysses.The 1922 Text*. Oxford World Classics, Oxford University Press, Oxford 2008.

27 Claudio Magris, a relatively early scholar of Roth's life and oeuvre, significantly characterized the author as "an Austrian Odysseus." See Claudio Magris, "Der ostjüdische Odysseus," in: *Joseph Roth und die Tradition*, ed. David Bronsen, Agora Verlag, Darmstadt 1975, 181–226; quoted in: Christoph Parry, "Joseph Roth in den Augen der Nachwelt: Migration, Mythos, Melancholie," in: *Joseph Roth: Ein europäisch-jüdischer Schriftsteller und österreichischer Universalist*, 303–313, 307, n. 9. In contrast, the influential critic Marcel Reich-Ranicki remained half-hearted about Roth's work, labeling him "ein Snob mit ahasverischen Zügen" ("a snob with ahasveric features"). See Marcel Reich-Ranicki, *Nachprüfung: Aufsätze über Deutsche Schriftsteller von Gestern*, Deutsche Taschenbuch Verlag, München 1977, 210.

28 Larmore, Charles, *The Romantic Legacy*, Columbia University Press, New York 1996.

Indeed, whereas the Wandering Jew motif was in the seventeenth and eighteenth centuries distributed mainly via Christian discourses and expressive genres, from the nineteenth century onward this figure was frequently adopted by Jewish authors and visual artists.[29]

The figure of the Wandering Jew appears in various degrees of explicitness in Joseph Roth's work, including in *Juden auf Wanderschaf*, his essayistic treatment of Jewish mobility, and in several of his novels – especially *Die Flucht ohne Ende*[30] – about the rootless existence experienced by many Europeans after the First World War (in which the author had participated as an Austro-Hungarian soldier).

3 Roth's *Job* and *Leviathan*

In two of Joseph Roth's most brilliant works of fictional prose, the novel *Hiob* (first published in 1930)[31] and the novella *Der Leviathan*[32] (first published, in book form, in 1940), the Wandering Jew figure is grafted onto or, rather, intertwined with the figure of Job. The combination draws on European legend traditions as well as the mythical traditions of the Hebrew Bible, presenting the modern condition – and perhaps the human condition in general – with spe-

---

29 Hasan-Rokem, Galit "The Cobbler of Jerusalem in Finnish Folklore," in: *The Wandering Jew – Essays in the Interpretation of a Christian Legend*, eds. Galit Hasan-Rokem and Alan Dundes. Indiana University Press, Bloomington 1986, 119–153; Cohen, Richard I. and Rajner, Mirjam, "The Return of the Wandering Jew(s) in Samuel Hirszenberg's Art," in: *Ars Judaica* 33 (2011): 33–56.
30 Roth, Joseph, *Die Flucht ohne Ende. Ein Bericht*. Kiepenheuer & Witsch, Köln 2010 (originally published in 1927). Roth, Joseph, *Flight Without End*, trans. David Le Vay, The Overlook Press, Woodstock 2003 (originally published in 1977). This novel appeared in 1927, the same year as Roth's essayistic *Juden auf Wanderschaft* (see footnote 6).
31 See footnote 5. The novel was hailed by the critic and philosopher Heinrich Luetzeler (whom the Nazis later banned from teaching, due to his steadfast critical stance) as an exemplar of religious literature. In the same review Luetzler encouraged similar authorship among his fellow Catholics. See Heinrich Luetzeler, "Neue Romane," in: *Hochland* 29 (1931): 267–268.
32 Roth, Joseph, *Der Leviathan*, Kiepenheuer & Witsch, Köln 2005 (originally published, in 1938, in the *Pariser Tageszeitung*). Roth, Joseph, *The Leviathan*, trans. Michael Hofmann, New Directions, New York 2011 (originally published as "The Leviathan," in: *The Collected Stories of Joseph Roth*, translated and with an introduction by Michael Hofmann, W. W. Norton & Co., New York 2002). The *Pariser Tageszeitung* was established in 1936 as a sequel to the earlier *Pariser Tageblatt*. See Hélène Roussel and Lutz Winckler, eds., *Rechts und links der Seine. Pariser Tageblatt und Pariser Tageszeitung 1933–1940*, Niemeyer, Tübingen 2002.

cial reference to the dialectics of particularity and universality. The traditional, singularly non-Hebrew identity of Job among the heroes of biblical books, and the conceptualizing of the Wandering Jew as a pious Christian who is identified as "Jew," make these figures' related presence in the novels doubly echo the oscillation of European Jews between international, national and ethnic identities, especially as experienced in the nineteenth and early twentieth centuries.[33] The Wandering Jew component in certain characters pulls the biblical Joban figure from its extreme, Promethean, chained immobility and towards (likewise extreme) modes of mobility, giving rise to a wide semiotic and symbolical range between the traditional curse of wandering and the messianic or otherwise utopian movement towards deliverance.

Hiob, or *Job – the Story of a Simple Man*, is a commiserating elegy on the life of Mendel Singer. Roth's protagonist is, unlike the biblical Job, not a rich man, and the author opts to focus on, of all the tribulations faced by Job, the most difficult: the demise of his children, one after another. The disasters that befall Singer's children are characteristic of the relevant historical and social context: one son, a soldier in Russia – itself a fate that East European Jews associated with calamity and sought to escape, even with great sacrifices – does not explicitly die yet effectively disappears; another son emigrates to America, where he initially succeeds but is killed while serving as an American soldier. Whereas the births of Job's daughters born after the disaster and after God's revelation to him and their subsequent flourishing signify their father's recovery, Mendel's daughter, whose risqué lifestyle was the reason for his emigration to America, loses her sanity there, in what has been interpreted as a desperate attempt to liberate herself from the unbearable contradictions of her life.[34] Unlike the biblical Job, whose wife supports him during his most trying

---

33 Gershon Shaked has added substantially to the earlier important work of Claudio Magris in linking Roth's oeuvre to the textual traditions – especially the Hebrew canonical traditions – of Judaism; however, I do not share Shaked's idea that Roth's rich use of intra-Jewish intertextual references rendered him less accessible to non-Jewish readers. *The Leviathan*, for instance, offers an excellent example of how these traditions may in fact enhance the universality of the text. See Magris, "Der ostjüdische Odysseus"; and Gershon Shaked, *Identity: Jewish Literatures in European Languages*, Haifa University Press, Haifa 2006, 234–256 (Hebrew).
34 de Bruyker, Melissa, "Narratologie der Vergewaltigung: Der Erzähler und die Ikonografie der Tochter in Joseph Roths 'Hiob,'" in: *Zeitschrift für Germanistik* 16.1 (2006): 77–88, 84–88; Dos Santos, Isabel, "Grenzen in Heimat und Fremde: Zu Joseph Roths 'Hiob,'" in: *Acta Germanica* 34 (2006): 71–79. Ritchie Robertson, in contrast, blames Roth for being cheap in introducing "soft-porn" (his words) in describing Mirjam's conduct. See Ritchie Robertson, "Roth's *Hiob* and the Traditions of the Ghetto Fiction," in: *Co-existent Contradictions: Joseph Roth in Retrospect*, ed. Helen Chambers, Ariadne Press, Riverside 1991, 185–200.

times, Mendel's wife dies, leaving him without the potential of familial regeneration that characterizes the final stage of Job's life. Still, unlike Job, whose performance of calamity and suffering is characterized by promethean immobility, Mendel transports himself to the new world – in more than one sense. He builds a new – not necessarily happier – life in America, and abandons his traditional mores and behaviors, without seeming to adjust to his new environment. The only redemptive power is introduced by his youngest son, Menuchim, who, though initially considered totally inept, actually embodies the musical association of the family's last name – Singer; he becomes a musical genius, and mysteriously appears to herald the (for Roth atypical, yet still ambiguous) happy ending of the novel. Some critics have interpreted the novel's ending as revealing the impact of Hassidism on Roth.[35] Redemption via musical performance (such as whistling or singing a folk tune) of someone not versed in the canonical modes of worship is indeed extant in Jewish folk narratives, particular in Hassidic ones.[36] Yet Menuchim's reconnecting with his father also bears signs of a more collective version of redemption. The major such sign is Menuchim's sudden arrival on Passover Eve, reminiscent of the traditional miraculous advents of Elijah, the precursor of the Wandering Jew in Jewish tradition. Notwithstanding Elijah's transformation from the biblical zealot fighting the priests of Ba'al (I Kings chapter 18) into the more intimate, itinerant post-biblical helper extant in folktales and legends, the explicit association to Elijah points to a more mythical and collective dimension of redemption. The echo of Elijah's role in the eschatological script of Messianic hope, wherein he declares the emergence of the great Day of the Lord (Malachi 4:5–6; Hebrew Bible in Jewish tradition: 3:23), orchestrates the ending of the novel as a bleak shadow of redemption; yet it also provides a symbolical compensation for the obvious absence of revelation in a world in which divinity is ostensibly vanishing, hidden or hiding.[37]

---

35 See Esther Steinmann, *Von der Würde des Unscheinbaren: Sinnerfahrung bei Joseph Roth*, Niemeyer, Tübingen 1984, quoted in: Jürgen Koppensteiner, Review of Steinmann's *Von der Würde des Unscheinbaren*, in: *Monatshefte* 79.2 (1987): 275–276. See also: Shaked, *Identity: Jewish Literatures in European Languages*; and Dos Santos, "Grenzen in Heimat und Fremde," 75.
36 See Micha Joseph Bin-Gorion [Berdyczewski], "The Pipe," in: *Mimekor Yisrael. Selected Classical Jewish Folktales* (abridged and annotated edition), ed. Emanuel Bin Gorion, trans. I. M. Lask, Indiana University Press, Bloomington 1990, 336. I thank Dan Ben-Amos for the reference.
37 True to his contradictory shifting between beliefs and ideologies, Roth could also express staunch belief in just retribution: for example, in 1937, reflecting on the Spanish Civil War, he noted "the sentence of the fathers that goes: 'The Court of the Lord is in continuous session, here an earth and in the hereafter.' Centuries may pass – but the judgment is ineluctable." See Roth, *The Wandering Jews*, 118.

In various Rabbinic sources Menahem, the comforter, is the name of the Messiah (e.g. Lamentations Rabbah 1, 1).[38] This name may well hide behind the Galician pronunciation – Menuchim – represented in Roth's orthography. Moreover, the father's name, Mendel, is the most common Yiddish colloquial form for the same Hebrew name, Menahem. This particular combination was given literary fame by the author Shalom Aleikhem (Rabinovitch), in one of his unforgettable (anti)heroes, the *luftmentsh* Menahem Mendl, who, like Roth's Mendel Singer, travels from Eastern Europe to America, the *goldene medine*. The dual appellation in Roth's novel may be another example of Roth's limited literacy in Jewish culture, as Jewish fathers and sons are almost never given the same name, and definitely not among Ashkenazi Jews.[39] But Roth's figurative language and multi-layered narrative may also be credited for rendering an effect similar to the midrashic semiotics of multiple layers of meanings (different from the effects of inter-textuality).[40] Thus the parallelism in the identically named father and son may allude to the Father and Son "family romance" of the Christian tale of salvation. This is hardly implausible, given Roth's intense interest in Catholicism and probable conversion towards the end of his life.[41] But it may also encode a Jewish mystical belief in *gilgul*,[42] the transformative migration of souls often marked by name (for example, Moses' soul transmigrating into Maimonides', etc.). In Roth's *Hiob* it would signify the redemptive option whereby the tortured soul of father Mendel is delivered into the soaring and singing soul of his son Menuchim. This is another emblematic representation of the novel's latent messianic theme. The various applications of different forms of the name Menahem – the comforter – could certainly be read as an expression of a strong need to be comforted.

Most Roth scholars dwell on the author's lamenting of the fall of the Austro-Hungarian Empire and its multi-ethnicity, viewing the First World War as the great divide between the ideal past and the hopeless present of the twenties

---

38 Hasan-Rokem, *Web of Life*, 153.
39 An oft-cited example is Roth's mistaken translation of *batlen* ("loiterer") as "jester" (*badhen*). See Roth, *The Wandering Jews*, 77.
40 See Hasan-Rokem, *Web of Life*, 22–27.
41 Carl Steiner considers *Hiob* the first novel in Roth's "religious turn" and suggests that Roth's adoption of Catholicism should be seen within the context of his love of Paris and France. See Carl Steiner, "Frankreichbild und Katholizismus bei Joseph Roth," in: *The German Quarterly* 46.1 (1973): 12–21, 13.
42 Scholem, Gershom, *On the Mystical Shape of the Godhead: Basic Concepts in the Kabbalah*, trans. Joachim Neugroschel, Schocken Books, New York 1991, 197–250.

and the thirties. Much of Roth's work, such as his novel *Radetzkymarsch*[43] (*The Radetzky March*), first published in 1932, is devoted to the social and emotional repercussions of the Empire's demise. Yet his is no simple nostalgia; rather, it is a bittersweet look back, one that feeds, in Alan Bance's insightful wording in his introduction to the English translation, "[Roth's] own modern awareness of the mythopoetic processes at work in the self-creation of the Hapsburg myth, to which he is nonetheless retrospectively contributing. It is his irony and ambiguity which make the novel so different from a mere self-indulgent exercise in nostalgia."[44] For Roth, the Empire's fall is never a thing in itself without deep connections to the particular hardships of Jews, even in this most Austro-Hungarian of his works, in which the Jews are still represented ethnographically as a group[45] rather than as individuals. Roth, in this novel and elsewhere, also directs social criticism against the condition of minorities, in particular of the Jews, in the Habsburg Empire and even expresses a kind of local patriotism for his Galician native soil. Likewise, though he laments the idealized Emperor Franz Joseph and his rule, he grieves more acutely for the tribulations of the Wandering Jews and indeed of the wandering modern human. The question whether suffering as a human condition is intensified in the Jewish condition remains unresolved in Roth's narrative universe. And, as with the hero of his post-First World War I text par excellence, *Die Flucht ohne Ende*[46] (*Flight without End*), first published in 1927, which traces the identity puzzles and roaming through Europe of a soldier who has survived the first of the great slaughters of modernity – the trauma which Roth himself shared – mobility itself becomes part of the disaster. However, as in his novel *Job*, Roth may actually be pointing at mobility as the protagonist's existential rebellion against impending calamity. God – about whose existence there is no certainty save omnipresent suffering – remains the major adversary of humans in all of Roth's Joban transformations.[47]

Nonetheless, among Roth's works it is not *Job*, its title notwithstanding, that resonates most powerfully the mythical motifs from the biblical namesake, but rather a relatively unknown (and definitely under-researched) short story or novella, *The Leviathan*, first published as "Der Leviathan," in 1938, in the

---

43 Roth, Joseph, *Radetzkymarsch,* Kiepenheuer & Witsch, Köln 2005 (originally published in 1932). Roth, Joseph, *The Radetzky March*, trans. Joachim Neugroschel, Alfred A. Knopf, New York 1996

44 Bance, Alan, Introduction, in: Roth, The Radetzky March, xviii.

45 For example, see Roth, *The Radetzky March*, 312, 314.

46 See footnote 30.

47 Cf. Larrimore, *The Book of* Job, xx.

Pariser Tageszeitung daily, one of the most active German-language exile publications in Paris.[48] Its posthumous publication as a novella, in 1940, makes it one of Roth's latest works; it has most often been printed in collections, alongside other shorter works by Roth. The opening paragraphs of both *Job* and *The Leviathan* echo their biblical forebear in slightly different tones.[49] In *Job*: "Many years ago there lived in Zuchnow a man named Mendel Singer. He was pious, God-fearing and ordinary," and, unlike Job, "an entirely everyday Jew."[50] In *The Leviathan*: "In the small town of Progrody there lived a coral merchant who was known far and wide for his honesty and quality of his wares."[51] The Jewishness of the latter protagonist, except as indicated by his name, Nissen Piczenik (a name that occurs in two other works of Roth, for characters who share some of the same traits), is disclosed only some pages later.[52] The phonetic affinity between the fictional Progrody and Roth's own birthplace, Brody, lends this late tale a particular pathos and a tentative autobiographical effect. However, Brody, where Roth grew up, was a large city in the northeasternmost corner of the Austro-Hungarian Empire; this was the realm of Kaiser Franz Josef, whom authors saluted in their works as "the Emperor, may his glory rise." (S. Y. Agnon, another great twentieth-century Jewish writer from an Eastern Galician town (Buczacz), would always acknowledge the monarch thusly in his texts.)[53] Brody was saturated with Jewish culture of various strains: religious Orthodoxy, Hassidic and otherwise; Haskala Enlightenment philosophy; Hebrew; socialism; Yiddish; Zionism. In contrast, Roth describes the fictional townlet of Progrody as an insignificant spot at the end of the world; unlike Brody it is not under the rule of the Emperor but rather in the Tsardom of Russia. The only concrete likeness that I have been able to

---

48 See footnote 32.

49 These opening sections have been referred to in claiming Roth's "folk narrative" style, often without attention to the fact that it is the biblical Book of Job that begins as a folktale. See Robert F. Bell, "The Jewish Experience as Portrayed in Three German Exile 'Novellen,'" in: *South Atlantic Bulletin* 42.4 (1977): 3–12, 4; and Alexander Ritter, "Über das 'Gleichwicht zwischen der Tischplatte und ihrer künstliche Verlängerung': Zu kulturkritische Antithese 'Amerika' der Lebensbalance in Joseph Roths *Hiob* (1930)," in: *Joseph Roth: Ein europäisch-jüdischer Schriftsteller und österreichischer Universalist*, 87–100, 93.

50 Roth, *Job*, 9

51 Roth, *The Leviathan*, 3.

52 Roth, *The Leviathan*, 6.

53 Among the many references to Roth's appreciation of the relative tolerance in the Habsburg Empire Stefan Zweig's eulogy of him stands out in its clarity. See Stefan Zweig, "Joseph Roth," in: *Stefan Zweig: Europäisches Erbe*, ed. Richard Friedenthal, Fischer Taschenbuch Verlag, Frankfurt am Main 1994, 267–280, 268; quoted in Parry, "Joseph Roth in den Augen der Nachwelt," 308–309.

detect between the two towns, except for the proportionally large Jewish population in each place, is that both are near marshland.[54] Roth thereby undermines the authorial autobiographical association before the reader has even constructed it; such ambivalence is truly his dominant mode of expression. This tale's consequence is primarily not its historical or biographical connections, but rather its strongly symbolical resonance in which coalesce the Wandering Jew figure in its modern symbolical twentieth-century manifestation and the Book of Job as a mythical echo.

From the beginning the tale spins around the peculiar rootedness and immobility – Job! – of the protagonist, to whom farmers and their wives travel on market days, shopping for ornaments and amulets. On these days Progrody changes from a marginal locale and into a destination of noted interest for villagers from distant places. The walking steps of such villagers accompany the opening of the novella. Other travelers, "beggars, traveling musicians, gypsies and men with dancing bears"[55] are referred to condescendingly by the protagonist and the authorial narrative voice, particularly for their lack of interest in Nissen Piczenik's corals, which soon become the emotional, economical and symbolical epicenter of the narrative.[56]

Parallel with the quotidian descriptions of small-town life the short tale is early on imbued with Joban and other mythological motifs; these focus on the charismatic, and later fatal, presence of the corals in Piczenik's life: "For corals are the noblest plants in the oceanic underworld; they are like roses for the capricious goddesses of the sea, as inexhaustible in their variety as the caprices of the goddesses."[57] The fatalness of the corals is further emphasized by their comparison to blood, arteries and the heart.

The Book of Job surfaces most strongly in Roth's novella with the appearance of the Leviathan that constitutes the work's title and via which the recurring messianic theme is from the outset interwoven into the text. The first mention of Leviathan is associated with the creation of the world – and with God: "Now, the ancient god Jehovah had created everything [*selbst* – by himself], the earth and the beasts who walked upon it, the sea and all its creatures. But

---

54 The ubiquitous croaking of frogs in Roth's descriptions of nature, which Robertson deems "formulaic," may thus resonate real memories. See Robertson, "Roth's *Hiob* and the Traditions of the Ghetto Fiction," 198–199.

55 Roth, *The Leviathan*, 4

56 Does the resemblance of the coral chains to rosaries perhaps reflect Roth's intense involvement with Catholicism towards the end of his life, such that their critical transformation into fake corals suggests inconstant feelings about this involvement?

57 Roth, *The Leviathan*, 5.

for the time being – namely, until the coming of the Messiah – he had left the supervision of all the animals and the plants of the sea, and in particular of the corals, to the care of Leviathan, who lay curled on the seabed" (the German original uses the more deeply mythological *Urgrund alle Wasser*).[58] It is not until later in the story – after Piczenik's return from Odessa, where he has just seen the sea (for the first time in his life) while visiting with the young sailor Komrower – that it emerges that his passionless routine of life in Progrody includes visits to the synagogue.[59] In Piczenik's world God clearly does not reside in the house of prayer but is instead a cosmic God, much like Job's God, who speaks from the whirlwind. And, like Job's God, Piczenik's God rules over the great sea beasts. Moreover, the myth of the Leviathan is effectively and trans-religiously, universally, transmitted: "All the inhabitants of Progrody and its surroundings were convinced that corals are living creatures, and that the great fish Leviathan was responsible for their well-being under the sea. There could be no question of that, since Nissen Piczenik said so himself [*selbst* erzählt hatte]."[60] God has created the world, and Nissen Piczenik has disseminated the myth about Leviathan's task since the creation. Like Job's fate, Piczenik's and Leviathan's fate is in the (unsentimental) hands of God.

Significantly, the old God Jehovah appears in the tale in his most universal role, that of the God of the gentile Job, not the national God of Israel or the Jews of Progrody. The text reveals the sort of ambivalence of modulated awe towards Leviathan and other immense sea creatures as was formulated by M. D. Cassuto and others in the wake of his work. This ambivalence, the hallmark of their monotheistic bridling in Genesis 1:21,[61] is marked via pointing out that God created even the largest sea creatures, and, in Psalm 104:26, staging Leviathan as the Creator's plaything. The immensity of God's power is highlighted by the enormity of Leviathan as described in Job 40:25–41–26.

But Nissen Piczenik, as if he were God of the Psalm, treats Leviathan with a certain playfulness and slight reproach. The reproach concerns Piczenik's great passion, corals, which for him are the epitome of perfection; thus when he finds some that are less than perfect the blame must fall on someone: "There were some corals that ... had holes. The sloppy [*sorglose*] Leviathan couldn't have been paying attention"; this reflection ends with Piczenik's "shaking his head, as though he could not comprehend how such a powerful

---

58 Roth, *The Leviathan*, 7; Roth, *Der Leviathan*, 17.

59 Roth, *The Leviathan*, 37.

60 Roth, *The Leviathan*, 8; Roth, *Der Leviathan*, 18.

61 Cassuto, Umberto, "Baal and Mot in the Ugaritic Texts," in: *Israel Exploration Journal* 12.2 (1962): 77–86 (see especially page 84, on the sea monsters).

God as Jehovah could have left such an irresponsible [*leichtsinnige*] fish as the Leviathan in charge of all the corals."[62]

The personal catastrophe hinted at through recurrent mention of Joban motifs enters an active phase when Piczenik's dreams about the mighty sea and Leviathan are turned into his active wandering to the sea with Komrower, the young Jewish sailor (on shore leave from the Imperial Russian Navy). The description of their visit to a local pub prior to the trip to Odessa intensifies the presence of alcohol. (Roth himself, during the writing of the novella, was already being ravaged by alcoholism.) Alcohol is introduced earlier in the narrative as being a necessary ingredient of Piczenik's business: "Because once we have got a drink or two inside us, all good honest men are our brothers ... and there is no difference between farmer and merchant, Jew and Christian"[63] – a passage that carries echoes of Saint Paul's message "There is neither Jew nor Greek, etc." (Galatians 3:28). In Piczenik's mind the desperate utopia of universal brotherhood is wedded to drink and unbridled passion for the sea; however, when this wandering Jew first reaches the sea it is revealed that his homelessness is in fact a fatal longing for the depths foreboded in his coral red hair and beard, likened by the narrator to a sea god's.[64]

The scene at the Odessa harbor again recalls the Book of Job. As Piczenik is shown about the Russian warship on which Komrower serves, Roth paraphrases Job's praise of wisdom by which humans invent myriad sorts of innovations (Job, chapter 28) and proclaims the eternal, divine wind (*der ewige Wind*) "out of the very depths of the sea."[65] From this great cosmic wind Job heard God's voice; Piczenik, however, hears only his own longing for the sea and the corals.[66]

As in the Book of Job, in Roth's *Leviathan* the catastrophe is propelled through the plot by another mythological figure, namely Satan, the devil. In Roth's novella he is Jenö Lakatos, an itinerant Hungarian merchant selling artificial corals. Lakatos also resembles the traditional wandering Jew figure, at least in his almost supernatural gift to learn the languages of whatever place

---

62 Roth, *The Leviathan*, 8–9; Roth, *Der Leviathan*, 19.

63 Roth, *The Leviathan*, 14.

64 Roth had a special interest in red-haired Jews. See for example: Roth, *The Radetzky March*, 309, 312. Red hair is in Jewish tradition attributed to Cain and Esau but also to David.

65 Roth, *The Leviathan*, 33; Roth, *Der Leviathan*, 49–50.

66 Nissen, in his desperate love of the true corals, parallels the protagonist of a novella by another Galician author, Agnon, whose Jacob Rechnitz, in *Betrothed*, is obsessed with seaweeds. See Ilana Pardes, *Agnon's Moonstruck Lovers: The Song of Songs in Israeli Culture*, University of Washington Press, Seattle 2013, 73–74.

he arrives.[67] His asymmetric feet recall the variously described deformed feet and peculiar gait of the Wandering Jew in folk beliefs.[68] However, unlike the biblical Job, Piczenik falls into Satan's trap and "thereby betrayed both himself and the real corals."[69] This betrayal consists in his succumbing to the temptation to sell the false corals that Lakatos had begun selling in a neighboring town. Yet it is not the increased profits that drive Piczenik, not least as he has little use for money, especially after his wife's death. Rather, he succumbs to the flawless beauty of the ersatz corals, which do not have the holes and other asymmetries that real corals acquire in being carelessly tended by Leviathan. The yearning for total perfection in a state preceding true redemption is gravely inadequate, to say the least. Thus powers much greater than himself govern Piczenik's fate.[70] As in Roth's *Job,* a hardly believed-in God is charged with being an invisible torturer of humankind.

With regard to Satan, the parallel to the Book of Job is explicit, although there is a discernible wink towards a parallel between Piczenik and Jesus and thus perhaps a Christological backlighting of his sufferings: "And that was how the Satan first came to tempt the coral merchant Nissen Piczenik."[71] This may have been inspired by Roth's closeness to Catholicism at the time he was writing *Leviathan.*

Piczenik and his unloved wife (who dies prematurely) have no children but he compensates for his paternal yearnings by providing children, especially those of non-Jewish women, with various cures and blessings made possible from his corals. (This sorrow of childlessness may echo Roth's own childless marriage, although unlike Piczenik he apparently loved his wife, Friederike Reichler, quite keenly; she had been ill since at least 1920 and was eventually institutionalized, yet outlived her husband. She was murdered by the Nazis in 1940.) Once Piczenik starts to market the imitation corals as real ones, however, he becomes guilty for the deaths of children whom the fake corals did not save from a diphtheria epidemic. He may thus be seen as the carrier of

---

67 Another devilish figure with the name of Lakatos – meaning "locksmith" in Hungarian and associated with the Hungarian Roma population – appears in Roth's *Confessions of a Murderer* (2003), originally published as *Beichte eines Mörders* (1936). There are a number of recurring figures in Roth's fiction (such as Kapturak, the smuggler of humans, who appears in *Job* and elsewhere), reminding us of the fictional world that interlinks Balzac's various works.
68 See Hasan-Rokem, "The Cobbler of Jerusalem in Finnish Folklore."
69 Roth, *The Leviathan,* 43.
70 Cf. Stefan H. Kaszynski, "Die Mythisierung der Wirklichkeit in Erzählwerk von Joseph Roth," in: *Text und Kritik* 243–244 (1990): 137–143.
71 Roth, *The Leviathan,* 43; cf. Matthew chapter 4.

disaster, a role often assigned to the Wandering Jew in European folk beliefs.[72] Piczenik's sin is not only the faking of real corals but rather the intermixing of the real and the fake corals, robbing each, especially the real ones, of their true identity, thereby propagating the troubling theme of undistinguished identities. Should we infer from this that Roth did not necessarily celebrate his composite identity (which included being an East European Jew, a Central European intellectual, and a Parisian exilic writer of German, among other elements), or what might be more adequately described as a fractured identity? Or does the novella reflect that Roth had a troubled mind, stemming from his being caught between his Jewish roots and his Catholic yearnings? The uprootedness arising from Roth being orphaned at an early age (following the death of his mother; he never knew his father, who was institutionalized shortly before Roth was born) coupled not least with the tragic fate of his mentally ill wife, doubtlessly served as fertile soil for his unique oeuvre; however, it also would also have surely wreaked what would became for Roth incessant existential and concrete suffering. These were likely a major reason for Roth's succumbing to the devilish compulsion for alcohol – his reaper.

Let us now return to the uncannily parallel events of Roth's *Leviathan*: following the death of his wife, Piczenik's destruction – also involving alcohol – transpires rapidly. Like so many other East European Jews at the turn of the nineteenth and twentieth centuries, and like the protagonist of Roth's novel *Job*, Piczenik chooses to pursue a new start in another land – a social migration that helped reinforce the continuously rekindled image of the Wandering Jew.[73] In Hamburg, Piczenik boards a steamship named, with a strong tinge of irony, the *Phoenix*, thereby introducing into the short but intense narrative another Joban mythical being, per the traditional Jewish interpretation of the biblical text (Job 29:18).[74] The *Phoenix* departs for Canada but sinks four days into its journey; 200 people perish, including Piczenik, who drowns, perhaps deliberately. Unlike Mendel Singer, Piczenik never arrives in the western hemisphere, and thus does not recover even slightly from his disasters, as do Singer

---

72 About the spreading of disease in particular, see the most famous nineteenth-century literary text referring to the Wandering Jew, Eugène Sue's *Le Juif Errant* (serialized, in *Le Constitutionnel*, in 1844–1845). See Eugène Sue, *Le Juif Errant*, Robert Laffon, Paris 1983.

73 Hasan-Rokem, Galit, "Jews as Postcards, or Postcards as Jews: Mobility in a Modern Genre," in: *Jewish Quarterly Review* 99.4 (2009): 505–546.

74 JPS translation: "I thought I would end my days with my family / And be as long lived as the phoenix," is corroborated by the correlative tradition from BT Sanhedrin 108b, further quoted by RaSHI's interpretation, from where Roth could have learnt it. The Hebrew word for "phoenix" (ḥol) is translated as "palm tree" in the Septuagint and the Vulgate; in Luther's German Bible and the King James Version the translation is "sand."

and the biblical Job. Instead, he lies at the bottom of the sea, blessed by the narrator: "May he rest in peace beside the Leviathan until the coming of the Messiah."[75]

4 The Signs of the Times

The timelessness of Piczenik's death may remind us of the most common German sobriquet of the Wandering Jew, namely the Eternal Jew, a term which in general emphasizes the temporal element of the endless, cursed wandering of Ahasver and perhaps more strongly underscores his sin. But Piczenik, who, like the Eternal Jew, is stricken by a violent God, has ceased wandering; he remains frozen in an immobility and passiveness that reminds us more of Job's situation at the point between his erstwhile affluence and his recovery than of his final state. I must strongly disagree with interpretations that view *The Leviathan* as a moral tale or parable of sin and punishment, especially as punishment for assimilatory desire.[76] I assume that Roth's worldview was not only far more tragic than that but also closer to the central problematic of the biblical Book of Job, namely the suffering of the innocent or the irrationality of suffering, a problematic that remains unmarred by the book's absurd happy ending.

If Roth's *Job* ends somewhat like its biblical model, with a legendary or even almost fairytale happy ending, his *Leviathan* ends with a consistently mythical and rather grim eschatology. In this posthumously published novella Roth seems to have finally carried out the pessimistic consequences hinted at in the deeply moving preface he penned for the second edition of his *Juden auf Wanderschaft*, published in 1937. The book, written as a series of journalistic essays and in a mix of ethnographic and social critical styles, oscillates between a rejection of the lifestyle of East European Jews and strong feelings of empathy for what Roth describes as their misery. The new preface's closing reverberates with agonizing intuition. I quote it verbatim to emphasize my reading's historical contextualization of his seemingly timeless novella:

> I wish I had the grace and the insight to suggest some way out of our present difficulties. But honesty, one of the often unsung muses of the writer, forces me to bring this second foreword of mine to a pessimistic conclusion:
> 1. Zionism can bring only a partial solution to the Jewish question.

---

75 Roth, *The Leviathan*, 52
76 Shaked, *Identity: Jewish Literatures in European Languages*; Garloff, Katja, "Femininity and Assimilatory Desire in Joseph Roth," in: *Modern Fiction Studies* 51.2 (2005): 354–373, 359.

2. Jews will only attain complete equality, and the dignity of external freedom, once their "host-nations" have attained their own inner freedom, as well as the dignity conferred by sympathy for the plight of others.

3. It is – failing some divine intervention – hardly possible to believe that the "host-nations" will find such freedom and dignity.

Pious Jews may be left with the consolation of the hereafter.
As for the rest, it's *"vae victis."*

Joseph Roth [handwritten signature][77]

This complex ending of the preface, with its excruciating "woe to the vanquished," parallels the ending of the novella *Leviathan* in more than one way. Roth's initial recognition of the lack of grace (*Gnade*) sounds very much like despair of ever receiving the consolation offered by Christian theology to the suffering individual. His skepticism expressed in the phrase "failing some divine intervention" is in deep harmony with the silent and non-intervening God of both *Job* and *Leviathan*. The dead end of "present difficulties" holds painfully true for Piczenik and Roth, as well for as the hampered Jewish masses of Eastern Europe. Roth's harsh intuitions regarding Zionism[78] and the quality of life afforded to Jews by their "host-nations" in Europe could (with few exceptions) hardly have been more accurate. The preface's final thought, about the consolation of piety – the Messianic expectation – sinks, like the body of Nissen Piczenik, into mythical depths under the raw weight of *"vae victis."* Indeed. The first publication of the story as a novella, in 1940, was thus posthumous in both the personal and collective sense.

It thus seems that in this, one of his final narratives, and as in his own life, Roth had entirely given up any hope that history would serve as an arena of possible liberation from suffering – Jewish and human – and had let his expectations and his Wandering Jew recede into the depths of the mythical,

---

77 Roth, *The Wandering Jews*, 136–137.

78 See Mark H. Gelber, "'Juden auf Wanderschaft' und die Rhetorik der Ost-West-Debatte im Werk Joseph Roths," in: *Joseph Roth: Interpretation – Kritik – Rezeption*, eds. Michael Kessler and Fritz Hackert. Stauffenberg Verlag (Stauffenberg Colloquium volume 15), Tübingen 1990, 127–135; and Gelber, "Zur deutsch-zionistischer Rezeptionsgeschichte," especially page 204. Lunzer-Talos quotes Roth's intriguing argument (at the end of his "Der Segen des ewigen Juden" essay) that the Jews are more ancient than the concept of the nation and that their mission has been to "give God" to the world rather than attach themselves to a specific piece of land. See Lunzer-Talos, "Der Segen des ewigen Juden: Assimilation und Exil," 35. Yet Roth, at the same time as he praised the Yishuv in Palestine for taking the refugees of – the not yet murderous – Nazism into their fold, also warned Zweig about allying himself with the Zionists. See Zweig, "Joseph Roth," 267–280, 268, quoted in Parry, "Joseph Roth in den Augen der Nachwelt," 308–309.

Joban, ocean. This was a bitterly ironic parallel to the German culture that he was an inherent, if in some ways foreign, part of, a culture that was sweeping into the whirlwind of mythos where, alas, no voice of God was heard, and if Leviathan was present it was in the fearfully beastly manifestation known from Job 4:25–41:26.

Although I have nowhere in Roth's work found reference to Carl Schmitt, or vice versa, I find the coincidence of the latter's Der Leviathan in der Staatslehre des Thomas Hobbes[79] being published in 1938, more or less in parallel to the initial, serial publication of Roth's *Der Leviathan*, too striking not to mention. I have argued elsewhere that not only is Schmitt's irrationally irate criticism of Hobbes' choice of the Joban Leviathan as the symbol of the sovereign based on a misreading of the English philosopher – a misreading that overlooks the biblical interpretations that serve as the basis of Hobbes' monumental book; acknowledgment of such biblical elements would hardly have suited Schmitt's claim that Hobbes' text is in fact a secularized theological document – but that, moreover, Schmitt erases the figure of the Wandering Jew as he erases Spinoza's claim to the term "political theology". Likewise, Schmitt's description of the elements destructing the state – elements that include border crossers and bearers of ambiguous identities – not only implicitly designates Jews in general (whose elimination he at least tacitly supported), but possibly, and in a more concrete form, the legendary figure of the Wandering Jew.[80]

This mutual – perhaps unconscious yet not insignificant – mirroring of Roth's and Schmitt's respective Leviathans reveals yet another side of Roth's tragic predicament: he wished to be universal, not in spite of being a Jew but as a Jew, at the moment when European culture allowed for this arguably less than at any other moment in history, a moment when the Schmittian demarcation between friend and foe was in the process of becoming concretely manifested in a murderous selection.

As mentioned earlier, Roth's desperate vision had already been specifically expressed in his novel *The Radetzky March*, which he had written through his identity as an Austro-Hungarian, an identity whose disappearance had

---

79 Schmitt, Carl, *The Leviathan in the State Theory of Thomas Hobbes. Meaning and Failure of a Political Symbol*, transs. G. Schwab and E. Hilfstein, Greenwood Press, Westport 1996.

80 Hasan-Rokem, "Carl Schmitt and Ahasver." In an earlier text Schmitt had presented the Roman Catholic Church as the only institution carrying forth the European tradition of politics that he professed. See Carl Schmitt, *Römischer Katholizismus und politische Form*, Klett-Cotta, Stuttgart 2008; and Carl Schmitt, *Roman Catholicism and Political Form*, trans. G. I. Ulmen. Greenwood Press, Westport 1996.

doomed masses of Galician Jews to indescribable homelessness. In the two texts that have been the focus of this essay Roth's desire to be universal as a Jew, and even because a Jew, is forcefully recounted through the mythology of Job, the exemplar of suffering (and who is characterized as non-Jewish), and the Wandering Jew, the legendary paragon of eternal wandering, whose identity bridges Christian and Jewish. The realities of Roth's world denied him the fulfillment of the potential models of composite identity afforded by myth and legend, at a moment when legendary beliefs and mythical programs were dimming the humane options of European consciousness. All of this left Roth no other alternative but a degraded death on the threshold of Europe's brutal ruins. Reading Roth's work as part of the exegetical (in the wide sense of the term) tradition of the Book of Job, and as a link in the European narrative and figurative tradition of the Wandering Jew, sharpens its expression of universal values and its reflection of a particular Jewish fate, in striking parallel with the central tension expressed in these two forebears. It also tells us about the particular intuitive power of great literature to see into the depth of its time and beyond it.

Bibliography

Anderson, George K. *The Legend of the Wandering Jew*. Providence RI: Brown University Press, 1965.

Augustimovic, Agostino. *'El-khadr' and the Prophet Elijah*. English translation by Eugen Hoade. Jerusalem: Franciscan Printing Press, 1972.

Bakhos, Carol. "Figuring (out) Esau: The Rabbis and Their Others." *Journal of Jewish Studies* 58.2. Oxford: Oxford Centre for Hebrew and Jewish Studies, 2007. 250–262.

Bell, Robert F. "The Jewish Experience as Portrayed in Three German Exile 'Novelle.'" *South Atlantic Bulletin* 42.4. Atlanta: South Atlantic Modern Language Association, 1977. 3–12.

Bin-Gorion [Berdyczewski], Micha Joseph. *Mimekor Yisrael. Classical Jewish Folktales*. Abridged and annotated edition. Ed. Emanuel Bin Gorion, trans. I. M. Lask, introduction and notes by Dan Ben-Amos. Bloomington: Indiana University Press, 1990.

de Bruyker, Melissa. "Narratologie der Vergewaltigung: Der Erzähler und die Ikonografie der Tochter in Joseph Roths 'Hiob'". *Zeitschrift für Germanistik* 16.1. Berlin: Humboldt-Universität zu Berlin, 2006. 77–88.

Cassuto, Umberto. "Baal and Mot in the Ugaritic Texts." *Israel Exploration Journal*, 12.2. 1962. 77–86.

Cohen, Richard I. *Jewish Icons: Art and Society in Modern Europe*. Berkeley: University of California Press, 1998.

Cohen, Richard I. "The 'Wandering Jew' from Medieval Legend to Modern Metaphor." *The Art of Being Jewish in Modern Times*. Eds. Barbara Kirshenblatt-Gimblett and Jonathan Karp. Philadelphia: University of Pennsylvania Press 2007, 147–175.

Cohen, Richard I. and Mirjam Rajner. "The Return of the Wandering Jew(s) in Samuel Hirszenberg's Art." *Ars Judaica* 33. 2011, 33–56.

Daube, David. "Ahasver," *Jewish Quarterly Review* 45.3. 1955. 243–244.

Dos Santos, Isabel. "Grenzen in Heimat und Fremde: Zu Joseph Roths 'Hiob'." *Acta Germanica* 34. 2006. 71–79.

Fisch, Harold. *A Remembered Future: A Study in Literary Mythology*. Bloomington: Indiana University Press, 1984. 44–45, 61–80.

Fredriksen, Paula. *Augustine and the Jews: A Christian Defense of Jews and Judaism*. New York: Doubleday, 2008.

Garloff, Katja. "Femininity and Assimilatory Desire in Joseph Roth." *Modern Fiction Studies* 51.2. 2005. 354–373.

Gelber, Mark H. "Zur deutsch-zionistischer Rezeptionsgeschichte: Joseph Roth und die *Jüdische Rundschau*." *Von Franzos zu Canetti: Jüdische Autoren aus Österreich*. Neue Studien. Eds. Mark H. Gelber, Hans Otto Horch, Sigurd Paul Scheichl. Tübingen: Max Niemeyer Verlag, 1996. 201–209.

Gelber, Mark H. "'Juden auf Wanderschaft' und die Rhetorik der Ost-West-Debatte im Werk Joseph Roths." *Joseph Roth: Interpretation – Kritik – Rezeption*. Eds. Michael Kessler, Fritz Hackert. Stauffenberg Colloquium Bd. 15. 1990. 127–135.

Greenblatt, Stephen. *Marvelous Possessions: The Wonder of the New World*. Chicago: University of Chicago Press, 1992.

Harel-Fisch, Harold. "Elijah and the Wandering Jew." *Rabbi Joseph Lookstein Memorial Volume*. Ed. L. Landman. New York. 1980. 125–135.

Hasan-Rokem, Galit. "The Cobbler of Jerusalem in Finnish Folklore", *The Wandering Jew – Essays in the Interpretation of a Christian Legend.* Eds. Galit Hasan-Rokem and Alan Dundes. Bloomington Indiana: Indiana University Press, 1986. 119–153

Hasan-Rokem, Galit. "*Homo viator et narrans* – Medieval Jewish Voices in the European Narrative of the Wandering Jew." *Europäische Ethnologie und Folklore im internationalen Kontext*. Festschrift für Leander Petzoldt. Ed. Ingo Schneider. Frankfurt am Main: Peter Lang, 1999. 93–102.

Hasan-Rokem, Galit. *Web of Life: Folklore and Midrash in Rabbinic Literature*. Stanford CA: Stanford UP, 2000a.

Hasan-Rokem, Galit. "*Ex Oriente Fluxus*: The Wandering Jew – Oriental Crossings of the Paths of Europe", *L'orient dans l'histoire religieuse de l'Europe: L'invention des origins*. Eds. Mohammad Ali Amir-Moezzi et John Scheid. Turnhout: EPHE & Brepols, 2000b. 153–164.

Hasan-Rokem, Galit. "L'Image du juif errant et la construction de l'identité européenne." *Le juif errant: un témoin du temps*. Eds. Laurence Sigal-Klagsblad et Richard I. Cohen. Paris: Adam Biro & Musée d'art et d'histoire du Judaisme, 2001. 45–54.

Hasan-Rokem, Galit. "To Be or Not to Be – Job in Aggadic Literature?." *Mehqerei Talmud: Memorial Volume for Ephraim E. Urbach*. Eds. Yaakov Sussman and David Rosenthal. Jerusalem: Magnes Press, 2005. 385–402 (Hebrew).

Hasan-Rokem, Galit. "Carl Schmitt and Ahasver: The Idea of the State and the Wandering Jew". *Behemoth, A Journal on Civilization* 2. 2008. 4–25. http://www.behemoth-journal.de/archive/volume-1-no-2/galit-hasan-rokem/ (accessed November 2013).

Hasan-Rokem, Galit. "Jews as Postcards, or Postcards as Jews: Mobility in a Modern Genre". *Jewish Quarterly Review* 99.4. 2009. 505–546.

Hasan-Rokem, Galit. "Ahasver – The Enigma of a Name". *Jewish Quarterly Review* 100.4. 2010. 544–550.

Hasan-Rokem, Galit. "The Wandering Jew and the European Imagination: Self Image and the Image of the Other in Lion Feuchtwanger's Jud Süss". *Icons and History for Richard I. Cohen*. Ed. Ezra Mendelsohn (forthcoming; Hebrew).

Kaszynski, Stefan H. "Die Mythisierung der Wirklichkeit in Erzählwerk von Joseph Roth." *Text und Kritik* vol. 243–244. 1990. 137–143.

Koppensteiner, Jürgen. "Review of Esther Steinmann, *Von der Würde des Unscheinbaren: Sinnerfahrung bei Joseph Roth.*" *Monatshefte*, 79.2. 1987. 275–276.

Ladner, Gerhart B. "Homo Viator: Mediaeval Ideas on Alienation and Order." *Speculum* 42.2. 1967. 233–259.

Larmore, Charles. *The Romantic Legacy.* New York: Columbia University Press, 1996.

Larrimore, Mark. *The Book of Job; A Biography.* Princeton: Princeton University Press, 2013.

Lehnardt, Andreas. "Leviathan und Behemoth: mythische Urwesen in der mittelalterlichen jüdischen Tradition". *Tiere und Fabelwesen im Mittelalter.* Ed. Sabine Obermaier. Berlin: De Gruyter 2009. 105–129.

Luetzeler, H[einrich]. "Neue Romane". *Hochland* 29. 1931. 263–268.

Lunzer-Talos, Victoria. "Der Segen des ewigen Juden: Assimilation und Exil". *Joseph Roth: Ein europäisch-jüdischer Schriftsteller und österreichischer Universalist. Conditio Judaica* 82. Eds. Johann Georg Lughofer und Mira Miladinović Zalaznik. Berlin: De Gruyter, 2011. 23–38.

Magris, Claudio. "Der ostjüdische Odysseus." *Joseph Roth und die Tradition.* Ed. David Bronsen. Darmstadt: Agora 1975. 181–226.

Neubaur, Leonhard. Die Sage vom Ewigen Juden, Leipzig, 1893.

Pardes, Ilana. *Agnon's Moonstruck Lovers: The Song of Songs in Israeli Culture.* Seattle: University of Washington Press, 2013.

Parry, Christoph. "Joseph Roth in den Augen der Nachwelt: Migration, Mythos, Melancholie." *Joseph Roth: Ein europäisch-jüdischer Schriftsteller und österreichischer Universalist. Conditio Judaica*, 82. 2011. 303–313.

Reich-Ranicki, Marcel. *Nachprüfung: Aufsätze über Deutsche Schriftsteller von Gestern.* München: Deutsche Taschenbuch Verlag, 1977.

Ricoeur, Paul. *Interpretation Theory: Discourse and the Surplus of Meaning.* Fort Worth: Texas Christian University Press, 1976.

Ricoeur, Paul. "Philosophical Hermeneutics and Biblical Hermeneutics." *From Text to Action: Essays in Hermeneutics* II. Trans. Kathleen Blarney and John B. Thompson. Evanston: Northwestern University Press, 1991.

Ritter, Alexander "Über das 'Gleichgewicht zwischen der Tischplatte und ihrer künstlichen Verlängerung': Zur kulturkritischen Antithese 'Amerika' und der Lebensbalance in Joseph Roths *Hiob* (1930)". *Joseph Roth: Ein europäisch-jüdischer Schriftsteller und österreichischer Universalist. Conditio Judaica* 82. Eds. Johann Georg Lughofer and Mira Miladinović Zalaznik. Berlin: De Gruyter, 2011. 87–100.

Robertson, Ritchie. "Roth's *Hiob* and the Traditions of the Ghetto Fiction." *Co-existent Contradictions: Joseph Roth in Retrospect.* Ed. Helen Chambers. Riverside CA: Ariadne Press 1991. 185–200.

Roth, Joseph. *Die Flucht ohne Ende. Ein Bericht.* 1927. Köln: Kiepenheuer & Witsch, 2010.

Roth, Joseph. *Flight Without End.* 1977. Translated by David Le Vay. Woodstock NY: The Overlook Press, 2003.

Roth, Joseph. *Juden auf Wanderschaft.* 1927. Preface for 2nd edition 1937. Köln: Kiepenheuer & Witsch 2000.

Roth, Joseph. *The Wandering Jews.* Translated by Michael Hofmann. New York NY: W. W. Norton & Co., 2011.

Roth, Joseph. *Hiob. Roman eines einfachen Mannes.* 1930. Wiesbaden: Marixverlag, 2010.

Roth, Joseph. *Job. The Story of a Simple Man*. 1931. Translated by Dorothy Thompson. Woodstock NY: The Overlook Press, 2003.

Roth, Joseph. *Job. The Story of a Simple Man*. Translated by Ross Benjamin. Brooklyn NY: Archipelago Books, 2010.

Roth, Joseph. *Radetzkymarsch*. 1932. Köln: Kiepenheuer & Witsch, 2005.

Roth, Joseph. *The Radetzky March*. Trans. Joachim Neigroschel, introduction by Alan Bance. New York NY: Alfred A. Knopf Everyman's Library, 1996.

Roth, Joseph. "Der Segen des ewigen Juden: Assimilation und Exil." *Werke* vol. 3, Köln: Kiepenhauer & Witsch, 1989. 527–532. Originally published in *Die Wahrheit* 13.30. Prag 1935. 4–5.

Roth, Joseph. *Werke in sechs Banden* hrsg. und Nachwort von Fritz Hackert, Bd. 3. Köln: Kiepenheuer & Witsch, 1989.

Roth, Joseph. *Der Leviathan*. In. *Pariser Tageszeitung*, 1938. Köln: Kiepenheuer & Witsch, 2005.

Roth, Joseph. *The Leviathan*. Trans. Michael Hofmann. 2002. New York NY: New Directions 2011.

Roth, Joseph. *The Collected Stories* of. Trans. and with introduction by Michael Hofmann. New York: W. W. Norton & Co., 2002.

Roussel, Hélène, Lutz Winckler Eds. *Rechts und links der Seine. Pariser Tageblatt und Pariser Tageszeitung 1933–1940*. Tübingen: Niemeyer, 2002.

Schirmann, Jefim [Hayim]. "The Battle between Behemoth and Leviathan according to an Ancient Hebrew Piyyut." *Publications of Israel Academy of Sciences and Humanities*, 4. Jerusalem: Israel Academy of Sciences and Humanities, 1970.

Schmitt, Carl. *The Leviathan in the State Theory of Thomas Hobbes. Meaning and Failure of a Political Symbol*. 1938. Trans. G. Schwab and E. Hilfstein. Westport, CT: Greenwood Press, 1996.

Schmitt, Carl. *Römischer Katholizismus und politische Form*. 1923. Stuttgart: Klett-Cotta, 2008.

Schmitt, Carl. *Roman Catholicism and Political Form*. Trans. G. I. Ulmen. Westport, CT: Greenwood Press, 1996.

Scholem, Gershom. *On the Mystical Shape of the Godhead: Basic Concepts in the Kabbalah*. Translated from the German by Joachim Neugroschel. New York: Schocken Books, 1991.

Schönborn, Sibylle. "Zwischen Lemberg und Marseille: Joseph Roths Europa als 'Dritter Raum'." *Rivista di letteratura e cultura tedesca* 7. 2007. 49–56.

Shaked, Gershon. *Identity: Jewish Literatures in European Languages*. Haifa: Haifa University Press, 2006. 234–256 (Hebrew).

Steiner, Carl. "Frankreichbild und Katholizismus bei Joseph Roth". *The German Quarterly* 46.1. 1973. 12–21.

Steinmann, Esther. *Von der Würde des Unscheinbaren: Sinnerfahrung bei Joseph Roth*. Tübingen: Niemeyer, 1984. Quoted in Koppensteiner 1987.

Wiener, Aharon. *The Prophet Elijah in the Development of Judaism: a Depth-psychological Study*. London: Routledge & Kegan Paul, 1978.

Zweig, Stefan. "Joseph Roth." *Stefan Zweig: Europäisches Erbe*. Ed. Richard Friedenthal. Frankfurt am Main: Fischer Taschenbuch Verlag, 1994. 267–280. Quoted in Parry, 2011. 308–309.

יוזף רות, **יהודים נודדים** תרגם מגרמנית והוסיף הערות: יונתן ניראד; עורך ראשי: אוריאל קון; עריכת תרגום: דיטה גוט, ירושלים: סמטאות, 2011.

Robert Alter
Hebrew Poems Rewriting Job

I feel obliged to begin by explaining a point of literary culture that will be self-evident to any literate Hebrew reader but that may be slightly perplexing to anybody else. The Bible, though standing at a remove of two and a half to three millennia from the contemporary world, remains a potent presence in Hebrew poetry. Perhaps the closest analogy in English would be Shakespeare, though there is, I think, a difference at least in degree. Admittedly, biblical literacy in Israel and therefore engagement in the Bible are not what they once were, but the Bible is still the strong and perennially relevant foundation on which subsequent strata of Hebrew expression have been constructed. There are obviously many Hebrew poets now, minimalist or otherwise, who avoid any reference to the Bible, yet one suspects that it takes a certain conscious resolve to do so. It is hard, writing in Hebrew, to think about outrageous or unreasonable sacrifice without referring to the Binding of Isaac; to contemplate the futility of human endeavor without alluding to Ecclesiastes; to celebrate the joy of erotic experience without recalling the Song of Songs; to confront the manifest injustice of the world order and its terrible toll of undeserved suffering without invoking Job. A literary person in Israel of course may be moved by all sorts of writers outside the framework of Hebrew tradition, from Homer to Proust to Faulkner. Accessible in his or her own language, however, are the Psalms, the great narrative of David, the poetry of Isaiah, and much else – all of which is as good as it gets in any literature. There are, one must concede, some hindrances, but for the most part only minor ones, to this linguistic accessibility. I would say that the distance between the language of the Bible and modern Hebrew is roughly like that between Elizabethan and modern English. There is a vast wealth of vocabulary that the language has acquired after the Bible, from the rabbinic period to the day before yesterday. The grammar is slightly different, and some biblical words have changed in meaning. The verb that in modern Hebrew means "to think," for example, in the Bible means "to plan" or "to devise"; so a contemporary reader could misconstrue certain statements, just as a contemporary English reader might think that "meat" in Shakespeare was something bought from a butcher and not a general word for food. Notwithstanding such bits of static in the transmission of the biblical language to the modern ear, a Hebrew poet in the twentieth century or even in the twenty-first can read, say, the sublime celebration of creation that is Psalm 8 or the somber, mesmerizing prose-poem that begins Ecclesiastes and be immediately moved by its language, perhaps even drawn to use it in some way.

It is instructive that the generation of Hebrew poets who became active in the 1950s, though they had agendas that might have led them away from the Bible, reverted to it with surprising frequency. This is true of Natan Zach, whose role in the literary scene I will explain momentarily; it is true of Dalia Ravikovich; it is true of early and late Yehuda Amichai, who at the end of his career devoted an entire section of his final volume of poetry to contending with the Bible.

Natan Zach has long been a cultural eminence in Israel (in one of the poems we will look at, he even describes himself as having been enlisted, despite himself, as a national prophet), but he is a relatively unfamiliar figure elsewhere, so a few words of introduction are in order. He was born in Berlin, in 1930, and came with his parents to Palestine in 1935. (It is an odd coincidence, strictly the product of the historical circumstances of those years, that three of the leading poets of this generation – Zach, Amichai, and Dan Pagis – were native speakers of German.) At the beginning of the 1950s, he was part of a small group of young poets self-designated as *Likrat* ("Toward") that aimed to bring about a revolution in Hebrew verse. The poets who had been dominant in the 1930s and 1940s characteristically cultivated a high literary Hebrew, often exhibiting ingenious linguistic artifice, and favored metrically regular rhyming forms, influenced by Russian models. The Likrat poets, by contrast, enamored of Anglo-American modernist verse, aspired to make Hebrew poetry colloquial, in touch with the sounds and rhythms and lexicon of everyday life, in modes that were understated and ironic rather than rhetorical. Zach's role in Likrat, and in the years after its brief lifespan, was that of literary ideologue, sometimes excoriating the poets of the previous generation, and articulating a poetic agenda. He seems to have aspired to be a kind of Ezra Pound for his fellow modernizing poets and even claimed, against all evidence, to have been the mentor in style of Amichai, who would prove to be by far the greatest poet to emerge from this group. Zach himself has been a prolific poet over the years (his collected works take up three large volumes) but it is my candid opinion that much of the poetry is rather mediocre. Some of his poems, like many of Amichai's, have entered Israeli popular culture by being set to music; most of his poetic production strikes me as uninspired, however, more self-consciously willed than poetically imagined. In my view, he has been more a *figure* in Israeli poetry than a poet of the first order.

Yet Zach's engagement with the Bible has generated several of his most deeply interesting poems. It may not be an entirely anticipated engagement in a poet who advocated a vernacular idiom and sought to follow the path of Eliot, Pound, and Auden. Unlike Amichai, whose relation to the Bible is usually expressed through allusion and sometimes a kind of creative exegesis (often pointedly heterodox), Zach is more drawn to rewriting the biblical texts as a mode of personal expression. The three poems about Job that I would like to consider manifest three rather different ways of treating the biblical materials.

"For Job It Was a One-Time Thing" carries out a strategy that has often been deployed by the Anglo-American modernists in relating to classical texts. One might think of Eliot's "Sweeney Among the Nightingales," in which Aeschylus's *Agamemnon* is invoked in the Greek epigraph and in the final stanza; in this poem, however, the high dignity of Greek tragedy has been reduced to vulgar figures in a sordid setting – some sort of cheap pub – and Clytemnestra's modern avatar, "Rachel née Rabinowitz," is an animalistic creature that "Tears at the grapes with murderous paws." (The anti-Semitic innuendo is part of the contrast Eliot intends between lofty Greek tragedy and a fallen modern reality infested by vile Jews.) In Zach's poem, the aggressively colloquial diction, reflecting the speaker's modern, very post-biblical location, is flaunted from beginning to end.

For Job It Was a One-time Thing

For Job it was a one-time thing
While he was yet speaking, there came also another
first the cattle, then the camels and the sons and the daughters,
what can you say, good healthy blows.
Then came the eternal debates,
the claims and the blames, and the promises, the promises.

For me it's not so dramatic.
A tiny blow in the morning, sometimes just
a slap or an accidental tap.
Sometimes even a glitch, not divine.
And a little bruise, sometimes a black eye
or just sight problems, or forms,
or a landlord, work, or letters, a wife, in the evening.
And on Friday two blows, to pay your dues,
and on Saturday you rest and recover.

Once I was in another land,
where no one knew my name,
and God and the Adversary didn't compete over my righteousness
and altogether nobody made a fuss, *no breach and no shouting*, and
it was a bit boring but wonderful. And everything was
okay but not as it should be. And I returned to my place
and, look, I'm a prophet,
a nationalized Jobchik kicking and screaming
me me.

The italicized second line, of course, is a quotation from the point in the frame-story of Job when the messengers appear, each bearing successive ill tidings.

Everything else in the language of the poem, with one additional exception, is flaunted vernacular. The flaunting begins with the very first word, *etsel*, which is slightly lower in register than my English equivalent "for" and reflects a colloquial usage that derives from the homey Yiddish *bei*. The same register, of course, is manifested in "a one-time thing" (*had-pa'ami*). The opening line also nicely articulates a sharp contrast between two different orders of time: Job, a figure in a memorable literary narrative, moves through the linear time of a clear-cut plot in which one thing follows another until a resolution is finally achieved. His dreadful suffering occurs in a quick sequence of catastrophic events, triggering his debate with the three comforters, and then is reversed in the restoration of his fortunes at the end of the story. For the speaker of the poem, however, misery is both habitual and trivial, and time a cycle of banal repetitions. Instead of a catastrophic "blow" – in the Bible, *makah* often implies lethal force and is also a term for "plague" – what he receives is a *makonet*, "blow" with a diminutive suffix, represented in my translation as "tiny blow" because of the difficulty in English with diminutive endings. The suffering of Job's modern counterpart is a matter of routine – an annoying bump here or there, sight problems, landlords, paperwork, domestic difficulties.

The generalized modern ordinary man of the first two verse-paragraphs becomes explicitly autobiographical in the final one. Zach is no doubt alluding to his extended stay in England in the 1960s, some of it in the provinces. There he enjoyed the comfort of anonymity, being off-stage both from cosmic drama where Job's fate was played out and from Israeli culture. In this setting, "nobody made a fuss" (more literally, "bothered," *hitrid*), and, in the poem's other biblical citation, there was "no breach and no shouting" (Psalm 144:14). Not being the object of divine or human attention was obviously something of a relief, yet it also left the speaker with a sense of lack of reality – "everything was okay but not as it should be." The place to which he returns is of course Israel, where he finds himself a recognized cultural figure, a kind of prophet despite himself, "a nationalized Jobchik" – not Job, with his one-time suffering etched in narrative, but a Job with a comic diminutive suffix, a pygmy Job whose pain is devoid of dignity or drama. The biblical Job is an exemplary figure of human suffering. His diminished modern counterpart, dragged by his heels into the public arena, merely wants to be himself, to be left alone with his petty miseries, bearing no message, prophetic or otherwise, simply yelling "me me."

The second Zach poem I will consider, "Sometimes He Misses," does not trace the familiar modernist antithesis between contemporary reality and foundational text but instead expresses a relation to the biblical story that one can call midrashic. In keeping with this aim, the language of the poem is not flaunted colloquial, like that of "For Job It Was a One-Time Thing"; instead it exhibits a kind of modern middle diction, more literary than vernacular, in which the bits of biblical citations and echoes are seamlessly integrated rather than standing out in sharp contrast. It is worth noting that the biblical intertext for this poem is exclusively the frame-story of Job, not the debate and complaint against God that make up the poetic body of the book.

Sometimes He Misses

Sometimes God misses
His sweet servant Job. But he's dead.
Job is now far from God
as from other things, angels.
What should God do?

He's reading – believe it or not –
in Psalms. He still doesn't know it by heart,
and the words there are so soothing:
so many poems.
A great and wide sea and numberless
beasts great and small
and trees, lots of trees, and always water.

There is no darkness nor shadow of death,
He recites to Himself in a faint voice
and then remembers something in loving rebuke:
God is already weeping,
refusing to be consoled, He has no consolation
for His sweet servant Job, the sweetest of servants,
each of whose eyeballs was like an Eden,
there's been none like His servant Job, to this day, in all times.

We recall that in the frame-story God repeatedly refers to Job, with pride and satisfaction, as "My servant Job," both in His initial exchanges with the Adversary and in His closing affirmation of Job's righteousness. Yet the God of the biblical story remains a remote and rather enigmatic figure. If He is so pleased with His devoted servant, why does He agree to the perverse wager that the Adversary proposes? What does He feel about the hideous chain of afflictions that the man He supposedly cherishes is made to undergo? Biblical narrative in general famously abounds in unexplained gaps, a trait spectacularly evident in the frame-story of Job. One of the characteristic operations of midrash is to fill in these gaps, thereby offering explanation and motivation where none is provided, thereby fleshing out what is unstated in the biblical text. In Zach's poem, this process of filling in the gaps begins when the seemingly unfeeling God of the biblical tale is said at the outset to "miss" (or "long for") Job; in the next line the poet inserts the adjective "sweet" into the biblical epithet "My servant Job." An implicit problem in the biblical book is the immense distance between God and Job. (The Zelda poem, as we shall see, highlights this feature.) Determinations about Job's fate are made in the celestial assembly far above him, of which he cannot have the slightest inkling. In the poetic body of the book, God does not answer any of Job's complaints and accusations until His thundering speech from the whirlwind, which is hardly an intimate response.

The God of Zach's poem does not express remorse or sorrow over Job's sufferings but rather painful regret that Job has died, as all people must. God, it seems, has missed an opportunity, as most of us do in our loving relationships: when Job was with Him, He could have been close to His sweet servant; on the evidence of the biblical text, however, He failed to do so. Now Job is gone, and God, who for better or for worse is immortal, struggles to come to terms with the loss. The fitting – and also amusing – source of consolation He seeks is Psalms, another of the various books He has inspired, though He confesses that He does not yet know it by heart. At this point, the poem glides smoothly into quotation and reminiscence of the biblical book in question. God reads a verse from the great panoramic ode to creation that is Psalm 104 – in the King James Version of verse 24, cited here, "this great and wide sea, wherein are things creeping innumerable, both small and great beasts." Perhaps if He can no longer enjoy the presence of Job, He can at least contemplate the teeming riches of the wonderful creation He has made. The many trees invoked recall the trees of the forest that in other psalms sing out joyously, just as the water alludes both to the streams, in the very first psalm, by which the flourishing tree of the righteous is planted, and to the repeated references to the breakers of the sea, over which God holds sway.

The concluding verse-paragraph begins with a quotation not from the Book of Psalms (which God has been reading) but from Job 34:22: *there is no darkness nor shadow of death*. In a strategy not uncommon in classical midrash, these words are recontextualized to mean something quite different from what they mean in their biblical source. The entire verse in Job reads: "There is no darkness nor shadow of death where the workers of iniquity may hide themselves." Zach, omitting the latter part of the verse, represents the bereaved God as seeking in the biblical words a consoling notion that death will have no dominion. God's voice, however, is faint – He really doesn't believe it. In a crescendo of repetitions of the loving epithet, Job at the end is not only a sweet servant but "the sweetest of servants." His preciousness to God is concretized in the penultimate line, "each of whose eyeballs was like an Eden." This slightly odd locution is probably a transmogrification of an idiom, found in both

Hebrew and English, for great affection (*kevavat eyno*, "like the apple of his eye") and is encouraged by the paired alliterations of ***galgal ayin*** and ***gan adanim***, which my translation tries to emulate with **e**ach / **e**yeballs / **E**den.

In the end, the gap in the biblical text that Zach's poem fills is not a matter of explanatory detail or motivation but an emotional gap. He transforms the remote God of the Book of Job into a compassionate, loving God. This deity, however, is not a loving God in any Christian sense but instead a thoroughly humanized figure. If in fact He had great feelings of fondness (not expressed biblically) for His servant Job, He now is inconsolable in missing him, just as we ordinary humans are when we have lost a loved one, with the added anguish that He will go on missing Job forever because, unlike the flesh-and-blood bereaved, His existence is without end.

If the first of these three Zach poems is colloquial and the second cast in middle diction, the third is entirely biblical. Indeed, it presents a limit-case for literary allusion, for its twelve lines contain not a single word that is not a quotation from the Bible – specifically, from Psalms, Genesis, and Job. What is remarkable is that through the simple strategy of repetition, syntactic variation, and interweaving three biblical texts Zach has created a haunting original poem.

Man As the Grass His Days

Man as the grass his days.
His days as the grass.
The days of man as the grass
his days.
Fear not.

Man unto trouble is born.
Is born unto trouble.
Man is born unto trouble
is born.
Fear not.

And the sparks fly upward.
Upward the sparks.

My translation throughout uses the phrasing of the King James Bible, the English version most familiar to readers of a literary bent. The Hebrew, one should say, is more arrestingly compact than the English, a reflection of the powerful concision of biblical Hebrew that is difficult to reproduce in any modern Western language. The poem's first line, just three words in the Hebrew, is taken from Psalms 103:15; withering grass as an image of ephemerality is a poetic commonplace in the Bible and occurs with slightly different wording in Isaiah and elsewhere. The next verse in Psalm 103 continues this somber meditation on the frailty and brevity of life: "For the wind passeth over it, and it is gone; and the place thereof shall know it no more." The poem's second, third, and fourth lines each repeat the first, merely changing the order of the words. The effect is to transform the three biblical words initially cited into a kind of mantra on mortality: the poem turns "man," "days," and "grass" round and round in a mesmerizing spell, making the reader deeply absorb their message of human transience. The two words of the fifth line introduce a counterpoint. "Fear not," *al tiyra*, appears numerous times in the Bible, usually spoken by God in reassurance to a human being. Its first occurrence is in Genesis 15:1: "Fear not, Abram: I am thy shield." The speaker, confronted through the text from Psalms by the bleak terror of mortality, seeks, perhaps desperately, for consolation in these two reassuring words found in other biblical texts.

The phrases from Psalms and Genesis are then juxtaposed, for the remaining seven lines of the poem, with a verse from Job (5:7): "Man is born unto trouble, as the sparks fly upward." This, of course, is still another unsettling image of man's existential plight. Zach again uses the strategy of repetition to produce an almost hypnotic intensification of the already somber biblical words. "Trouble" is repeated three times and "is born" (one word in the original Hebrew) four times, the fourth coming at the end of the sequence; these repetitions invite us to focus on the ill-starred condition of being born, the entering from the womb into the cycle of futility and mortality that is the lot of humankind. This bleak perspective, like the one from Psalms, also needs the urgent counterpoint of "Fear not." The poem's final two lines pick up the second part of the verse from Job. There may be an implicit linkage between the image of sparks and the image of grass – flying sparks can ignite withering grass – so that the metaphors combined transfigure human transience and trouble into an altogether combustible condition. The penultimate line is an exact quotation of Job, with the miniscule difference that instead of "as," *ke*, Zach uses "and," *ve*. Then in the final line he once more turns around the syntax, eliminating the verb "fly," *uf*. The effect is slightly disorienting: the sparks rise up (*yagbihu*), but are denied actual flight; the poem's final image is disembodied sparks rising into the void.

The decision to weave "Man As the Grass His Days" entirely from phrases from the Bible is an unusual one, yet its execution is a tour de force. It places the Book of Job, with its dark sense of suffering as humanity's ineluctable fate, in dialogue with the psalmist's notion of the ephemerality of human life, and then strives to set God's two-word assurance to His chosen ones against both of these. By emphatic, artful repetition, the chasm between the biblical texts and the modern reader is bridged: the biblical words that constitute the poem become both the poet's and ours as readers of the poem.

Zach, as I have indicated, is a perfectly secular poet to whom the Bible, and the Book of Job in particular, speaks strongly in a variety of ways. I would now like to take up the instructive counter-example of a seriously devout poet who also proves to be a boldly challenging reader of Job. Zelda (born Zelda Schneerson) (1914–1984) was from a distinguished Hasidic family; she was a cousin of Zalman Schneerson, the Lubavitcher rebbe, some of whose followers consider him, even after his death, to be the messiah. Though I doubt that Zelda ever entertained such notions about her cousin, she certainly remained a pious ultra-Orthodox woman all her life. She was also a remarkable poet, with a sensibility that often seems daringly modern – not what one usually thinks of as Orthodox. It is revelatory that Amos Oz, in his autobiographical *A Tale of Love and Darkness,* reports that when she was his teacher in a religious elementary school in Jerusalem, she took him aside, recognizing him as a student with literary gifts, and would read with him works by Uri Zvi Greenberg and other Hebrew modernist poets. She also had no difficulty in befriending the younger feminist poet Yona Walloch, famous, among other things, for writing an erotic poem that involved the paraphernalia of male prayer in the act of sex.

Unlike the Zach poems, there are no quotations from Job in Zelda's "Be Not Far"; indeed, there is no unambiguous indication that the poem has anything to do with Job until the revelation in the final line makes clear that the entire poem is a profound and illuminating response to the biblical book.

Be Not Far

The comforters come into the outer
court
standing by the gate
that faces the valley of the shadow of death
and its terror all around.
To stand by the gate is all
the comforters can bear.
My soul, too, is thousands of leagues
from the self of the weeper. A divine decree.

Creator of nights and wind,
is not this terrible weeping before You,
be not far –
let not millions of light years
stand as a barrier
between You and Job.

The first word of the poem, *hamenahamim,* "the comforters," provides a minimal clue about its the relation to Job. Eliphaz, Bildad, and Zophar are not explicitly termed comforters in the Bible but rather *re'im*, "companions" or "friends." But they are linked with the verb "to comfort" when they first come to visit Job after the disasters that befall him. In any case, the initial setting of the poem looks distinctly contemporary, not something from the land of Uz. The house, with its outer court surrounded by a gated wall, sounds like the sort one would find in Meah Shearim, the prominent ultra-Orthodox quarter in Jerusalem. The speaker of the poem, evidently standing outside and looking at the comforters, who appear to have come to the home of the bereaved in observance of the mourning practice of *shivah,* is herself part of this contemporary scene.

In the fourth and fifth line, however, Zelda effects one of the startling shifts of perspective that characterize much of her poetry. Beyond the gate there may or may not be an actual valley, but here it becomes a mythic vista, "the valley of the shadow of death / and its terror all around." The term for "terror," *eimah,* is more than mere fear, and is associated in biblical usage with the awesome might of the deity and with the panic-inducing fright of devastating defeat and death. We then return to the comforters, their hesitation in standing at the gate an expression of their incapacity to cross the chasm and enter into the anguish of the bereaved person. Here we might well begin to think of Job's comforters and their abysmal failure to understand what he has undergone.

At this point, the speaker of the poem explicitly introduces herself, defining her distance from the mourner – pointedly, he is not called this but rather is identified as someone weeping – not as the distance from the gate to the house but, psychologically and emotionally, as thousands of leagues. (The Hebrew term used here inscribes a small but effective midrashic gesture, amplifying the mythic thrust of the poem, because *parsa'ot,* "parasangs," which I have rendered as "leagues," has a distinctive coloration of early rabbinic literature.) The phrase at the end of the first verse-paragraph, "A divine decree," *gezeirah hi,* points to a kind of theological nuance in this remarkably efficient and concise poetic vehicle. It is how a pious person would say, "Well, that's the way things are." The problem is that there is something disturbing about the way things are as, presumably, God has determined them to be. Built into human nature itself, as the speaker painfully realizes through unflinching introspection, is a kind of monadic egoism. We may aspire to deep empathy with others in their suffering, but each of us is imprisoned in his or her own self, unable to bridge the gap, despite the best of intentions, between self and other. If this is how God has decreed things to be, one might be drawn to question the decree. This sort of questioning returns us to the Book of Job, to the behavior of the comforters and to God's own seeming impassivity. The second verse-paragraph then turns directly to God.

Zelda's phrasing in the first three lines of her address to God reflects the ease with which she works with traditional Hebrew while making it something quite new. The words of the poem's title, *al tirhaq,* "be not far," occur frequently in psalms of supplication (again, I offer them in the King James Version) as the expression of a desperate sense of abandonment by God, and here that feeling of God's being far away is given startling poetic realization. "Creator of nights and wind," *yotseir leylot varuah* (the last word could also mean "spirit") sounds biblical, but it is biblical with important differences. It appears to build on an epithet for God in Amos 4:13, *yotseir harim uvorei' ruah,* "shaper of mountains and creator of wind." In the poem, however, Instead of "mountains" we have "nights" in the plural – not the night that with day constitutes the diurnal cycle but the nights when each of us is alone with his or her fears and grief. The full force of "the weeper" at the end of the first verse-paragraph now becomes evident: the speaker, standing by or outside the gate, has been hearing a terrible sound of weeping from within the house. Can God, who we are told is merciful, remain distant from this intolerable suffering? The speaker's sense of her distance, and that of the comforters, from the mourner's anguish is in the poem's second movement extrapolated to God's apparent distance. Another small verbal choice brilliantly articulates the distance: the speaker's removal at thousands of leagues becomes the divine removal at millions of light years. Here, the midrashic and biblical frame of reference explodes into a modern scientific vision of a vast cosmos millions of light years in breadth.

The end of the poem, where Job's name finally appears, offers a searching perception of the biblical text. In the poetic debate, Job's anger and anguish are repeatedly focused on his feeling that God remains remote from him in his suffering. He would like to confront God face to face, to exact from Him some answer, judicial or otherwise, about why he has been subjected to such catastrophes. In Zelda's reading, God has interposed a barrier of millions of light years between Himself and Job – and, by implication, between Himself and every human sufferer – and the speaker, invoking the two-word phrase from the psalms of supplication, implores God to cross that terrible distance. It is hard to imagine how a biblical text could be put to more powerful use: the poet makes Job's comforters into an image of the distance between the present-day comforters and herself and the bereaved person's grief; identifying with Job, she picks up Job's desperate sense of a vast unspannable chasm between himself and the God whom he feels must somehow be responsible for what has befallen him.

It should be evident from these examples how the Book of Job – the plot of its frame-story, the substance of its poetic argument, bits of its language – becomes a rich resource for both these modern Hebrew poets. Intertextuality, moreover, as has often been observed, is a two-way street. The poets, exploiting the biblical text in unanticipated ways, also end up throwing light on it. Job has been the object of endless philological analysis and of literary and theological interpretation, some of it even instructive. Yet one might argue that certain aspects of the ancient text become most urgently alive through the modern literary remakings of it. In the exemplary instance of *Moby-Dick*, Melville understood – and made us see – with far greater penetration than the scholars the radical implications of the rejection in Job of the anthropocentric view of creation. Zach's three poems respectively illuminate the contrast between the high drama of Job's suffering and the banality of our everyday equivalent; the missing element of divine compassion in God's reported relationship with His favored servant; and the full, frightening power of the Job poet's vision of human life as relentless trouble, transience, and instability. Zelda's poem helps us to understand more keenly the existential isolation that is inseparable from Job's suffering: the friends who ostensibly come to console him have no access to his zone of anguish, and the God to whom he addresses his pleas remains remote, hidden, inscrutable. Any foundational literary work continues to live most amply in its imaginative interpretations and transformations by subsequent writers. These two modern Hebrew poets, who directly engage the Book of Job in its original language, make that vividly clear in their respective poems.

Freddie Rokem
The Bible on the Hebrew/Israeli Stage: Hanoch Levin's *The Torments of Job* as a Modern Tragedy[1]

> Finally Job cried out:
> God damn the day I was born
> and the night that forced me from the womb.
> On that day – let there be darkness;
> let it never have been created;
> let it sink back into the void.
>
> *The Book of Job*[2]

In order to understand the importance of Hanoch Levin's adaptation of the biblical Book of Job, *The Torments of Job* (first performed in 1981), which I consider a modern tragedy with profound and uncanny, even nihilistic, implications, it is necessary to present certain basic contexts of the Zionist and Israeli culture – in particular of the theatre – within which Levin's play was written and performed and to which it reacts with such brilliance. Levin's adaptation – which in every sense is an original play by Levin – was first performed in the early 1980's; thus the play and its performance (as well as much of Levin's previous and subsequent work) constituted a radical critique of mainstream Zionist-Israeli culture and its basic values. These values were initially inspired by a strong sense of ideological and physical continuity between the Bible and the state of Israel; however, after the 1967 Six Day War as well as after the 1973 October War these presuppositions gradually came to face more open interrogation.

I begin this essay by exploring the more comprehensive cultural and aesthetic contexts of the Bible as a Hebrew "classic," which, under certain condi-

---

1 I have examined different aspects of Hanoch Levin's adaptation of the Book of Job in some of my previous publications: see Freddie Rokem, "The Bible and the Avant-Garde: The Search for a Classical Tradition in the Israeli Theatre," in: *European Review* 9.3 (2001): 305–317; Rokem, "Narratives of Armed Conflict: Tragedy and History in Hanoch Levin's *Murder*," in: *Theatre Journal* 54.4 (2002): 555–572; Rokem, Introduction, in: Levin, Hanoch, *The Labor of Life: Selected Plays*, trans. Barbara Harshav, Stanford University Press, Palo Alto 2003, ix–xxxv; and Rokem, "Job's Soul and Otto Weininger's Torments: Jewish Themes In The Theatre of Hanoch Levin and Yehoshua Sobol," in: *Jewish Theatre: A Global View*, ed. Edna Nahshon, Brill, Boston 2009, 257–268. My basic understanding of the play has not changed over the years. In *Performing History*, I presented a detailed analysis of another Levin play with a similar structure, *The*

tions, can serve as a rich source of inspiration for different genres of avant-garde arts, in this case the theatre. I continue my discussion by presenting some general observations about Levin's critical stance to the hegemonic Zionist culture. The analysis of *The Torments of Job* is preceded by a general discussion of the relationships between tragedy and logic, which will serve as the theoretical basis for my analysis of the play and the performance of it that Levin directed in 1981. I argue that the play is a modern tragedy, and one that confronts in particular the ethical aspects of what it means to be human.

1 Cultural and Dramaturgical Contexts for Biblical Theatre

There are several features that distinguish Israeli theatre from most other national theatre traditions. First, it is a young tradition. The Habima Theatre, the

---

Boy Dreams, focusing on the narrative structure of threats as well as their characteristics as speech acts; see Rokem, *Performing History: Theatrical Representations of the Past in Contemporary Theatre*, University of Iowa Press, Iowa City 2000. In *Philosophers and Thespians*, I attempted to theorize the relations between wishes, promises and threats; see Rokem, *Philosophers and Thespians: Thinking Performance*, Stanford University Press, Stanford 2010. In this article, I return to several of the ideas presented in my previous publications on the Hebrew and Israeli theatre as well as the work of Hanoch Levin; here I contextualize them from a much wider perspective, mainly trying to define an aspect of modern tragedy which, as I argue, has previously not received due attention. The general framework for the analysis of tragedy that I propose was first presented at the Drama and Philosophy conference at the New University of Lisbon in January 2013; an earlier version of this particular analysis of *The Torments of Job* was presented at the symposium "The Book of Job: Aesthetics, Ethics and Hermeneutics," held at Princeton University in October 2012. Parts of the present version have previously been published as "The Logic of/in Tragedy: Hanoch Levin's Drama *The Torments of Job*," in: *Modern Drama* 56.4 (Winter 2013): 521–539. I wish to thank the participants at these conferences for their valuable comments and the editors of *Modern Drama* for their permission to publish the article here. For additional articles in English on Levin's *The Torments of Job*, see Sharon Aronson-Lehavi,"Transformations of Religious Performativity: Sacrificial Figures in Modern Experimental Theatre," in: *Performance and Spirituality* 3.1 (2012): 57–70, http://www.utdl.edu/ojs/index.php/pas/article/view/43 last accessed Nov 23, 2013; Yael Feldman, "Deconstructing the Biblical Sources in Israeli Theater: *Yisurei Iyov* by Hanoch Levin," *AJS Review* 12.2 (1987): 251–77, http://journals.cambridge.org/action/displayAbstract?fromPage=online&aid=4497552; and Matthias Naumann, *Dramaturgie der Drohung. Das Theater des israelischen Dramatikers und Regisseurs Hanoch Levin*, Terctum, Marburg 2006.

2 *The Book of Job*, trans. Stephen Mitchell, Harper Perennial, New York 1986, 13; all passages quoted are from this translation.

first professional Hebrew theatre – meaning that the people who founded it considered the art of the stage to be their major profession as well as a spiritual vocation – was founded in 1917, in Moscow, in the wake of the Bolshevik Revolution and the Spring of Nations, reinforcing the initial multi-cultural and multi-national ideals of these events. Only in the mid-1930s, however, after the Habima Theatre collective had settled in the steadily growing city of Tel Aviv, and after several other theatres had been established among the Jewish settlers, did the Hebrew theatre – which, in 1948, became the Israeli theatre, following the declaration of the independence of the state of Israel – begin to have a somewhat more significant influence on the cultural life of the Jewish population of what was, from 1917 to 1948, British Mandatory Palestine. Today – 66 years later – the Israeli theatre has developed into a complex system of established theatres and includes a broad range of more avant-garde fringe groups, including other live performing arts, including ballet/dance and opera. The Habima Theatre, founded in Moscow as an avant-garde theatre collective, was declared the Israeli national theatre in the mid 1950's.

Owing to its relatively young age, the Israeli theatre lacks an indigenous tradition of classical plays which could be regularly included in the repertoire. Beginning with the establishment of the state, but particularly since the 1960's, a remarkable number of Israeli plays have been written and performed; in most cases, however, these have been performed only once, in a single production, after which most have become more or less forgotten. No more than a handful of plays written in Hebrew have been performed more than once and become "canonized" within this young tradition.[3] Theatre traditions with longer history usually have a significant reservoir of "classical" plays, to which young theatre makers feel a need to return and reinterpret in new contexts. And although many plays had been written in Hebrew before the revival of Hebrew as a spoken language at the end of the nineteenth century and the beginning of the twentieth century – a project in which Habima and the other theatres played an important role – they were as a rule not suited for staging. These were "literary" plays, written in a literary language, whereas the theatres served as a model for how Hebrew sounds and communicates when spoken.

Most of the classics that were performed on the Hebrew stages were translations of foreign plays, from other dramatic and theatrical traditions. Such "foreign" classics are, of course, performed in all countries, albeit usually in combination with productions of "local" or "native" works. Besides presenting

---

3 See Yael Zarhi-Levo and Freddie Rokem, "Criteria for Canonization in Israeli Theatre: Re/evaluating the Identity of Hebrew Drama," in: *Writing and Rewriting National Theatre Histories*, ed. Steve Wilmer, University of Iowa Press, Iowa City 2004, 174–200.

some of these foreign classics the Hebrew theatres also staged plays written in Yiddish, where the characters and their fictional world as a rule stemmed from various Jewish sources familiar to the Jewish audiences. S. Ansky's *The Dybbuk*, composed first in Russian and later translated into Yiddish (or re-composed in Yiddish with some additions, as in the fictional world depicted the characters would have spoken Yiddish), was, following Constantin Stanislavski's recommendation, performed by the Habima Theatre, after being translated into Hebrew by the national poet Chaim Nachman Bialik. *The Dybbuk*, directed by the Armenian director Evgeny Vakhtangov, premiered at the Habima Theatre in January 1922, after it had been performed (in Yiddish) by the Jewish avant-garde theatre *Die Vilnaer Truppe*, in 1920. The Habima Theatre's production of *The Dybbuk* can be regarded as the paradoxical point where an indigenous theatre tradition in Hebrew was created.

It is of course possible to ask why such a classical tradition in the indigenous language is at all necessary. Is it not more productive for a new theatre tradition to develop without the burden of a classical heritage? Certainly, one of the reasons for the extraordinarily creative development of the Israeli theatre is that it did not carry the "burden" of a "classical" tradition. Yet an existing tradition can also become an element of resistance, that is, an already existing theatrical tradition usually serves as a kind of mental or cultural space, a horizon of expectations or a system of norms on the basis of which – following the theories of the Russian Formalists – innovations can take place. For many Israeli theatregoers (and I am referring to the period after the Second World War), as well as for the Israeli theatrical establishment itself, these norms were, for a long time – and to some extent still are – the London West End theatres and even Broadway.

One way to compensate for this lack of a playwriting tradition was by turning to the Bible, both as a general source of inspiration and as a reservoir for concrete narrative materials. When Habima was founded in Moscow, it was mainly through the initiative of Nachum Zemach, who contacted the famous Russian director Constantin Stanislavski to support the establishment of a Hebrew theatre; it was suggested that the new "Studio" (as the theatre groups working under Stanislavski's leadership were called) should be named the "Biblical Studio," thereby drawing attention to this classical tradition. And on many of the early posters of the newly founded theatre this is the name that appears. Besides drawing inspiration from the Hebrew Bible, the founders of Habima also considered the actors to be a new form of prophet, who obviously would speak in the language of their ancient predecessors.

This biblical trajectory was also reinforced by the choice of the more official name of the theatre: "Habima." The Hebrew word for "stage" is *bima* (*Ha-*

Bima means "the stage"), with the stress on the first syllable. However, and also in daily speech, by stressing the second syllable – *bima* – one usually refers to the elevated, canopied platform situated in the center or at the front of the synagogue, where the weekly portions of the *Tora* – the five books of Moses – are recited every Sabbath as part of the prayer rituals. The Habima Theatre transformed this elevated "stage" in the synagogue – where the Bible, the classical Hebrew text *par excellance*, is read –into an artistic space where the language itself is "biblical" and the stories presented draw inspiration from biblical themes.

The Bible holds a central position in the 1922 Habima production of *The Dybbuk*. The first act, when the two lovers meet, takes place in a synagogue, with the *Tora* shrine situated as the focal point of the stage's one-point perspective. (The stage designer was the painter Natan Altman.) In front of the shrine the canopied stage for reading the *Tora* is clearly visible. A short biblical quote is hanging over the stage in each of the three acts. This obviously reinforces the role of the Bible within the theatrical world created on stage, indirectly implying that the art of the theatre is an act of revelation in which the words of God are literally materialized on stage, hanging overhead.

On the one hand this aesthetic transformation of the Bible into theatre no doubt replaced the dramatic canon which I noted above. Instead of plays written during the Renaissance, the budding Hebrew theatre drew on an even more ancient text. This transformation also accorded with the basic notion that the Bible was a major source of inspiration for the ideology of the Zionist movement. These ancient texts, written in a Hebrew language that could be understood by contemporary speakers and readers, were even considered as a proof for the ancient biblical land having been promised to the Jewish people. Of course, in 1922, in the post-revolutionary context of Moscow, such an aesthetic and ideological agenda could hardly be taken for granted. Therefore, at the same time as the Zionist/Jewish subtexts were transmitted through use of the Bible, the Habima production of *The Dybbuk* had also developed a clear revolutionary, Communist agenda, for example by using a red canopy for the wedding ceremony where Leah – the young bride who is refused permission to marry her true lover, Hanan – revolts against the groom that her rich father has chosen for her. This is the moment when the Dybbuk of Hanan (who, at the end of the first act, had died before the Tora shrine upon hearing about the match) enters her body and speaks, quoting from the Song of Songs and addressing Leah through her own mouth. This act of revolt and subversion, prepared by the beggars even before the wedding itself, constitutes the proletariat protesting against the Capitalist system to which Leah has been subjected by her father.

This performance of *The Dybbuk* combined Bolshevik/Revolutionary messages with Jewish ones, relating to Jewish customs and religious beliefs as well as the ongoing cultural changes signaled by Zionism. Such combinations included performing in Hebrew, but in the Sephardic accent which was gradually becoming the accent of everyday Hebrew speech among the Jews who had settled in Mandatory Palestine. There is no doubt that the performance's simultaneous multiple coding (or "radical ambivalence"), its presenting ideological positions which in fact contradict each other – even if for a short period the Spring of Nations and Zionism were considered compatible – eventually made it impossible for the Habima Theatre to remain in Moscow, especially with the ideological unification of the Soviet Union becoming more stringent under the leadership of Stalin. The theatre departed Moscow, in 1926, but their performances at the time were also not warmly received in Tel Aviv. The ending of *The Dybbuk* – Leah dies, during an attempt to exorcise the Dybbuk from her body, and is united with her dead lover in the next world – is an expression of this complexity. Where can the two (now dead) lovers become unified as their social world disintegrates? From the Zionist perspective this is the *Igra Rama*, the mystical high abode to which their souls ascend (making *aliah*) in an afterlife that is at the same time a homecoming to the land of the Bible. This *Igra Rama* has not yet been given any specific qualities, however, and – at least at that point in time – it remained an abstraction. These forms of Jewish mysticism on which *The Dybbuk* relies were not easily accepted among the Jewish settlers in Mandatory Palestine, and acceptance of this production after the Habima Theatre had made Tel Aviv its home was gradual.

Yet, despite these problems, the contradictory perspectives of traditional Jewish culture presented by *The Dybbuk* and its simultaneous multiple coding have remained an important source of inspiration for avant-garde experimentation and ideological radicalism in the arts in Israel. Such a contradictory scenario must be kept in mind while analyzing Levin's *The Torments of Job*, as well as much of his writing both before and after this play. There have also been various other performances of works based on biblical materials. These works have been, for different reasons, avant-garde in this sense, and include Nissim Aloni's *Cruelest of all the King*, which premiered, at the Habima Theatre, in 1953[4] and was directed by Shraga Friedman; *Jehu*, by Gilead Evron, and directed by Hanan Snir at the Habima National Theatre in 1992; and Rina Yerushalmi's renowned Bible Project in two parts, with *Va-Yomer/Va-Yelech* ("And He said and He walked," 1996) and *Va-Yishtahu/Va-Yera* ("And they Bowed and

---

4 For a discussion of the canonization process of this play see Zarhi-Levo and Rokem, "Criteria for Canonization in Israeli Theatre."

he Feared," 1998).[5] Throughout the short history of the Hebrew and the Israeli theatre there have been more than thirty-five productions based on biblical themes or biblical texts. This category of plays has been far more frequent in the Israeli theatre than in any other national theatre tradition of which I am familiar. But only a handful of these productions can be considered to have been avant-garde in the sense that I am discussing here, that is, in drawing attention to the subversive ideological potentials of the biblical text, which itself is hegemonic.

Before focusing more directly on Levin's *The Torments of Job* it is important to refer to another context in which the Bible and the theatrical stage intersect, namely, the holiday of Purim. Even in the most traditional Jewish orthodox contexts, in which theatre is banned, there is exception for Purim. Indeed, according to orthodox Jewish faith, theatre as an art form is actually forbidden, yet there is an existing Jewish tradition and practice which had afforded room for such a transformation, namely, performing biblical narrative in a parodic manner. Purim celebrates the miraculous rescue of the Jews from the Persian ruler Ahasver, as commemorated in the short biblical novella *Esther*. During this holiday, it is the custom (begun in the sixteenth century) to dramatize biblical stories in a humorous or even subversive manner. Since Purim was a carnivalesque holiday, it was the only day during the year that, according to Jewish religious laws, it was permissible to play theatre. The Israeli theatre has, in a way, adopted this carnival spirit as a yearlong phenomenon, while at the same time frequently engaging in ideological debates over the significance of these canonical texts.

2 Hanoch Levin

I will now gradually move on to the analysis of Hanoch Levin's adaptation of the Book of Job, beginning with a brief presentation of Levin and certain aspects of his work. Besides prose and poetry, Levin (born in 1943) wrote almost sixty plays, for which he directed over twenty of the thirty-plus productions staged before his death, at the age of fifty-six, in 1999. As a dramatist and a director, albeit one who directed only his own plays, Levin has had a crucial impact on the development of the Israeli theatre. He also directed the production of his adaptation of the Book of Job, which premiered in 1981 at the Cameri Theatre, in Tel Aviv; this play was entitled *Yesurei Iov* (יסורי איוב) in Hebrew,

---

5 For an analysis of these additional examples see Rokem, "The Bible and the Avant-Garde."

which translates as the "torments," the "agony," the "suffering," and even the "Passion" (in the Christian sense of this term) of Job.

Levin had emerged, in the late 1960s, as the preeminent *enfant terrible* of the Israeli theatre, harshly criticizing Israeli society in the wake of the 1967 Six Day War, especially through his satirical reviews and grotesque domestic comedies.[6] His satirical review *The Queen of the Tub*, staged in 1970 at the Cameri Theatre, where Levin's adaptation of the Book of Job would be performed eleven years later, turned Levin into a nationally known writer; moreover, it exposed him as a rebel who dared criticize not just the political establishment but also the country's accepted foundational myths. The production became a scandal, which ended only when the theatre decided to close it. The main, though hardly only, reason for the harsh reception was that the performance featured a parody of the *Genesis* story of Abraham's sacrifice of his son Isaac. The scandal had actually commenced before the premiere, when one of the national newspapers, *Ma'ariv*, published certain sections from the planned performance which had been censored. (One of *Ma'ariv*'s editors was also chairman of the governmental censorship board.)

According to Levin's rendering of the biblical narrative of Abraham's planned sacrifice of Isaac, on their way to the mountain Abraham informs Isaac about the true purpose of their outing and asks his son to forgive him, because, as he says, he is only doing what God has asked him. Isaac, however, tells his father not to have a bad conscience, for he understands that this is God's will, and therefore his father should not feel culpable about what he is about to do. As they approach the mountain where the sacrifice will take place, the angel of God, just as in the story told in *Genesis*, calls out to save the youth; Levin's Abraham, however, has poor hearing and does not hear the voice of the angel. Had it not been for Isaac's ability to convince his father that God in fact wants him to save his son, the incident, as Levin's short dialogue between

---

6 During its initial stages of development, Israeli playwriting and theatre basically stood in the service of the national Zionist ideology, sometimes raising problematic moral issues connected with the Zionist enterprise, but mainly in agreement with its hegemonic ideology. The aesthetic needs were somehow always subordinated to the ideological ones. This situation gradually began to change following the 1967 Six Day War. This was a grand victory in military terms; however, the ensuing Israeli occupation of the West Bank and the Gaza Strip – with their population of over a million Palestinians who, at that time, lived without prospects for political independence – as well as of Egyptian and Syrian territories brought about a process of ideological discord and growing critique within the Israeli society. This process was further reinforced by the 1973 October War, after which it became clear that Israeli culture in general (and the Israeli theatre in particular) was becoming an important form for expressing the breakdown of the ideological consensus.

the father and the son concludes, could easily have ended badly for everyone involved. The dialogue concludes with Isaac asking what will happen if other fathers who are about to sacrifice their sons are unable to hear the voice of the angel, assuming that it is God's will not to sacrifice children for any ulterior purpose.

The song following this parody of the well-known biblical story is sung by a dead boy addressing his father from the grave:

> Father dear, when you stand over my grave,
> Old and tired and forlorn here,
> And you see how they bury my body in the earth
> And you stand over me, father dear,
>
> Don't stand then so proud,
> And don't lift up your head, father dear,
> We're left flesh facing flesh now,
> And this is the time to weep, father dear.
>
> So let your eyes weep for my eyes,
> And don't be silent for my honor here,
> Something greater than honor
> Now lies at your feet, father dear,
>
> And don't say you've made a sacrifice,
> For the one who sacrificed was me here,
> And don't say other high-flown words
> For I am very low now, father dear.
>
> Father dear, when you stand over my grave
> Old and tired and forlorn here,
> And you see how they bury my body in the earth –
> Then you beg my pardon, father dear.[7]

Even though Isaac had been saved, just as in the biblical story, Levin presents here a victim whose father apparently did not hear the angel of God. Written shortly after the 1967 Six Day War this song led to controversies and was initially censored. It can also be seen as a precursor to Job mourning his dead children in Levin's *The Torments of Job*, which ends with the children singing to the living, paraphrasing a key scene from Anton Chekhov's *Uncle Vanya*. I will return to this scene later; for now it is important to stress that Levin was no doubt consciously developing his own agenda, constantly experimenting with different forms of expressing mourning for dead children, a theme that appears in many of his plays.

---

7 Quoted in Rokem, Introduction, xix–xx.

The parody of the biblical text as well as the song sung by the dead son show, already at this early stage of Levin's career, his sensitivity to the source text, which he then undermines in a gesture of ideological subversion and political protest. The censorship board considered his interpretation of the Bible and the dead son addressing his father to be offensive to the parents of the soldiers serving in the army. The theater appealed to the court; the censorship was cancelled the next day, and the dialogue was included in the performance. But the publicity that the performance received and the criticism it raised – in particular among certain religious members of the Tel Aviv city council, who threatened to withdraw their support for public funding for the Cameri as a municipal theatre – forced the board of the theatre to close *The Queen of the Bath* after nineteen performances. The actors, who had also felt threatened by the sometimes violent and aggressive reactions from spectators, agreed to this decision.

After a decade of writing satirical reviews and grotesque comedies about domestic life in a Tel Aviv-like fictional milieu, Levin turned to mythical narratives like the Book of Job, extending and deepening his ideological and philosophical critique not only of contemporary developments in Israel but also of the Israeli/Zionist ethos and its foundational narratives. In his adaptation of the Book of Job, Levin created a modern tragedy of extraordinary scope; and at the same time, he touched a sensitive streak of nihilism in Israeli culture, which, when identified, is inevitably criticized and even suppressed or denied.

Levin's approach to the biblical text opens a hermeneutic space of juxtaposed and interrelated, even contradictory, interpretations of Job's suffering and its meaning. It raises issues that touch the inner fibres of Israel society and its culture: for example, how can the fact that Job initially loses his children and all his possessions be justified, or even explained, in a modern world where a God can hardly be said to exist? And how does the Jewish experience of the Shoah and the establishment of the State of Israel influence our understanding of the kind of extreme human suffering Job endured? As for the children, they are prefigured by the biblical story of Abraham and Isaac, which is also related to the death/sacrifice of Hanan in *The Dybbuk*. And with regard to the Shoah-related context, a Dybbuk is the soul of a person who has not been properly buried and who returns to the living by entering the body of a living person. Israel, Levin implies with his play about Job, is a country haunted by those dead souls which – according to Levin – drive Job to insanity and finally to his death, after having become the central attraction in a circus.

The Book of Job holds a unique position in the Hebrew Bible. Its action takes place in Uz, a strange, completely unknown country; it is a diasporic, unidentified locality, about which we know nothing. Moreover, Job, the protagonist, is not directly identified as an Israelite. The Book of Job also has an unmistakeable dramatic structure, not at all typical for biblical texts; this structure is based on concrete situations and dialogue between the characters involved in conflicts – what the Greeks termed *agon*. It is a text that is closely related to classical Greek drama in many ways.[8] It also contains quite subversive messages, like the opening lines of chapter three – quoted as the epigraph for this article – where Job damns the day he was born, calling upon God to "uncreate" the world and let it sink back into the darkness and the chaotic void from which it was initially formed – a lament that sounds uncannily modern to a twentieth- and twenty-first-century reader.

When examining Levin's dramatic adaptation of the Book of Job, we must also consider the horizon of expectations of the ancient biblical narrative, according to which, after having endured extreme suffering and loss, Job was "rewarded" with a new family and his wealth restored, as if he was in some way a Holocaust survivor. Israeli readers and audiences are keenly familiar with Job as the biblical source of suffering, endurance, and compensation, and Levin no doubt had a subversive agenda when approaching this ancient text, undermining its basic ideological and theological assumptions. The complex interactions and tensions between, on one hand, a contemporary understanding of suffering and, on the other, the ideologically charged source of the Bible situate Levin's play at a crucial intersection in contemporary Israeli culture.

In the Book of Job, every new rhetorical move of the dialogic interactions between Job and his friends (who are justifying what happens to him) must be logically motivated on the basis of previous positions and statements. As narrated in the Bible, the only "character" in this cosmic drama who does not have to justify his position (until the very end) is the metaphysical protagonist of the text, God himself, who has sacrificed all of Job's possessions and even his family and children, all in a questionable wager with the "Accusing Angel" (as Stephen Mitchell terms "Satan" in his translation).

3 Logic and Tragedy

Besides its basic agonistic, dramatic structure, the Book of Job is also, like many classical tragedies, frequently based on the application, critical examina-

---

8 For more detailed accounts of these similarities, see H. M. Kallen, *The Book of Job as a Greek Tragedy*, Moffat, Yard & Co. New York 1918; and Eli Rozik, "The Book of Job: A Dialogue between Cultures," in: *Hellenic and Jewish Arts: Interaction, Tradition and Renewal*, ed. A. Ovadia, Ramot, Tel Aviv 1998.

tion, and even subversion of basic laws of logic. The logical laws that are most commonly embedded in such ancient tragedies, and which therefore can also be extracted from them, are the syllogism (the form of reasoning through which a conclusion is reached on the basis of two given or assumed premises, where at least one of the premises is a universal statement) and the law of the excluded middle (pointing out the impossibility that something can simultaneously have contradictory qualities).

My basic assumption for examining the Book of Job as well Levin's adaptation of it is that these basic laws of logic serve as a kind of grid through which the tragic dimensions of such texts gradually emerge, by challenging the logical structures embedded in them. This approach – of examining the ways in which tragedy defies logic – can probably be applied more universally, as a distinguishing feature of tragic narratives, though here I will present just a general outline of such an analysis. Such an approach, which argues that the tensions between logical structures and dramatic narratives are an important aspect of tragedy, has not yet received the critical attention it deserves. This approach is not intended to replace the existing approaches to tragedy; rather, it presents an additional perspective that, I believe, will enable us to understand the tragic dimensions of contemporary dramas (for example, Bertolt Brecht's *Lehrstücke* ("Learning Plays")), for which the Aristotelian and other paradigms seem insufficient but which still resonate with what Paul Hammond calls "the strangeness which tragedy fashions," where "through the estrangement and the decomposition of the tragic protagonist we are brought face to face with the fragility of our identity, and the fragility of the languages through which we make sense of that identity."[9] Thus, in analysing Levin's adaptation of the Book of Job, I hope to show that the approach suggested here can provide critical tools for analysing a contemporary tragedy in which the biblical narrative and its inner logic are subverted and replaced by an alternative logic, based on the nihilism and abjection of Levin's play.

The interactions between protagonists and antagonists in classical Greek tragedy, and between the characters in the Book of Job, can be viewed as a series of conflicting syllogisms. These syllogisms create a weave of universal propositions (which cannot and need not be proven empirically), like "God exists" or "God punishes only those who have sinned," combined with particular statements, like "Job is punished." In this example, Job has, according to the syllogistic logic applied by the three comforters, in effect sinned. Job, however, clearly holds another view, arguing that he has been unjustly punished.

---

9 Hammond, Paul, *The Strangeness of Tragedy*, Oxford University Press, Oxford 2009, 9.

But even if he considers himself to be treated unjustly, he never doubts God's existence. In the Book of Job, the syllogistic arguments are immersed in contexts where they become subjected to novel and unexpected shifts of meaning, such as when the comforters arrive and explain to Job that he has sinned, thereby infuriating Job.

Readers of the biblical text, who have "witnessed" the wager between God and the Accusing Angel which opens the book, know that Job is indeed a righteous man, who is unjustly punished and tested. Knowing this increases our identification with him and his constant doubts about whether God, in fact, punishes only those who have sinned. After a series of confrontations, beginning with Job's cursing the day he was born and wishing that he was dead, God appears; in the following monologue (the longest delivered by God in the Bible) spoken from the "whirlwind," it is God himself who, in effect, proves his own existence, leaving Job speechless. Nature could never function the way it does without "my" intervention, God basically argues. Therefore, according to the logical thinking that the comforters have previously applied, it is impossible to "think" the world without God's existence.

The interactions between logical thinking and dramatic structure also offer my analysis a point of departure for exploring the relations between philosophical thought, on one hand, and performance, theatre, and drama, on the other. The principles of logical thinking – in particular, the theory of deduction as exemplified by the syllogism as well as the law of the excluded middle – had already been embedded in and thus can also be extracted from classical Greek tragedies like *Antigone* and *Oedipus Tyrannos* which have been formative for western theatrical traditions. Aristotle was obviously familiar with these plays when he formulated the basic principles of logic, more than two generations after the plays had been written. By analysing the principles of logic activated through the narrative structures and dramatic conflicts of these plays, as well as through the actions and words of their protagonists, it is possible to deepen our understanding of the interaction between philosophical and performance discourses. This is a field of investigation that has recently become the focus for a broad range of studies – here, in this particular case, drawing attention to the intricate relations between philosophical thinking and dramatic structure, exploring their common ground in logic.

Before substantiating my claim about Levin's dramatic adaptation of the Book of Job – itself a completely new play, in fact – as a modern and even nihilistic tragedy, not merely an adaptation, I wish to make some ad hoc distinctions between a literary work and the formal, logical structures of the syllogism. The so-called deductive syllogism (which will be the focus of my discussion here) was a major topic of study within the classical academies of learning. It is typically a brief "narrative" consisting of at least three statements. The first sentence is usually a universal statement – for example, "all humans are mortal" – which is typically followed by two statements making particular claims. The first of these would usually name an individual – for example, "Socrates is a human" – while the second particular statement draws the inevitable conclusion – in this case, that "Socrates is mortal." Thus, (1) all humans are mortal; (2) Socrates is human; (3) Socrates is mortal. This form of deductive syllogism, called the Barbara syllogism, emerges from the dynamics between universal and particular statements; this dynamics was a major concern of classical philosophy and logic, and, as I argue, was a central feature of classical tragedy. This relation between the universal and the particular was also a central concern in metaphysical contexts, as perhaps seen most forcefully in the interaction, expressed in Plato's theory of pure forms, between the eternal ideas and particular, individual realizations of these ideas.

According to Christopher Shields:

> In Aristotle's logic, the basic ingredients of reasoning are given in terms of *inclusion* and *exclusion* relations /.../. He begins with the notion of a patently correct sort of argument, one whose evident and unassailable acceptability induces Aristotle to refer to is as a 'perfect deduction' (*APr.* 24b22–25). Generally, a *deduction* (*sullogismon*), according to Aristotle, is a valid or acceptable argument. More exactly, a deduction is 'an argument in which when certain things are laid down something else follows of necessity in virtue of their being so' (*APr.* 24b18–20).[10] (Citations in the original)

And, adds Shields, "a deduction is the sort of argument whose *structure* guarantees its validity, irrespective of the truth or falsity of its premises."[11] By combining at least three statements, on the basis of exclusions and inclusions, like the partly overlapping circles of a Venn diagram, a deductive syllogism constitutes a narrative "skeleton," "scaffold," or "prism," just as the representation of an action, or *mimesis*, which Aristotle theorizes in the *Poetics*, is based on principles of selection (exemplified by a range of inclusions and exclusions) and combinatory strategies, constituting the narrative "syntax" of a certain play or narrative.

As far as I know, Aristotle himself never makes any explicit comparison between such syllogistic "narratives" and tragedy, the dramatic genre he analyses in the *Poetics*, with *Oedipus Tyrannos* serving as his prime example. But

---

10 Shields, Christopher, "Aristotle," in: *The Stanford Encyclopedia of Philosophy*, ed. Edward N. Zalta, http://plato.stanford.edu/archives/sum2012/entries/aristotle/ last accessed Dec 15, 2012.
11 Shields, "Aristotle."

the seemingly self-evident, even trivial formulation, in the seventh chapter of the *Poetics*, that a tragedy must have three parts (a beginning, middle, and end) in order to be complete must not be understood naïvely, as if Aristotle were considering three acts in a play; rather they should be read as an implied reference to the three parts of the deductive syllogism. In Aristotle's own formulation from the *Poetics*:

> A beginning is that which does not itself follow anything by causal necessity, but after which something naturally is or comes to be. An end, on the contrary, is that which itself naturally follows some other thing, either by necessity, or as a rule, but has nothing following it. A middle is that which follows something as some other thing follows it. A well constructed plot, therefore, must neither begin nor end at haphazard, but conform to these principles. (Part 7, par. 2)[12]

Defining the beginning of a tragedy as "that which does not itself follow anything by causal necessity, but after which something naturally is or comes to be" connects it to the initial universal statement of the deductive syllogism, which serves as the basis for the thought experiment or fictional construction that is continued by the second statement, which, in turn, serves as a bridge to the final conclusion that "has nothing following it."

A deductive syllogism establishes a direct causal relationship between a general or universal assumption that we have good reasons to accept but that does not necessarily have to be empirically true: for example, "all humans are mortal" or "the sun rises in the east every morning and sets in the west" but also "all unicorns have a horn on their forehead." Such assumptions are followed by at least two statements, which, together with the initial assumption, form a syllogistic narrative kernel of three tightly interconnected links of the narrative chain. The syllogism, with its complex relations between universal and particular statements, can be reformulated in the form of a conditional statement: "If all x's are y, and S is an x, then S is y." The abstract logical structure of the deductive syllogism (all x's are y, S is an x, and thus S is y) and its complementary conditional deep structure (If A and B, then y) becomes a narrative construct when the logical structure of the syllogism is embedded within a specific context. When the logical formula is contextualized through the mortality of all humans in combination with the fact that Socrates is a human, it becomes a narrative about the death of Plato's admired teacher and the main speaker in most of his dialogues, whose life and lack of fear about his own death serve as a model of excellence for philosophical activity.

---

12 Aristotle, *Poetics*, trans. S. H. Bucher, *The Internet Classics Archive*, http://classics.mit.edu/Aristotle/poetics.html, last accessed, September 13, 2012.

The narrative in which a syllogism has been embedded could also be about a man of perfect integrity, called Job, who lived in the land of Uz, and who was punished by God for no apparent reason and suffered as the victim of an almost arbitrary bet between God and the Accusing Angel. The Book of Job is based on the syllogism that (1) "God is omnipotent and makes those who have sinned suffer"; (2) "Job suffers"; (3) therefore "Job sinned." The question which the biblical book confronts, from several perspectives, is whether God makes *only* those who have sinned suffer, since it seems that he does not cause suffering for *all* those who have sinned. There is a "spillover" between sinning and suffering that upsets the initial syllogism of the biblical narrative but which is explained by the initial wager between God and the Accusing Angel, thereby creating a contingency beyond logic, at least from the perspective of Job. And from a logical perspective the reason why the syllogism becomes so problematic to solve for Job and the comforters is that it upsets the chronological sequence of events. In order for the "logic" to work the sinning must precede the suffering; otherwise the contradictions that appear cannot be resolved.

The crucial issue distinguishing between logic and tragedy is the extent and the manner in which the specific syllogistic/conditional structures embedded in the dramatic text have been contextualized. What I would term "dramaturgy" is the dynamic interaction or dialectics between the abstract logical structure of the syllogism (as well as other rule-related activities, like the game of chess[13]) and its "inner" causality, based on the set relations between, on one hand, its different statements, and, on the other hand, the specific historical and ideological contexts where these conditional structures, the "logical" narrative structure, are realized within a literary narrative. Literary narratives – and this is no doubt also true for narratives in other media – integrate complex "external" contexts, like changing social, historical and ideological conditions and contingencies that are not necessarily in full harmony with the syllogistic, logical features of the text. In some cases, these contextualizations even contradict the seemingly formal, logical structures of the syllogism and the law of the excluded middle. This means that, in the universe of tragedy, it is possible that an object or person is simultaneously something and its opposite (P and not-P).

One of the distinguishing features of the Book of Job is that it provides few details about such external contexts. The reader, as noted, is not even sure whether Job is an Israelite, and the text affords no sense of the social conventions of Uz or even where it is located geographically. The Book of Job does,

---

13 Rokem, Freddie, "Dramaturgies of Exile: Brecht and Benjamin 'Playing' Chess and Go," in: *Theatre Research International* 37.1 (2012): 5–19.

however, present several *agones*, wherein different worldviews, presented as valid syllogisms, confront each other. As opposed to the Book of Job, the biblical prophets, who present the wrath of God as the reason for human suffering, are always careful to contextualize divine punishment, arguing that it is the result of human sins in God's eyes. Classical Greek tragedy also carefully contextualizes logical structures within larger social, historical, and/or mythical contexts. In the Book of Job, however, the inner logical, syllogistic framework carries most of the weight in how the characters understand their respective situations and in the possibilities available to us for interpreting this text.

4 The Logic of Hanoch Levin's *The Torments of Job*

The basic dramaturgical strategy of Levin's adaptation of the Book of Job follows the Greek classical model, adding contexts rather than keeping them to an absolute minimum, as the biblical source narrative does. Levin situates his adaptation of the Book of Job in a specific historical and geographic context, in *Eretz Israel* (The Land of Israel), at the time of the Roman Empire, specifically during the life of Jesus. Levin's Job can even be seen as a Christ figure who is sacrificed (and willingly so) because of his belief in the God of the Jews, a belief that, in Levin's play, the new Roman emperor has outlawed (though the former rulers had accepted it). Unlike his three friends, who immediately deny the existence of God when they hear about the brutal punishment ("a spit stuck up their rear"[14]) to be inflicted on those who profess belief in God, Job publicly affirms his belief. He does this after having a vision of his dead father, whom he mistakes for God, and is immediately impaled by the law-abiding Roman soldiers. By this point, Job has nothing to lose, save for his life, which has become worthless after the loss of his children and possessions. Even the little kiosk he owns in Yaffo (originally a Palestinian town), the southern section of Tel Aviv, has been confiscated by the new emperor.

Levin's play situates the story of Job within the concrete historical context of the Roman Empire and the time of Jesus, when the Temple of Jerusalem was destroyed and the Jews were forced into exile. Job's torments on the pole also allude to the suffering of Jesus, which, according to Christianity, brings redemption to the world. But the play subverts the Crucifixion's claim to bring salvation. The Officer even cynically refers to "that nut / In the next village

---

14 Levin, Hanoch, *The Torments of Job*, in: Levin, *The Labor of Life*, 77.

who claims to be the son of god"[15] – obviously not the option chosen by the Jewish people. Instead, Levin offers an almost nihilistic version of the existential situation of the individual, as reflected in the Jewish historical experience of the twentieth century, where a belief in God such as Job's could easily be seen as an absurdity.

In parallel to these obvious contextualizations of a text that is completely non-contextualized, Levin's play provides a cynical, material proof, performed syllogistically, that God actually exists through the closure of the play (as will be discussed later). At the same time, Levin's adaptation also offers a biting critique of the Israeli valorization of Jewish victimhood – valorization that culminates in certain official forms of commemoration of the Shoah, which, together with the biblical heritage (on which the play is obviously based), are founding principles of the Jewish state. According to the Israeli Declaration of Independence, the Hebrew Bible (which the Jews "gave to the world") and the Shoah are the two main justifications for the establishment of a Jewish state.

Instead of presenting the basic message of the Declaration of Independence, Levin (who, in fact, grew up in an orthodox Jewish home in the slums of south Tel Aviv, near the location of the former central bus station), turns the suffering of Job into a circus show and belief in God into a travesty. Such belief, according to the play, is the result of delusion and of intentional iconoclastic distortion of how God has traditionally been perceived. But perhaps most importantly, giving additional weight to his radical ideological critique, Levin transforms the complex, almost impenetrable language of the biblical original – and Job is one of the most linguistically complex biblical books – into a remarkable poetic text, thereby implicitly showing that, even if the Shoah has become a "show" that presents the existence of God as a cynical travesty, the modern Hebrew language – as expressed in this and many of Levin's other plays – has achieved an extraordinary victory.

Levin's adaptation begins with Job and his friends sharing a meal, unlike the scene between God and the Accusing Angel (who are making a deal to test Job) that opens the biblical narrative. As the meal ends, Levin's Job praises God's generosity for giving them plenty of food. There is enough food, he adds, to satisfy the Beggars and the Beggars of the Beggars, who can now come and eat from the leftovers. Yet the third party in this formulation, the Beggarly Beggar, receives nothing this time, pointing out that:

---

15 Levin, *The Torments of Job*, 83.

The only time I get food is when
One of the middling beggars gulps down
The bones too fast, his throat rebukes,
A bone sticks in his gorge and he pukes.
I can swallow what he pukes without having to chew
And easily digest the thrown-up stew
Which is already half-digested.
And if I'm in luck, I find in the mess
A piece of what was once potatoes, beets, or cress.
Of course, that doesn't happen every day,
So I'm always weak, almost fade away.
Yet, never mind – you get used to it.
Be patient, my friend,
And somebody will surely puke in your hand.
Well, somehow we manage to live.
There's a God in the sky,
Tra-la-la, tra-la-lie.
Maybe they'll throw up for me on the way,
Tra-la-la, tra-la-lay.[16]

It is impossible, at this stage, even to imagine how this strange "prophecy" – that someone will eventually vomit and thereby feed the Beggarly Beggar – is going to be realized at the end of the play. Here, it is merely a playful fantasy. And it is no coincidence, I believe, that the beggars play such a central role in the subversion of God's existence, returning us to the revolutionary beggars in the opening of the second act of *The Dybbuk* and to the image of Jewish poverty which the Zionist project was supposedly going to end.

Just as Job's guests finish praising God for the abundance he has blessed them with, even feeding the Beggars, the Messengers of Poverty arrive, announcing the loss of Job's wealth. First, Job learns that his mines in Lebanon have been destroyed by an earthquake; that his ships en route to Alexandria have been lost in a storm; and finally, that per decree from the new Roman emperor, his small plot of land in Yaffo and all his personal belongings have been confiscated. Bailiffs arrive and empty the banquet hall, stripping Job to his underwear. When they have finished, Job offers a cynical, sarcastic remark, challenging them audaciously:

You forgot my gold teeth.
I've got some gold teeth in my mouth.[17]

---

16 Levin, *The Torments of Job*, 56.
17 Levin, *The Torments of Job*, 64.

The response from the Leader of the Bailiffs consists of a mixture of mythical narrative and ordinary life typical of Levin's writing:

> Don't be ridiculous.
> Don't try to make us into monsters.
> We're all just human, part of the group,
> We all go home to our wives at night,
> To our slippers and a hot bowl of soup.[18]

For an Israeli audience, this exchange recalls powerfully the Nazi persecutions of World War II, when mass murder was preceded by confiscation of property and followed by removal of gold teeth from the mouths of the dead. Yet the Bailiffs insist that *they* will not commit such atrocities: they are just ordinary folk, they claim, who enjoy the pleasures of everyday life, in common with the rest of humanity. Job's response shows how the despair of the biblical Job has been transformed into a modern, almost Beckettian gesture of existential despair, while also alluding to the formulations of the biblical text:

> Naked came I from my mother's womb and naked came my mother
> From her mother, too.
> Shuddering, we emerge, one from another,
> A long line, naked and new.
> "What shall I wear?" asked my mother in the morning
> But when the day was done,
> Naked was she borne to the grave.
> Now I too stand naked, her son.[19]

At this point, the Leader of the Bailiffs sneaks back onto the stage without Job's noticing, grabs him by the throat, and yanks out his gold teeth with a pair of pliers:

> Here's a tooth – one!
> Another tooth – two! Three!
> Not a sound! Swallow your shout!
> It hurts? Your mouth is bleeding?
> Bite your lip! Swallow your shout!
> Help me get through this job and get out.[20]

This jailer, who moments earlier had claimed to be just another ordinary human being and someone who would certainly not want anyone to suffer in excess, has become a monster of extreme cruelty.

---

18 Levin, *The Torments of Job*, 64.
19 Levin, *The Torments of Job*, 64–65.
20 Levin, *The Torments of Job*, 65.

In this staged world, when Job challenges, or rather teases, his victimizers with the unimaginable threat of pulling his gold teeth, nobody can envision such an atrocity. Today, however, we know that such things have occurred. In Levin's play, Job's initial taunt is dismissed because the Bailiffs wish to go home to their wives, their slippers, and their warm soup, leaving Job to reflect on the meaning of his own life and that of his mother's. But then the Bailiff barges in and performs the actual abominable act that Job had spoken of as a bitter joke. It turns out that the advent of extreme cruelty had not actually been cancelled; it had merely been postponed. What had previously been an almost unconscious fear has suddenly become reality, its only warning the fear that it might happen. It is important to note that the biblical Job also lives in a world of uncertainty: as the narrator remarks, every year, after Job's children have come together, he summons them to be purified, because he fears, "Perhaps my children have sinned, and cursed God in their hearts."[21]

In his adaptation, Levin magnifies the modality of anxiety and potential threats, creating situations where the unexpected – what has already happened on a smaller scale or has just been subconsciously imagined as a potential threat, without any probability of being realized – suddenly occurs in reality. Levin's Job (or the allegorical reference to the Jewish people that the play gradually develops) is victimized, seemingly without reason – and, more importantly, without any warning that such violence is about to occur – and only afterwards learns that there is a new emperor in Rome. In many of his plays, Levin depicts both small, insignificant catastrophes and atrocities that simply happen, as well as large ones that change the fate of the individual. Thus, as in Job's confrontations with the Bailiffs, the fact that something terrible has been imagined and announced creates a hiatus, a pause, during which Job – and the spectators – believe the proposed scenario remains merely rhetorical and has thus been avoided; however, once the fear has been alleviated for a short moment, and the victim believes himself safe, the imagined horror suddenly becomes real. In terms of the logical structures of the syllogism and the conditional statement referred to earlier, the universal statement – or the first part of the conditional statement (the "if I am being punished ..." of "if, so, and then so") – has been suppressed or even negated. Or, it turns out to be so obvious that it does not merit being mentioned, while the consequences ("then they will pull out my teeth") are perceived as self-evident, no matter how atrocious, and require no explanation.

Levin's use of this narrative structure – presenting a consequence without specifying what its conditions are, thus subverting the syllogistic structure –

---

21 *The Book of Job*, 5.

is based not just on introducing a single misfortune or catastrophe, but also on a pattern that holds strong potential for repeating itself in the continuum of the text, thereby introducing new misfortunes. The Jewish "experience" of history, in particular during the twentieth century, which has been seminal for the creation of a collective Israeli cultural consciousness, serves as the basis for the narrative pattern used by Levin. Jews have, he claims, internalized the experience of irrational misfortunes initiated by others (not just natural catastrophes), misfortunes for which there had been no apparent reason or prior warning.

In Levin's play, the tooth-pulling scene ends with the appearance onstage of the Messengers of Death, each of whom announces the death of one of Job's children. With each announcement, the named (and now dead) child is carried onstage on a stretcher, until all are accounted for. Job is left alone with the bodies of his children, his own naked body convulsing with grief. Eliphaz, Bildad, and Zophar, Job's friends, arrive to "comfort" him, explaining that God is punishing Job for his sins. In response, Job takes refuge from his torments in a vision of his dead father as the ultimate comforter and fantasizes that his suffering is unreal and has been only a terrifying dream. His vision is interrupted by the arrival of an officer of the new emperor, who proclaims,

> The god of the Jews is null and void, wiped out.
> All who believe in him are heretics and rebels.
> To reinforce the new belief and make it crystal clear:
> All those who believe in the god of the Jews will have
> A spit stuck up their rear.[22]

Job's friends are in a difficult situation: if they stand by their religious beliefs, they will be tortured by the emperor's officials. In considering their options, they think of their fields, which must be harvested, of their children, who are young and need support and protection; and then, with some hesitation, they submit to the authorities and abandon their faith. Only Job stands firm. Levin has him mistake his envisioned father for God, a misapprehension that apparently gives Job courage not to deny the existence of God. Moreover, Job now has nothing left to lose, and so refuses to disavow his convictions; for this, he is literally placed on the aforementioned spit. For the rest of the performance, he remains impaled, an image of permanent suffering like that of the crucified Christ.

At this point, a Ringmaster from a circus arrives, pronouncing that it is a shame

---

22 Levin, *The Torments of Job*, 77.

For such a performance as this to go to waste.
All those potential tickets mutely crying out
Like the souls of unborn children dying out.
Not to mention the educational worth
For those who still think god exists on earth.
I've run musical circuses in all the most
Important capitals of Europe.
I can even say that I've run Europe.

...

Five hundred dinars to the royal treasury
For the right to put this man
In my circus.[23]

After tough bargaining with the officer, the Ringmaster acquires the "rights" to Job, and the torments of the "crucified" believer are made the main attraction of his circus. In the 1981 performance of Levin's play (which he himself directed), at the Cameri Theatre in Tel Aviv, scenographer Rut Dar staged a bone-chilling transformation. At the moment when the Officer and the Ringmaster struck their deal, a huge circus tent opened, parachute-like, over the stage, and, in an instant, the sight of the suffering, impaled Job was transformed into a display of vulgar sensationalism, something to entertain circus audiences; for the spectators watching Levin's performance, this was totally stunning. The implication, which is evident in Levin's script, is that this cynical exploitation of suffering is characteristic of contemporary theatre. The character who claims to have "run Europe" is also a theatre impresario working to transform suffering into spectacle; likewise, what was once seen as a noble art is now mere showmanship. More importantly, perhaps, is the implication that Job's loss, which in today's Israeli context has in many ways become an allegory of the Shoah, has become nothing but cheap and vulgar entertainment – perhaps even a Purim celebrating the rescue of the Jews from persecution in ancient Persia, as told in the biblical book that does not mention God's name but which offers an allowance for Jews to appear on the stage.

But there is one crucial problem for the Ringmaster with Job in his current state. He is quickly approaching death, yet the Ringmaster has not yet sold enough tickets to recoup his investment. As Job dies, the Ringmaster curses him; the circus then abruptly disperses. Job, alone with his final torments, vomits. As if on cue, the Beggarly Beggar of the first scene enters to lick the vomit, explaining,

---

23 Levin, *The Torments of Job*, 84–85.

Just like I said: a little patience
And somebody finally pukes. Yes,
Somehow we manage to live.
There's a god in the sky.[24]

This is apparently the ultimate form of "divine benevolence" and a proof of God's existence.

At the end of Levin's adaptation, after Job's death and the cynical assertion that vomiting is proof of the existence of God, only the song of the dead can be heard. This song, which paraphrases Sonya's final monologue in Chekhov's *Uncle Vanya*, is spoken/sung by Job's dead children:

But there is mercy in the world
And we are laid to rest.
Thus the dead lie patiently,
With silence are we blessed.
Grass grows on our flesh,
The scream dies in our breast;
But there is mercy in the world
And we are laid to rest.[25]

Maybe, finally, there *is* some kind of mercy in the world; unlike Chekhov, however, Levin envisions this mercy as something that can be experienced only as "we are laid to rest" (such that the "we" do not become dybbuks), when the world has nothing to offer those who have lived in the world, and we, the living, are left even more empty-handed, knowing that as long as we live there will be no mercy whatsoever.

In his adaptation of the Book of Job, Levin reverses the traditional syllogism, which begins with a universal statement. Instead, he begins with a particular statement about a particular person named Job, who one day, while enjoying his riches, suddenly loses everything. The play proceeds to show that, if this is the work of God, then all people are subject to the possibility that they will suffer for no apparent reason. Or, on another level, if the fact that vomiting proves that God exists, then there is no guarantee that all of us will not end up hoping for someone to vomit so as both to afford us something to eat and to reconfirm the existence of divine benevolence, for what it is worth. Indeed, the forms of suffering indicated by the syllogisms in Levin's *The Torments of Job* have no end.

---

24 Levin, *The Torments of Job*, 91.
25 Levin, *The Torments of Job*, 91.

5 What is Man?

The presence of syllogistic arguments in the Book of Job, in classical tragedy, and in many of Levin's other plays (where syllogisms are dramatized through conditional statements such that the first part – the "if" – is suppressed) points to close interactions between logical thinking and different forms of tragedy. Another aspect of this connection between philosophy – in particular, logical thinking – and drama is an insistence on characterizing what it means to be human and what the ethical dimensions of being human are. Without going into detail, it is possible to argue that, in trying to define and exemplify what it means to be human, regardless of how we understand and interpret the specific contents and contexts of these human qualities, tragedies activate a particular logic that can break or subvert the law of the excluded middle, a law generally considered to be universally applicable.

The most direct way to formulate the law of the excluded middle is to state that the proposition "P is true *and* not-P is true" is always false. This means that something cannot be described simultaneously both by a certain quality and by its opposite. Yet this is exactly what tragedy does in regards to what it means to be human: in short, to be human is to be characterized by P and not-P at the same time. The "Ode to Man" in Sophocles' *Antigone* is perhaps the most well-known example of this inner contradiction – the *deinon* which has become so central for philosophical thinking – in our understandings of human nature. According to the Chorus,

> There is much that is strange [*deinon*], but nothing
> that surpasses man in strangeness.
> He sets sail on the frothing waters
> amid the south winds of winter
> tacking through the mountains
> and furious chasms of the waves.
> ...
>
> Everywhere journeying, inexperienced and without issue,
> he comes to nothingness.
> Through no flight can he resist
> the one assault of death,
> even if he has succeeded in cleverly evading
> painful sickness.
> Clever indeed, mastering
> The ways of skill beyond all hope,

he sometimes accomplishes evil,
sometimes achieves brave deeds.[26]

The Book of Job, as well as Levin's adaptation, also juxtaposes the general understanding of what it means to be a human and the concrete experience of that understanding in terms of stark contradictions. The biblical Job formulates this in a number of his speeches, for example:

Man's life is a prison;
he is sentenced to pain and grief.
Like a slave he pants for the shadows;
like a servant he longs for rest.[27]

and:

Man who is born of woman –
how few and harsh are his days!
Like a flower he blooms and withers;
like a shadow he fades in the dark.[28]

In Levin's adaptation, Job defines what it means to be human in the first scene of the play, after he has finished the meal with his companions: he blesses God, not only for feeding his own household and his close friends as well as the beggars, but also for making it that we are hungry again after six hours, when the nourishment has made its full course through the intestines, thereby enabling us to be reborn – "A new man is born every six hours,"[29] as Job expresses it. The second time the play directly formulates what it means to be human is in lines spoken by two clowns who work in the circus where the "crucified" Job has become the main attraction. Job is now close to death – his actual death, as opposed to the temporary, "small" death that comes after eating a full meal or the analogous post-coital state from which the individual is quickly resurrected. In response to Job's death the Solemn Clown asks,

What is man: What he said yesterday?
What he cries now? His silence soon?
Is he his memories? His hopes?

---

26 Quoted in Martin Heidegger, "'The Ode to Man' in Sophocles' *Antigone*," in: *An Introduction to Metaphysics*, trans Ralph Mannheim, Yale University Press, New Haven 1959, 146–165, 86–87.
27 *The Book of Job*, 23.
28 *The Book of Job*, 36.
29 Levin, *The Torments of Job*, 54.

What he does or what is done to him?
His last scream on his deathbed?
Or his first scream between his mother's legs?
Or is he that awful, ridiculous muddle
Between one scream and the other?
Where is the thread that binds it all?
Where is the thread and what is meaning?
What is man? And what is life?
And the thread, gentlemen, tell me where is the thread?[30]

And the Cynical Clown, presenting the other side of the human complexity, immediately retorts, in a statement that is typical for the remarkable form of poetic and tragic nihilism Levin has given voice to in his dramatic adaptation of The Book of Job:

Who cares what is a man?
What is the world? Who gives a damn?
Ladies and gentlemen, you see
A man fall off a high roof, you stare –
His arms waving, spinning in the air,
His shattered scream reverberates in space,
You step back a bit so the blood won't spatter your clothes and face.
Hypnotized by his fall like lead,
Your expressions a blend of yearning and dread
For the final, unrepeatable moment when his body hits the ground.
Don't search for meaning.
Don't ask for a moral. Why try?
Just watch: a man falls, soon he'll die.[31]

If a man falls, *then* he will soon die. This is clear. But we will never really understand what the reasons for his fall are. What we know, however, is that that truncated causal relationship is the stuff from which tragedies are made.

Bibliography

Aristotle. *Poetics*. Trans S. H. Bucher, *The Internet Classics Archive*. http://classics.mit.edu/Aristotle/poetics.html (Sept 13, 2012).
Aronson-Lehavi, Sharon. "Transformations of Religious Performativity: Sacrificial Figures in Modern Experimental Theatre". *Performance and Spirituality*, 3.1. 2012. 57–70. http://www.utdl.edu/ojs/index.php/pas/article/view/43 (Nov 23, 2013).
The Book of Job. Trans. Stephen Mitchell. New York: Harper Perennial, 1986.

---

30 Levin, *The Torments of Job*, 89.
31 Levin, *The Torments of Job*, 89.

Feldman, Yael. "Deconstructing the Biblical Sources in Israeli Theater: *Yisurei Iyov* by Hanoch Levin." *AJS Review*, 12.2. 1987. 251–277 http://journals.cambridge.org/action/displayAbstract?fromPage=online&aid=4497552.

Hammond, Paul. *The Strangeness of Tragedy*. Oxford: Oxford University Press, 2009.

Heidegger, Martin. "'The Ode to Man' in Sophocles' *Antigone*." *An Introduction to Metaphysic*. Trans Ralph Mannheim. New Haven: Yale University Press, 1959. 146–165.

Kallen, H. M. *The Book of Job as a Greek Tragedy*. New York: Yard, Moffat, 1918.

Levin, Hanoch. "The Torments of Job." *The Labor of Life: Selected Plays*. Trans. Barbara Harshav. Palo Alto: Stanford University Press, 2003.

Naumann, Matthias. *Dramaturgie der Drohung. Das Theater des israelischen Dramatikers und Regisseurs Hanoch Levin*. Marburg: Tectum, 2006.

Rokem, Freddie. "The Bible and the Avant-Garde: The Search for a Classical Tradition in the Israeli Theatre." *European Review*, 9.3. 2001. 305–317 http://journals.cambridge.org/action/displayAbstract?fromPage=online&aid=81391.

Rokem, Freddie. "Dramaturgies of Exile: Brecht and Benjamin 'Playing' Chess and Go." *Theatre Research International*, 37.1. 2012. 5–19. http://journals.cambridge.org/action/displayAbstract?fromPage=online&aid=8480617.

Rokem, Freddie, *Introduction*. Levin, ix–xxxv.

Rokem, Freddie. "Job's Soul And Otto Weininger's Torments: Jewish Themes In The Theatre of Hanoch Levin and Yehoshua Sobol." *Jewish Theatre: A Global View*. Ed. Edna Nahshon. Boston MA: Brill. 257–268. http://booksandjournals.brillonline.com/content/books/10.1163/ej.9789004173354.i-308.27.

Rokem, Freddie. "Narratives of Armed Conflict and Terrorism in the Theatre: Tragedy and History in Hanoch Levin's *Murder*." *Theatre Journal*, 54.4. 2002. 555–572. http://muse.jhu.edu/login?auth=0&type=summary&url=/journals/theatre_journal/v054/54.4rokem.html.

Rokem, Freddie. *Performing History: Theatrical Representations of the Past in Contemporary Theatre*. Iowa City: University of Iowa Press, 2000.

Rokem, Freddie. *Philosophers and Thespians: Thinking Performance*. Stanford: Stanford University Press, 2010.

Rozik, Eli. "The Book of Job: A Dialogue between Cultures." *Hellenic and Jewish Arts: Interaction, Tradition and Renewal*. Ed. A. Ovadia. Tel Aviv: Ramot, 1998.

Shields, Christopher. "Aristotle", *The Stanford Encyclopedia of Philosophy*. Ed. Edward N. Zalta. http://plato.stanford.edu/archives/sum2012/entries/aristotle/ (Dec 15, 2012).

Zarhi-Levo, Yael and Rokem, Freddie. "Criteria for Canonization in Israeli Theatre: Re/evaluating the Identity of Hebrew Drama." *Writing and Rewriting National Theatre Histories*. Ed. Steve Wilmer. Iowa City: University of Iowa Press, 2004. 174–200.

Leora Batnitzky
Beyond Theodicy? Joban Themes in Philip Roth's *Nemesis*

Is it possible to read the Book of Job without reference to theodicy – defined simply as the attempt to justify God's goodness or wisdom or purposiveness in the face of the seeming evils of this world? Of course, this is not a new question. As the essays in this volume show, Job has had a long afterlife, not just in religious circles but also in literature, art, and music. Job has also enjoyed an important place in twentieth-century European philosophy and remains, second perhaps only to Saint Paul, the religious darling of post-Christian European philosophers. Here we need but mention not only the centrality of Job to Rene Girard's thought but also Job's significance for thinkers as diverse as Paul Ricœur and Slavoj Žižek. In the context of what Hent de Vries has helpfully described as twentieth-century philosophy's turn to religion, the turn to Job is not surprising.[1] After all, if twentieth-century philosophy turned to religion it did so largely in response to the particular horrors of the murder of millions of innocents. As Jacques Derrida observed, "The possibility of *radical evil* both destroys and institutes the religious."[2]

Girard, Ricœur, and Žižek's readings of Job are relevant to the question of whether it is possible to read Job without reference to theodicy. To reformulate Derrida's statement, their respective readings of Job both destroy and institute theodicy, albeit each in a different way. Girard, Ricœur and Žižek, in other words, despite their efforts to move beyond theodicy in their readings of Job, reinstitute a kind of theodicy even as they attempt to destroy it. For this reason, I wish to suggest, they illustrate the difficulty of reading Job without reference to theodicy *even outside of explicitly religious contexts.*

There are important and subtle differences between Girard's, Ricœur's, and Žižek's respective readings of Job. For the purposes of this article, we need but focus on one theme common to their respective interpretations: namely, that all three read the Book of Job as attempting to sever the connection between suffering and divine retribution. Girard calls this fissuring of the relation between suffering and retribution "ethical" as opposed to "mythological." The

---

1 de Vries, Hent, *Philosophy and the Turn to Religion*, Johns Hopkins University Press, Baltimore 1999.

2 Derrida, Jacques, "Faith and Knowledge: The Two Sources of 'Religion' at the Limits or Reason Alone," in: *Religion*, eds. Jacques Derrida and Gianni Vattimo, Stanford University Press, Stanford 1998, 40–101, 65–66.

Book of Job's teaching, according to Girard, is ethical because it affirms the truth of Job's innocence. Girard contends that Job, against Eliphaz in particular, in maintaining his innocence in the face of his suffering, is not denying God. On the contrary, "in the Gospels, Jesus very explicitly claims as his own all Job's criticisms of retribution."[3] As such, Job prefigures Jesus: "Job foretells Christ in his participation in the struggle against the God of persecutors. He foretells Christ when he reveals the scapegoat phenomenon that envelops him, when he attacks the system of retribution, and above all when he briefly eludes the logic of violence."[4]

Whereas for Girard the Book of Job is fundamentally ethical, Ricœur claims that it is precisely the ethical character of the Old Testament that the Book of Job opposes. According to Ricœur, the Old Testament as a whole reflects the view that "History is a tribunal, pleasure and pains are retribution. God himself is a judge ... the whole of human experience assumes a penal character."[5] However, as Ricœur notes, the suffering of the innocent is a problem only if God is understood as a just judge. Job, for Ricœur, is a harbinger of "a faith that wanders in the darkness in a 'new night of understanding' ... before a God who has not the attributes of 'Providence.' ... Beyond this night, and only beyond it, will be recovered the true meaning of the God of consolation, the God of the Resurrection."[6] Thus, despite the differences between Girard's reading of Job as affirming the ethical character of the Hebrew Bible, and Ricœur's reading of Job as denying the ethical character of the Hebrew Bible, we see that both describe Job as attempting to break the cycle of suffering and retribution, a rupture that is only fully realized in Jesus.

Like Girard and Ricœur, Žižek also regards Job as an internal break within the Old Testament. However, for Žižek, Job not only anticipates Christ: the crucified Jesus who is forsaken by his father *is* Job.

> What Job suddenly understood, was that it was not him, but God Himself, who was actually on trial in Job's calamities, and He failed the test miserably. Even more pointedly, I am tempted to risk a radical anachronistic reading: Job foresaw God's own future suffering – "Today it's me, tomorrow it will be your own son, and there will be no one to intercede for him. What you see in me now is the prefiguration of your own Passion!"[7]

It is important to recognize that although Girard, Ricœur, and Žižek each link Job with the anticipation of Jesus, their interpretations are not offered as decla-

---

3 Girard, René, *Job: The Victim of His People*, Stanford University Press, Stanford 1987, 155.

4 Girard, *Job: The Victim of His People*, 166.

5 Ricœur, Paul, *Symbolism as Evil*, Beacon Press, Boston 1986, 314.

6 Ricœur, Paul, *Conflict of Interpretations*, Northwestern University Press, Chicago 2007, 88.

7 Žižek, Slavoj, *The Puppet and the Dwarf*, MIT Press, Cambridge 2003, 126–127.

rations of Christian faith. Rather, for each of these thinkers Job's anticipation of Jesus and Jesus himself reveal something important about what it means to be human as such. For Girard, Job and Jesus expose the scapegoat mechanism that, Girard argues, undergirds much of human behavior. For Ricœur, Job's experience of "the inscrutable God of terror" reflects the modern predicament of the atheist who, in order to move forward, must completely abandon the beliefs of the past. For Žižek, Job expresses, simply yet bluntly, what it is to be a human being, to be at once abandoned and whole.

Based on these claims, it might seem that Girard, Ricœur, and Žižek have moved beyond theodicy. After all, their shared contention is that Job begins to break what they view as the Old Testament framework in which God rewards the just and punishes the sinful. Yet these post-theological readings of Job, I would argue, nonetheless retain a theodic orientation. Immanuel Kant's definition of theodicy is helpful here. In his important essay of 1791, "On the Failure of All Philosophical Efforts in Theodicy," Kant defines theodicy as "the defense of the highest wisdom of the creator against the charge which reason brings against it for whatever is counter purposive in the world."[8] Kant's term "counter purposive" captures the intrinsic problem facing any interpreter who wishes to emphasize Job's innocence: namely, the temptation to ascribe *a purpose* to Job's "counter purposive" suffering (or what Emmanuel Levinas terms "useless suffering").[9] Perhaps inadvertently, Girard, Ricœur, and Žižek each find a purpose in Job's suffering. This purpose, rather than being punishment for sin, is in fact a profound insight into the meaning of our humanity, be it the human tendency to scapegoat, the human experience of God's terror (experience which may open a new space for faith), or the human experience of the abandoned Christ. Girard, Ricœur, and Žižek, in finding a purpose and hence a reason for Job's suffering, thereby destroy yet at the same time institute theodicy.

Part of the problem here is the very nature of philosophy and theology, however post-metaphysical or post-theological. Philosophers and theologians offer reasons or explain the purpose of things, even when arguing that there are no reasons or purposes (an argument, it should be noted, not presented by Girard, Ricœur, and Žižek). Theodicy is a philosophical and theological construct; for this reason anti-theodic claims, and anti-theodic readings of the Book of Job, always remain theodic simply because they are still explanations,

---

8 Kant, Immanuel, *Religion and Rational Theology*, in: *The Cambridge Edition of the Works of Immanuel Kant*, eds. and transs. Allen W. Wood and George di Giovanni, Cambridge University Press, New York 2001, 24.
9 Levinas, Emmanuel, "Useless Suffering," in: *Entre-Nous: On Thinking-of-the-Other*, transs. Michael B. Smith and Barbara Harshav, Columbia University Press, New York 1998.

even if the explanation is that there is no explanation. Of course, in contrast to philosophical or theological treatises on the problems of suffering and evil, the Book of Job is a literary work. As such, it would be a fundamental disservice to the text, and indeed to the reader, to read the figure of Job as offering a final, or even a single, answer to the meaning of Job's suffering (and again, this would include the claim that Job's suffering is meaningless).

For this reason, it should not be surprising that art and literature have offered far more compelling and provocative interpretations on the Book of Job than have philosophers and theologians. Among contemporary literature's most interesting meditations on the Book of Job is Philip Roth's novel *Nemesis*, published in 2010. For various reasons, Roth and *Nemesis* may strike some as unlikely candidates for a reading of Job. While his life's work has had much to say about various forms of modern Jewish identity, Roth has had almost nothing to say about religion or theology, beyond depicting them as, at best, relics of a long-ago past. And *Nemesis* itself, as will be discussed in greater detail, resembles not biblical literature but, if anything, Greek tragedy. These two reasons may seem to preclude any consideration of Joban themes in *Nemesis*. Yet these apparent objections to reading *Nemesis* for its Joban themes are based upon two assumptions about the Book of Job that a reading of *Nemesis* actually helps to call into question: the first assumption is that the Book of Job is a book about religion and theology; the second, which builds upon the first, is that the Book of Job does not include tragic elements. Both assumptions, as I suggest in the conclusion of this article, are directly tied to theodic readings of the Book of Job, religious or otherwise.

Let us begin this consideration of Roth's *Nemesis* by returning briefly to Girard's well-known distinction between Job and Oedipus. Girard labels Job "a failed scapegoat" and Oedipus "a successful scapegoat."[10] As noted, Girard argues that the theme of the Book of Job is Job's innocence in the face of his friends' condemnations. Girard contrasts Job's innocence to what he claims is Oedipus's guilt. In Girard's succinct summary: "The city of Thebes is ravaged by a plague epidemic. A religious oracle announces that one single individual inside the city is responsible for the disaster: A culprit is sought and a culprit is found. He is the new king. He has no knowledge of his own horrendous crimes and yet he really committed them."[11] Oedipus's suffering, according to Girard, however tragic it may be, is nonetheless just.

At first glance, Roth's *Nemesis* appears to fit Girard's characterization of Oedipus rather well. Let me briefly summarize the plot. It is the summer of

10 Girard, *Job: The Victim of His People*, 35.
11 Girard, René, *Oedipus Unbound*, Stanford University Press, Stanford 2004, 107.

1944. Bucky Cantor is a twenty-three-year-old gym teacher in Newark, New Jersey. He has poor eyesight, which has rendered him unable to fight in the war. Due to shame and guilt over not being able to join the war effort, Bucky chooses to work as a playground director in the sweltering city rather than join his girlfriend at an affluent summer camp in the Poconos. The children worship Bucky's physical prowess, athletic skills and commitment to sportsmanship. A polio epidemic erupts in Newark, affording Bucky a chance to fight, even if only on the domestic front: "This was real war too, a war of slaughter, ruin, waste and damnation, war with the ravages of war – war upon the children of Newark." The causes of the outbreak are unknown, and panic ensues. When boys from another neighborhood threaten the children on the playground with antisemitic taunts blaming the Jews for the epidemic, Bucky responds calmly and bravely.

A number of children fall ill. Some are hospitalized and placed in iron lungs. Some die. In the face of mounting crisis, uncertainty, and fear, Bucky remains steadfast in his devotion to the children and to their grieving families. As the situation continues to deteriorate, Bucky becomes worn down by his unstinting efforts to provide a small piece of normality at the playground, visit hospitals, call on families of sick children, and attend increasing numbers of funerals. Encouraged by his grandmother to take a few days off and go to the shore, he instead visits his girlfriend, in the Poconos; while there he decides to take a job at the camp, so as to replace a young man who has left to fight in the war. However, the camp's oasis of peace is short lived, both for Bucky and everyone else. Polio strikes a camper, and Bucky learns that, despite not having had any symptoms, he himself is a healthy carrier of the disease. Other children become sick and the camp is evacuated. Bucky also falls ill; he survives, but loses use of an arm and a leg. He blames himself for spreading polio at the camp, and despite his girlfriend's plea that they remain together, rebuffs her. He lives the rest of his life a lonely, bitter man.

Bucky would indeed seem to be a modern-day Oedipus. Like Oedipus, Bucky has no knowledge of his crime (namely, that he is a healthy carrier of the polio virus), yet he is still guilty of infecting children in the Poconos and perhaps even on the playground. As Girard says of Oedipus, we might also say of Bucky Cantor: his suffering is tragic but it is also just. The novel's title would seem also to make such a reading likely. As J. M. Coetzee notes in a review of *Nemesis*, "Behind *nemesis* (via the verb *nemo*, to distribute) lies the idea of fortune, good or bad, and how fortune is dealt out in the universe."[12] Like

---

12 Coetzee, J. M., "On the Moral Brink," in: *The New York Review of Books* 57.16 (October 28, 2010): 13–15.

Oedipus, Bucky is unable to escape his fate, despite his almost heroic attempts to do so. In the course of the novel we learn that Bucky's mother died in childbirth and that his father was a thief and gambler who went to prison, leaving Bucky's impoverished, hardworking, and elderly grandparents to raise him. And it is through their example that Bucky tries to escape the physical and moral weaknesses that fate seems to have bestowed upon him. Bucky tries to impart to the playground children what his grandfather taught him: "toughness and determination, to be physically brave and physically fit and never to allow themselves to be pushed around or, just because they knew how to use their brains, to be defamed as Jewish weaklings and sissies."[13] Yet, like Oedipus, Bucky cannot escape his fate. In the end, all his hard work is useless. Despite his weak eyes he made himself strong and athletic, only to be rendered a cripple from polio. Likewise, despite his father's degenerate character, Bucky made himself the embodiment of decency and commitment; the illness, however, leaves him a criminal.

Yet the similarity between *Oedipus Rex* and *Nemesis* ends when we consider how Oedipus and Bucky each responds to his suffering. Oedipus, acknowledging his failure to have seen the truth, blinds himself, crying: "No more shall you look on the misery about me, The horrors of my own doing! Too long have you have known the faces of those whom I should never have seen, too long been blind to those for whom I was searching! From this hour, go in darkness!"[14] But Bucky, who has been only too aware of his poor eyesight, proclaims the truth of what he sees and experiences. Here he resembles Job far more than he does Oedipus. Indeed, rather than accepting his fate, Bucky rallies against it.

Job attributes his suffering to God: "For Shaddai's arrows are in me – their venom my spirit drinks. The terror of God beset me" (6:4).[15] Bucky likewise claims that God is responsible for the suffering he sees and experiences:

> it suddenly occurred to Mr. Cantor that God wasn't simply letting polio rampage through the Weequahic section [of Newark] but that twenty-three years back, God had also allowed his mother, only two years out of high school ... to die of childbirth. ... So too was his father's being a gambler and a thief something that was meant to happen and that couldn't have been otherwise. But now that he was no longer a child he was capable of understanding that why things couldn't be otherwise was because of God. If not for God, if not for the nature of God, they would be otherwise.

---

13 Roth, Philip, *Nemesis*, Houghton Mifflin Harcourt, New York 2010, 28.
14 Sophocles, transs. Dudley Fitts and Robert Fitzgerald, *The Oedipus Cycle: Oedipus Rex, Oedipus at Colonus, Antigone*, Mariner Books, New York 2002, 69.
15 All translations of the Book of Job are from Robert Alter, *The Wisdom Books: Job, Proverbs, and Ecclesiastes: A Translation with Commentary*, W. W. Norton & Company, New York 2010.

... His anger [was] provoked ... not against whatever cause, however unlikely, people, in their fear and confusion, might advance to explain the epidemic, not even against the polio virus, but against the source, the creator – against God, who made the virus.[16]

Job's suffering transforms him and forces him to question his former view that God punishes the wicked and rewards the just. Thus he asks: "What is my offense that I have done to You O Watcher of man? Why did you make me Your target, and I became a burden to You? And why do You not pardon my crime and let my sin pass away?" (7:20–21). In perhaps his most provocative statement, Job proclaims: "It's all the same, and so I thought: the blameless and the wicked He destroys" (9:22). Like Job, Bucky rethinks his worldview as he tries to understand his suffering. Whereas Job reconsiders his previous understanding of God's justice and forgiveness, Bucky rethinks his previous secularist commitments:

He was struck by how lives diverge and by how powerless each of us is up against the force of circumstance. And where does God figure in this? Why does He set one person down in Nazi-occupied Europe with a rifle in his hands and the other in the Indian Hill dining lodge in front of a plate of macaroni and cheese? Why does He place one Weequahic child in polio-ridden Newark for the summer and another in the splendid sanctuary of the Poconos? For someone who had previously found in diligence and hard work the solution to all his problems, there was now much that was inexplicable to him about why what happens, happens as it does.[17]

Rather than affirming his secularist, perhaps even atheist, worldview, Bucky responds to his suffering and the suffering around him by condemning God. In this sense, the formerly independent, self-assured Bucky comes to affirm God's existence: God exists for Bucky and he is cruel.

Just as Job's claims about God upset his friends, Bucky's announcement of God's cruelty disturbs those around him. Despite, or perhaps because of, the consternation that they each cause, Job and Bucky are compelled to speak their truth. Responding to his friends, Job professes: "As for me, I will not restrain my mouth. I would lament with my spirits in straits. I would speak when my being is bitter" (7:11). Job continually declares the truthfulness of his words as well as his ability to tell the truth: "Is there injustice on my tongue? Does my palate not taste disasters?" (6:30). "To my righteousness I cling, I will not let go, my heart has not caused reproach all my days" (27:6). Similarly, Bucky insists on challenging the beliefs of those closest to him. Witness the following

---

16 Roth, *Nemesis*, 125–127.
17 Roth, *Nemesis*, 154.

conversation between Bucky and his girlfriend, Marcia, upon Bucky's arrival at camp.

> *Marcia:* "I thought you were going to become paralyzed and die! I couldn't sleep, I was so frightened. I'd come out here whenever I could to be alone and pray to God to keep you healthy ..."
> *Bucky:* "Do you really think God answered your prayers? ..."
> *Marcia:* "I can't really know, can I? But you're here, aren't you? ..."
> *Bucky:* "That doesn't prove anything ... Why didn't God answer the prayers of Alan Michaels's parents? They must have prayed. Herbie Steinmark's parents must have prayed. They're good people. They're good Jews. Why didn't God intervene for them? Why didn't He save their boys?"[18]

Marcia's response to Bucky echoes Bildad's answer to Job. Bildad counters Job by declaring his friend's words about God empty: "How long will you jabber such things? – the words of your mouth, one huge wind" (8:2). And Marcia contends that Bucky does not know what he is talking about.

> *Marcia:* "Your attitude toward God – it's juvenile, it's just plain silly."
> *Bucky:* "Look, your God is not to my liking, so don't bring Him into the picture. He's too mean for me. He spends too much time killing children."
> *Marcia:* "And that is nonsense too! Just because you got polio doesn't give you the right to say ridiculous things.[19]

We have discussed three parallels between the characters of Job and Bucky: each holds God accountable for his suffering; as a result of this suffering, each questions his previous views of God; and each is compelled to articulate the truth of his experience of suffering. In *Nemesis*, these three affinities become all the more powerful when we realize – first, in passing, about a third of the way through the novel, and then in greater detail in the final forty pages – that the narrator is not in fact Bucky but rather Arnie Mesnikoff, one of the children from the playground who had been stricken with polio. We learn at the end of the novel that the adult Arnie had run into Bucky; they have lunch together, and it is from the ensuing conversation and Arnie's memories that he tells Bucky's story.

It is Arnie, more so than Marcia in her opposition to Bucky's claims about God, who plays the role of Job's friends. In the context of Roth's early twenty-first-century America, Marcia's view of a benevolent but mysterious God is at best a thin and naïve theology. It is Arnie who, like Eliphaz, gives greatest

---

18 Roth, *Nemesis*, 168–170.
19 Roth, *Nemesis*, 260–261.

expression to the dogma of the day. Eliphaz seeks to defend God's justice: "Recall, pray: what innocent man has died, and where were the upright demolished. As I have seen, those who plow mischief, those who plant wretchedness, reap it" (4:7–8). Similarly, Arnie seeks to defend today's creed that, in his words, "Sometimes you're lucky and sometimes you're not ... the tyranny of contingency – is everything." In making their claims, Eliphaz and Arnie seek to silence Job and Bucky.

As Edward L. Greenstein has argued, "even more than about issues and themes, [Job] is about the ways that we talk about them."[20] Greenstein notes that "Wind (ruah), empty speech, is a key term in the dialogues between Job and his companions." Job and his friends accuse each other of empty speech. This is especially important for understanding Eliphaz, according to Greenstein: "Contrary to what is usually claimed by commentators, Eliphaz does not contend that Job is guilty of anything. He explains that he simply cannot remain silent in the face of Job's deficient discourse."[21] Arnie also cannot remain silent in the face of what he claims is Bucky's refusal to recognize the contingency, and in this sense the meaninglessness, of his suffering. As Arnie summaries his view:

> His [Bucky's] conception of God was of an omnipotent being who was a union not of three persons in one Godhead, as in Christianity, but of two – a sick fuck and an evil genius.
>
> To my atheistic mind, proposing such a God was certainly no more ridiculous than giving credence to the deities sustaining billions of others; as for Bucky's rebellion against Him, it struck me as absurd simply because there was no need for it. That the polio epidemic ... was a tragedy, he could not accept. He has to convert tragedy into guilt. He has to find a necessity for what happens ... . He has to ask why. Why? Why? That it is pointless, contingent, preposterous, and tragic will not satisfy him. Instead he looks desperately for a deeper cause, this martyr, this maniac of the why ... .[22]

We can now return to the title of the book – *Nemesis*. The word is ambiguous. On one hand, as mentioned earlier, nemesis indeed refers to fortune and fate. Yet, at least in American popular culture, nemesis can (in keeping with its Greek origins) also refer to an avenger. (The term nemesis – and even arch nemesis – is often used in superhero comics and movies). The difference in these two meanings goes to the heart of the question posed by the novel *Nemesis*: Is there a reason for why things happen as they do? Understanding nemesis

---

20 Greenstein, Edward L., "Truth or Theodicy? Speaking Truth to Power in the Book of Job," in: *The Princeton Seminary Bulletin* 27 (2006): 238–258, 239.
21 Greenstein, "Truth or Theodicy?" 244.
22 Greenstein, "Truth or Theodicy?" 264–265.

as fate means that asking for such reasons is beside the point. However, understanding nemesis as an avenger means that there is a reason for why things happen as they do, even if, as is the case with Bucky, that reason points to God's cruelty. Roth's novel demonstrates the difficulty of even recognizing the ambiguity of nemesis in twenty-first-century America.

Nemesis, like the Book of Job, shows how challenging it is for the individual to truthfully express what is, for him, the reality of his suffering in the face of the prevailing dogmas of the day. Job attempts to speak the truth of his experience of underserved suffering against the prevailing biblical view that God is just. And Bucky attempts to speak the truth of his experience of undeserved suffering against the prevailing secularist view that the course of a person's life is largely contingent. The dialogical character of each work remains essential to the tension between the individual's experience and the normative assumptions against which he tries to speak. What matters here is not the resolution of the theological or philosophical problem of innocent suffering but rather the individual's struggle to give voice to his suffering.

By way of conclusion, I would like to return to the previously mentioned two reasons as to why Roth and *Nemesis* may initially seem unlikely candidates for Joban themes: namely, that Roth has had little to say about religion or theology, and that *Nemesis* would seem to resemble not so much biblical literature but, if anything, Greek tragedy. As noted, these objections to reading *Nemesis* for its Joban themes are based upon two assumptions about the Book of Job: first, that the Book of Job is a text about religion and theology; and second, building upon the first, that Job does not have tragic elements. As I suggested earlier, both of these assumptions are tied directly to theodic readings of Job, religious or otherwise.

If, as I have argued here, Job and *Nemesis* are indeed dramatic enactments of the individual's attempt to voice the truth of his experience against prevailing assumptions, then what matters is not the ultimate answer to the question of why the innocent suffer (the question of both theodicy and anti-theodicy), a question which neither the Book of Job nor *Nemesis* provides an answer, but rather the individual's struggle to speak the truth. Greenstein's reading of the Book of Job is again helpful. As he notes, "It almost does not matter to what degree Job's theological constructions and his friends beliefs are acceptable ... Job has made a valiant effort to speak his mind honestly."[23] I would add that God's response to Job may well be the best answer the Book of Job offers to the question of innocent suffering. It may well be the truth about God. Like-

---

23 Greenstein, "Truth or Theodicy?" 258.

wise, Arnie, who survives polio and later marries and devotes himself to designing homes for disabled people, may well offer the best non-theological response to the suffering of the innocent. Yet neither the Book of Job nor *Nemesis* resolves the question of why the innocent suffer. And it is this lack of resolution that both silences and amplifies Job's and Bucky's voices.

Does this mean that Job and *Nemesis* are tragedies? Nietzsche's characterization of tragedy as "Bravery and composure in the face of a powerful enemy, great hardship, a problem that arouses aversion" indeed applies to both.[24] Their bravery and composure in the face of a powerful enemy mark Job and Bucky as tragic heroes of sorts. Yet, as we have seen, neither Job nor Bucky succumbs to his fate, as Oedipus does.[25] On the matter of fate – of *nemos* – neither book offers a final answer. What is at stake is the individual's voice. But this voice can exist only in relation to other voices. The lack of resolution expressed in the dialogical character of both the Book of Job and *Nemesis* shows why almost any philosophical or theological attempt to explain what the Book of Job is really about, including those that claim to be anti-theodic, will always succumb to theodicy.

Bibliography

Alter, Robert: *The Wisdom Books: Job, Proverbs, and Ecclesiastes: A Translation with Commentary*. New York: W. W. Norton & Company, 2010.
Coetzee, J. M. "On the Moral Brink." *The New York Review of Books* 57.16. October 28, 2010.
Derrida, Jacques. "Faith and Knowledge: The Two Sources of 'Religion' at the Limits or Reason Alone." *Religion*. Eds. Jacques Derrida and Gianni Vattimo. Stanford: Stanford University Press, 1998.

---

24 Nietzsche, Friedrich, *Twilight of the Idols*, trans R. J. Hollingdale, Penguin Books, New York 1990, 93.
25 The topics of tragedy and Job as tragedy are of course large ones. As Harold Fisch suggests, "The [biblical] text summons the reader to respond in an accustomed literary fashion to a familiar form but at the same time undermines that response. The forms will be there but the text will encourage the reader to call them into question" (see Harold Fisch, *Poetry with Purpose: Biblical Poetics and Interpretation*, Indiana University Press, Bloomington 1990, 5). See also Richard Sewall's discussion of Oedipus, Job, and tragedy in: Sewall, Richard, "The Vision of Tragedy," in: *The Review of Metaphysics* 10.2 (1956), 193–200, especially his definition of tragedy as "this sense of ancient evil, of the blight man was born for, of the permanence and the mystery of human suffering, that is basic to the tragic sense of life," (see Sewall, "The Vision of Tragedy," 198).

Fish, Harold. *Poetry with Purpose: Biblical Poetics and Interpretation*. Bloomington: Indiana University Press, 1990.

Girard, René. *Job: The Victim of His People*. Stanford: Stanford University Press, 1987.

Girard, René. *Oedipus Unbound*. Stanford: Stanford University Press, 2004.

Greenstein, Edward L. "Truth or Theodicy? Speaking Truth to Power in the Book of Job." *The Princeton Seminary Bulletin* 27. Princeton: University of Princeton, 2006.

Kant, Immanuel. "Religion and Rational Theology." *The Cambridge Edition of the Works of Immanuel Kant*. Eds. and trans. Allen W. Wood and George di Giovanni. New York: Cambridge University Press, 2001.

Levinas, Emmanuel. "Useless Suffering." *Entre-Nous: On Thinking-of-the-Other*. Trans. Michael B. Smith and Barbara Harshav. New York, Columbia University Press, 1998.

Nietzsche, Friedrich. *Twilight of the Idols*. Trans R. J. Hollingdale. New York, Penguin Books, 1990.

Ricœur, Paul. *Symbolism as Evil*. Boston: Beacon Press, 1986.

Ricœur, Paul. *Conflict of Interpretations*. Chicago: Northwestern University Press, 2007.

Roth, Philip. *Nemesis*. New York: Houghton Mifflin Harcourt, 2010.

Sewall, Richard. "The Vision of Tragedy." *The Review of Metaphysics* 10.2. Washington: The Catholic University of America, 1956.

Sophocles. *The Oedipus Cycle: Oedipus Rex, Oedipus at Colonus, Antigone*. Trans. Dudley Fitts and Robert Fitzgerald. New York: Mariner Books, 2002.

de Vries, Hent. *Philosophy and the Turn to Religion*. Baltimore: Johns Hopkins University Press, 1999.

Žižek, Slavoj. *The Puppet and the Dwarf*. Cambridge: MIT Press, 2003.

Notes on Contributors

Robert Alter is Emeritus Professor of Hebrew and Comparative Literature at the University of California, Berkeley, and Director of the Center for Jewish Studies there. He has written widely on literary aspects of the Bible, on modern Hebrew literature, and on the European and American novel.

Leora Batnitzky is Ronald O. Perelman Professor of Jewish Studies and Professor and Chair of Religion at Princeton University. She is the author of *Idolatry and Representation: The Philosophy of Franz Rosenzweig Reconsidered* (2000); *Leo Strauss and Emmanuel Levinas: Philosophy and the Politics of Revelation* (2006) and *How Judaism Became a Religion* (2011).

Moshe Halbertal is Professor of Jewish Thought and Philosophy at the Hebrew University of Jerusalem and the Gruss Professor of Law at New York University. His latest books are *On Sacrifice* (2012) and *Maimonides: Life and Thought* (2013).

Galit Hasan-Rokem is Max and Margarethe Grunwald Professor of Folklore and Professor (emerita) of Hebrew Literature at the Hebrew University of Jerusalem. Her books include: *Web of Life: Folklore and Midrash in Rabbinic Literature* (2000) and *Tales of the Neighborhood: Jewish Narrative Dialogues in Late Antiquity* (2003).

Ariel Hirschfeld is Professor of Hebrew Literature at the Hebrew University. His books include: *Notes on a Place* (2000), *Toward the Last of the Gods: The Fountains of Rome* (2003), *Notes on Epiphany* (2006), and *Reading S. Y. Agnon* (2011).

Vivian Liska is Professor of German literature, Director of the Institute of Jewish Studies at the University of Antwerp, Belgium, Distinguished Visiting Professor at Hebrew University in Jerusalem and on the Visiting Staff of the Graduate Center at NYU. Her publications include *Die Nacht der Hymnen* (1993), *Das schelmische Erhabene* (1998), *Giorgio Agamben's leerer Messianismus* (2008), *When Kafka Says We* (2009), and *Fremde Gemeinschaft. Deutsch-jüdische Literatur der Moderne* (2011). She is the editor of the book series *Perspectives on Jewish Texts and Contexts*, De Gruyter, Berlin.

Naphtali Meshel is Assistant Professor of Religion and Judaic Studies at Princeton University. His research pertains to the Hebrew Bible and to Israelite religion within a comparative framework. He is the author of *A 'Grammar' of Ritual* (2014), which examines the claim that rituals are governed by 'grammars' analogous to those of natural languages-an idea first perceived by the classical Sanskrit grammarians and pursued in recent anthropological studies.

Ilana Pardes is Katherine Cornell Professor of Comparative Literature at the Hebrew University of Jerusalem. She is the author of *Countertraditions in the Bible: A Feminist Approach* (1992), *The Biography of Ancient Israel: National Narratives in the Bible* (2000), *Melville's Bibles* (2008) and *Agnon's Moonstruck Lovers: The Song of Songs in Israeli Culture* (2013).

Yosefa Raz is a post-doctoral fellow at the Center for Jewish Studies at the University of Toronto. Her research focuses on biblical prophecy and its reception in modernist Hebrew poetry. She is also the author of a book of poetry, *In Exchange for a Homeland* (2004).

Freddie Rokem is the Emanuel Herzikowitz Professor for 19th and 20th Century Art and teaches in the Department of Theatre Studies at Tel Aviv University. His publications include *Performing History: Theatrical Representations of the Past in Contemporary Theatre* (2000), *Strindberg's Secret Codes* was published by Norvik Press (2004) and *Philosophers and Thespians: Thinking Performance, exploring the relations between the discursive practices of philosophy and performance* (2010).